Home Owne

Home Ownership
Buying and Maintaining

Nicholas Snelling LL B

Guild of Master Craftsman Publications Ltd

To my wife Lindsay and all my family – *nil desperandum!*

Acknowledgements

I would like to express my grateful thanks to the following, who gave freely of their advice and expertise, and without whom this book would not have been possible: Mike Bolt, Mike Bromley, Jonathan Bysh, Brian Davey, Geoff Ellis, Bryan Fearne, Tim Henson, Keith Hockridge, John Jenkins, Peter Lifford, Michael Logan-Wood, Geoff Looser, Henri Samy, Tom Sheldon, Eve Smith, Peter Snelling, and Allen Watters. I would also like to thank Liz Inman, Mary Chamberlain and Stephen Haynes for their editorial work.

First published 1997 by
Guild of Master Craftsman Publications Ltd,
166 High Street, Lewes, East Sussex BN7 1XU

© Nicholas Snelling 1997

ISBN 1 86108 067 0

Cover design by Guild of Master Craftsman Publications design studio 1997
Photography by Dennis Bunn

The right of Nicholas Snelling to be identified as the author of this work has been asserted in accordance with the Copyright Designs and Patents Act 1988, Sections 77 and 78.

Designed by John Hawkins

Set in Sabon

Printed and bound in Great Britain by Hillman Printers (Frome) Ltd

Contents

About the Author

Nicholas Snelling has been involved in building and renovation since childhood, and his family has been engaged in property development for some generations.

For ten years he ran his own contracting business in London, concentrating on the renovation of properties for both private and commercial clients. Much of the work involved prestigious, high-quality small works projects, and remedial work on buildings which had suffered structural movement was a particular speciality. Over the years, practically every form of small works building was undertaken.

Before starting his own business, Nicholas Snelling worked for some years as a litigation executive for a firm of West End solicitors. He has also had military experience, and has travelled widely. He has done logistics work in Afghanistan, and acted as an instructor on a major expedition in South America.

He is married with two children and lives in Essex.

Note

It must be emphasized that Scottish law differs in many respects from that of England, Wales and Northern Ireland. The major differences with respect to buying and selling property are covered in Appendix 1: Buying and Selling Property in Scotland. Except where otherwise stated, this book assumes English law to apply.

Introduction

PROBLEMS with property are universal. Almost everyone has suffered the intense stress involved in buying and selling property, and the difficulties of managing a building, or related project – be it having a bathroom or kitchen fitted, or the construction of an entire extension – receive their share of bad publicity. But perhaps it is not surprising that tensions run so high. Apart from property representing a person's most valuable possession by far, it is also usually their home and central to their emotional life. Indeed, along with bereavement, loss of a job and divorce, the buying and selling of a property is supposedly one of the most stressful of life's experiences.

What is surprising, however, given the importance of property, is the lack of knowledge that most people have at every level, and the almost cavalier attitude that is displayed when vital transactions are being undertaken, often with considerable amounts of money at stake. Few people know:

- how to define the work that they want carried out,
- how to employ a builder, or
- how to supervise and check any works done.

Indeed, frequently a builder will be chosen, and negotiations will take place for him to do substantial works, with less care than would be taken when buying a household appliance. It is therefore hardly surprising that so many problems occur. Perhaps if some of those 'bad builder' stories that are so widespread were subject to closer examination, a number of 'bad client' stories might emerge.

Equally, there is general ignorance about the buying and selling of properties. All too often the purchase or sale of a property is an ill-planned and haphazard affair, rather than the coldly calculated operation that would be justified by the amount at stake.

This combination of ignorance and sensitivity amounts to a potentially disastrous cocktail, particularly if the property owner is unaware of the constraints under which the professionals are working, or if the builders or professionals involved are not of the highest calibre and integrity.

It is vital to know, in outline at least:

- the functions of the professionals,
- the stages of various specific operations, and
- whether matters are proceeding satisfactorily and to budget.

With this information you can monitor and manage a project to ensure that it proceeds to a satisfactory conclusion.

Knowing in advance what problems may arise can reduce the stress of the experience, and make you remarkably effective – rather than a mere frightened bystander.

This book sets out primarily to provide guidelines both on small works construction (loosely defined as works under £50,000), and on the general experiences you will encounter with regard to your property including buying and selling. The book is not intended to enable you to build your own property, nor to convey it. It will, however, provide sufficient information for you to understand the part you should play in any transaction, and the performance that should be expected of those you employ. It will show you:

- where problem areas lie,
- how to manage personally any matter relating to your property,
- when and how to start placing pressure upon the professionals involved in any work.

A secondary aim of the book is to provide general information on property. Some of the most common problem areas are dealt with, such as:

- property movement or subsidence,
- finance,
- regulations governing building work,
- obtaining or objecting to planning permission.

There is also a preliminary look at the legal process, and the options open when seeking redress against either a professional or a builder.

PART ONE

Buying and Selling your Property

1

Buying your Property

F EW events are more stressful than buying property. There is invariably a lot at stake, both emotionally and financially, and yet for much of the time you can find yourself hopelessly in the dark about the process. This chapter takes you through the most usual procedure, known as purchase by **private treaty**; the alternative of purchase by auction is covered in Chapter 3.

It is vital when buying a property that you are fully prepared, know roughly what the different stages are and can recognize the proper functions of the professionals working for both parties. If you understand the process then you can, to some extent, control it and monitor what is happening. This can relieve much of the stress and make the transaction greatly more efficient.

There are essentially two ways of owning property in the UK, **freehold** and **leasehold** (except in Scotland, as detailed in Appendix 1: Buying and Selling Property in Scotland).

FREEHOLD

In this situation the **title** (or ownership) of a property is not limited by any period of time. It is, in effect, valid for an indefinite term. This does not mean that the property is not subject to **covenants and restrictions**, such as rights of way. It does mean, however, that the actual ownership of the land is not subject to any artificially imposed time limit. It belongs to the freeholder for ever.

LEASEHOLD

This is a way of owning property for a fixed period of time, commonly 99 years, at the end of which all the rights of the property revert to the freeholder. The property is effectively held by the **lessee** under the terms of a contract called the lease, which gives both the **lessor** (the owner of the property) and the lessee very clearly defined rights and responsibilities over the property.

Leases are, on the whole, more complicated as regards **conveyancing** (legal transfer of ownership), and special attention is needed to ensure that the terms of any lease are acceptable to the person buying it. Particular attention should be paid by a buyer and his conveyancer to the conditions, restrictions and financial responsibilities imposed by the lease.

Regardless of whether you buy your property freehold or leasehold, there are five key stages:

- Planning and Preparation
- The Offer to Buy
- Co-ordination
- The Mortgage Offer
- The Legal Process

PLANNING AND PREPARATION

Before seriously going to look for a property, the buyer must establish the following criteria.

A Firm Budget

This will be affected by a number of factors:

- the amount of money that you will be able to contribute personally towards the cost of the new property;
- the amount of money that a bank, insurance company or building society (the **lender**) will provide, based on your income;
- the fees that will be incurred in any purchase; and
- a contingency sum for any unexpected expenses.

While it may be quite clear what amount you personally can put towards the cost of the property, the contribution of the lender is normally less clear and should not be guessed. Before deciding how much you can offer, you should meet with a registered broker or at least a couple of lenders (see Chapter 4: Mortgages). They will tell you the amount that they are likely to lend, in principle, on the type of property that you wish to buy – given your financial circumstances. You should also obtain a fairly accurate statement of the monthly payments that you will have to make on your proposed mortgage.

Try to establish how quickly the chosen lender will be able to react once an offer to buy has been made. The time they will take to advise you of a formal mortgage offer is critical.

The fees, disbursements and costs involved in any purchase should be investigated, with particular attention to the costs that you will have to bear in the first month, immediately after buying your property. The main expenses will be for:

- **Solicitors' fees and disbursements** for the conveyancing: Approximately £300–£350 for a £60,000 property.

- **Land Registry fee:** There is a variable scale, depending on the value of the property.

- **Stamp duty:** This is payable on any property bought for a value of over £60,000, and is chargeable at 1–2% of the purchase price.

- **Searches:** Typically £60–£125, depending on the local authority.

- **Building society valuation report:** Depending on the lender, this normally costs around £100 for a £60,000 property. Some lenders will refund this fee if you take out buildings insurance with them, and sometimes the fee is waived, as part of a lender's special offer to entice people to take a mortgage with them. More commonly, however, you may upgrade the valuation report to a **House Buyer's Report,** in which case the fee will be approximately £200 + VAT, or a full structural survey which can cost anything up to £350–400 + VAT – but these prices should be taken only as a rough guide.

- **Insurance:** A property must be insured as soon as exchange of contracts has taken place. Invariably, the charges for buildings and contents insurance can be paid by direct debit, so that your initial monthly fee should not be too great. Note that insurance companies will usually be reluctant to provide cover if the property is vacant.

- **Mortgage Payments:** Make sure that you will be able to make your first monthly payment, on top of all the one-off costs that you will sustain on any purchase.

If possible you should reserve a **contingency sum** of, say, £1,000 for unforeseen costs. It may well be, for instance, that a survey on the property suggests the necessity of a structural engineer's report, prior to purchase. This will certainly be the case if any trace of subsidence is discovered by a lender's surveyor. Following this it may be a condition of any mortgage offer that certain essential works are carried out as soon as the purchase has been completed. On a more basic level, you may have to pay reconnection charges for gas, electricity or telephone services if they have been disconnected. When buying leasehold, there may be apportionments of ground rent, service charges and insurance to be paid on completion.

Which Professionals to Use

There are two types of **conveyancer** available: either a qualified **solicitor** or a **licensed conveyancer.** Both can legally convey properties and must be properly insured. Solicitors still do by far the most of the conveyancing undertaken in the UK. In this book, except where otherwise stated, the term 'conveyancer' covers both.

It can be worthwhile making an appointment with your conveyancer before looking for a property, to discuss his likely charges and the advice and service you will get from him. He may also be able to advise you on any financing required for your property. Conveyancers can be quite well placed to do this as they are not allowed to take commission on any mortgage they arrange, without your prior agreement. You should never agree on any financial package, however, until you have researched at least a couple of other options. It is therefore essential that you arrange the financial package before deciding on a property; it is all too easy to be tempted to take the first package on offer if you are in a panic about securing a particular property.

If you are buying the property as a joint purchaser, i.e. with someone else, it is vital that your conveyancer should be asked for specific advice. This is all the more critical when you are unmarried, so you are aware of what could happen if you or your partner in the purchase wants to sell the property and the other does not. You must also decide what should happen to the property should one partner die, especially if you are unmarried; this is a good time to make a will. Make sure that any advice on this vital topic is backed up in writing, and that you fully understand the implications of buying with someone else before proceeding on any purchase.

You may need to find a **surveyor**, particularly if you do not need a mortgage. Make sure he is properly qualified and able to act quickly. Your conveyancer may be able to recommend one.

You may also want to find a **builder** who could go around the property in advance, to provide at least outline costs for any works that may need to be done straight away.

If you want to move quickly, you must ensure that the right people are in place before you start looking at properties.

THE OFFER TO BUY

When you have been shown the property that you wish to buy, you should make your offer verbally to the estate agent (assuming there is one). They will pass this on to the seller, who may or may not accept it, depending on how close it is to the asking price.

Except in Scotland (see Appendix 1), your offer to buy a property, even if accepted by the seller, is not binding. Invariably, it will be an offer 'subject to contract', meaning that the offer can be revoked at any time up until exchange of contracts. At this time, both you and the seller will sign a formal and binding contract, which is irreversible. Up to that point, you can drop out of any purchase, without giving the seller any notice or reasons whatsoever, and without being legally liable to the seller in any way. It is worth bearing in mind, however, that the same is true of the seller.

The main reason for this contractual anomaly is that traditionally it has always been difficult to establish the clear title (ownership) of a property and the right of the seller to sell it. Accordingly, a thorough investigation of the property's title, together with a formal contract, is required before a sale of property can occur. This is a vital protection which prevents you from buying a property that may in some way, and to some extent, be owned by someone other than the seller.

COORDINATION

Once an offer has been accepted you should ensure that you immediately and efficiently organize the following:

The Lender Funding the Purchase

Advise your broker or lender of the offer you have made to buy the property, the name and details of your conveyancer and that of the seller's estate agent. The lender will then require a cheque for the cost of their surveyor, who will need to do a survey of the property before the lender will make any formal mortgage offer.

This survey is not a thorough survey of the property and must not be relied upon as such. The lender's survey is essentially a valuation, taking into account the condition of the property and its location, which confirms to the lender that the property is good security, in terms of resale value, for any loan made. The report is likely to raise only obvious problems, such as bulging walls or serious cracking, that would affect the viability of any loan.

Your Solicitor or Conveyancer

Inform your solicitor or conveyancer of the offer made, the address of the property, and the details of the estate agent, the seller's solicitor or conveyancer and your intended lender. Finally, obtain written confirmation (if this has not already been supplied) of the potential cost of your solicitor's or conveyancer's fees and disbursements. A rough average cost will be some £300–£350 for a £60,000 property.

The Estate Agents for the Seller

Try to persuade the seller, or his estate agents, to take the property 'off the market'. This means that the agents will not actively market the property by continuing to advertise it, display the details or take people round the property. The last thing that you want is to lose the property because the seller has been encouraged to accept a better offer, thereby **gazumping** you. Not only will this cause emotional stress, it may also mean you lose money.

As soon as you embark on the purchase process, you will find that you start incurring costs, through your conveyancer, the lender or any surveyor. None of them will refund your money, or fail to invoice you, just because the sale has collapsed. So although the estate agents are legally entitled to keep the property *on* the market, you should use all your powers to persuade them otherwise.

Survey of the Property

There is no duty imposed on you to have a survey made of the property. Any institution preparing to lend money on it will always conduct a valuation survey, but this is mandatory for them, regardless of your wishes.

You have three options, escalating in cost and degree:

- To rely entirely on the **lender's valuation report.** This should pick up obvious major defects, but it is primarily used to confirm, or otherwise, that the value of the property is adequate security for the loan being made. It cannot be relied upon as a comprehensive survey.

- To request the lender, at your expense, to upgrade the valuation survey to a **House Buyer's Report.** This is a more detailed report which should itemize all the problems with the property as well as obvious major defects. While it is greatly preferable to a valuation report, it has the disadvantage of not being fully comprehensive, and can therefore fall between two stools.

- To commission a full structural survey from a surveyor or consulting structural engineer. This, if carried out with proper rigour, will involve a very detailed and comprehensive investigation of all aspects of the property. The surveyor or engineer will need access to the loft space, flooring and below the main floor itself. This requires the permission of the seller, who may not be too keen to give it if the house is fully furnished. Although a responsible owner who is serious about selling should allow your engineer the necessary degree of access, you should be prepared to place pressure on the seller if required.

The point of commissioning a full structural survey is that you are left with absolutely no doubts at all about the condition of your property, whether it is the state of the wiring, plumbing, drains, roof or any possible defect to the physical structure. The report will also consider any potential for movement, whether the roots of nearby trees or the type of ground upon which the building is constructed.

Wherever possible, employ a **consulting structural engineer** to produce the report, rather than a surveyor. If a surveyor does find structural faults it is likely that, as he does not specialize in this field, he will simply advise you to obtain a further report from an engineer.

When commissioning the survey, stress that you want a comprehensive report, and that if it means lifting carpets, for example, then this must be done. You must realize that surveyors and engineers must be able actually to *see* the areas that need investigating.

Generally, it is wise to obtain a survey on a property, rather than relying only on the valuation report. If you are going to the expense of obtaining a survey, then it is worth considering obtaining a full structural survey, particularly if the property is old or in a poor state. Although this may be quite expensive, it will stand as a definitive document on the condition of the property. At the end of the day, the additional expense of a full structural report is small, when the total purchase price, or perhaps the cost of unexpected building works, is taken into account.

The last thing you want is to find that the property you have bought has hidden defects not picked up in the House Buyer's Report. What you need are precise assertions as to the condition of a property, for which you must be prepared to pay extra, so that a surveyor or engineer can spend time and effort to investigate properly.

A further advantage of obtaining a full report is that as it is likely to suggest areas requiring building work (particularly if the property is old), you may justifiably get a reduction in price by showing it to the seller.

The Seller

Initially, at least, you should communicate directly with the seller to make absolutely certain that he is also processing his side of the sale. While this may cause some upset with the estate agents, it is vital to ensure that the seller is aware of the process ahead. You must know that he is, in turn, putting pressure on the estate agents and his own conveyancer to press ahead with the sale.

If a seller has heard directly from you that all is going ahead, it can prevent him from getting too nervous about the sale. If some kind of personal bond can be formed, the seller may be less likely, if the sale process does become tricky, to place the property on the market again without first speaking directly to you.

This direct communication can be fraught, and is not something that the estate agents or conveyancers of either party particularly like. There is a time and a place for it, however, and sometimes, if the professionals are not doing their job sufficiently well, this can be picked up by speaking directly to the seller. It can be a valuable way of monitoring the purchase, and is a safety valve that should not be ignored.

THE MORTGAGE OFFER

The formal mortgage offer will be submitted some time after the lender's valuation survey has been done. The offer is effectively the amount that the lender is willing to provide, using the property as security for the loan. The offer will include all details of the amount that will be lent, the time period for repayment, the redemption of the loan and any conditions of the loan. Make sure that you discuss the offer with your conveyancer, who should check it to see that the offer covers what you require and that there are no unusual conditions. Your conveyancer can be useful at this stage in advising you, if he believes you are being sold an inappropriate or risky mortgage. It is well worth asking his advice directly, particularly if you are unclear about any aspect of the loan, such as the amount of the repayments or the redemption of the mortgage.

Obviously, the offer (if you do need to raise a loan or mortgage) is a critical part of the purchase process. If the lender is not prepared to lend the amount that you require, then you may be unable to fund any purchase of the property.

The conditions of the loan should be looked at carefully, as these may also affect whether you can afford the property. The most material conditions, at this stage, may be those that require you, as a condition of the loan, to perform certain works on the property within a defined time period. If this is not done, then the lender may retain a proportion of the loan until the works are completed. Alternatively, if the works are not undertaken, the lender has a right to have the works done and add the cost onto your mortgage account. Sometimes no conditions will be set, but if the valuation report has picked up any problems or defects that may affect the safety of the property, or may be critical in allowing its decline in value, then the lender will require them to be rectified.

So, for example, if the electrical wiring is in a dangerous condition the lender may want this resolved within a short time period – the last thing they want is for the property, the security for their loan, to burn down. Equally, the guttering may be in poor condition, allowing water to degrade the outside walls. This may also have to be rectified, perhaps within a longer time period, as a lack of action will result in the fabric of the property deteriorating in condition, and thereby value.

Make sure that you can afford to carry out these repairs to the lender's satisfaction and in the time limits decreed. That said, most institutions are extremely tardy in checking that the remedial repairs or alterations are performed, and quite often you can get away without doing them for much longer than the set time limits. In reality, however, it is normally in your interest to do the works, as they are only specified by the lender if they are matters that badly need doing.

Maintain constant contact with the institution preparing to lend you the purchase money, and apply pressure as necessary. Banks and building societies can be notoriously slow in instructing surveyors to do a valuation report, and it can take an unaccountably long time to obtain the mortgage offer. Of course, until a mortgage offer is received the sale process cannot be completed, and this is often the source of nerve-racking delays for both you and the seller.

THE LEGAL PROCESS
(not applicable to Scotland; see instead Appendix 1)

The aim of the conveyance of any property is the transfer from one person to another of the title (ownership) to a clearly defined piece of property. This can only be done after careful investigation into the title to establish the ownership of the property, together with any matters that affect the property either adversely or beneficially – such as easements and restrictive covenants. It is this investigation and the drawing up of an unambiguous contract that makes the work of any solicitor or conveyancer so vital. Accordingly, the legal process can take some time to complete, and while it can be speeded up to a certain extent, some areas can be out of the effective control of the conveyancer – such as when he is awaiting information, instructions or (frequently) the mortgage offer from your lender.

The Conveyancer

Although it is possible for anyone to do the conveyancing on a property themselves, in reality, the vast majority of people wisely employ a trained conveyancer. Conveyancing, while often straightforward, can occasionally be very complicated and require all the skills of a qualified and experienced practitioner. Any mistake or detail overlooked during a conveyance can have very serious implications.

As with all professionals there are good and bad conveyancers, so take care who you appoint. This is not an easy matter, unless you can rely upon a recommendation – preferably from a friend or acquaintance, rather than from an estate agent with whom you have never dealt before. Even then, you must ensure that you are proactive in this relationship, and that right from the start there is a clear understanding concerning the demands and expectations of both parties.

Commonly, conveyancers complain of two matters with regard to their clients. Firstly, they often say that clients rarely have any understanding of the process, and therefore their demands on the conveyancer are often unrealistic. Secondly, conveyancers often complain that clients negotiate fees down, and yet still expect a conveyancer to give absolute priority to their case, regardless of the rest of their workload. On the part of buyers and sellers, common complaints revolve around the grinding slowness of some conveyancers, and a feeling that they are left in the dark about the actual process.

You should not expect your work to be given priority unless you are willing to pay at least a fair price and perhaps a premium. In the latter case, most conveyancers will sideline other work to concentrate on your better-paying affairs. Most conveyancers have a phenomenal case-load – quite often several hundred matters, all of which they will be dealing with personally. They are therefore normally under considerable pressure, not helped by the fact that conveyancing fees, in real terms, have dropped considerably over the years.

On the whole, most conveyancers' fees are fairly similar, dictated by a market rate, and if you try to get a conveyancer to do the work for less money it can simply result in his not giving it the priority that you expect. If you want a priority service, then be prepared to pay a higher price for the work (although you must attempt to agree the total sum beforehand) – most particularly if you want a bespoke service.

Either way, it is important to monitor the performance of your conveyancer, and you can only do this effectively if you have a broad understanding of the conveyancing process. With this information, you can assess whether or not you are being given excuses for the slow progress of the matter, and then intervene with other parties or place pressure upon your conveyancer as necessary.

As for all professionals, you should place any requests, queries, or instructions in writing (a fax will do if time is of the essence) and keep copies. They will be prompted into responding in kind and, in doing so, will necessarily set matters out briefly and clearly. Certainly a sign of a good conveyancer is when he regularly sends you letters, or copies of correspondence, sent by him to the other parties – thus keeping you up to date on what is being done.

Ensure, when setting out to appoint a conveyancer to act for you, that he is on the **panel**, the approved list of conveyancers of the institution that will be lending you the money for the property. Then your conveyancer will be able to act for the lender as well as yourself. This is important, as otherwise you could find yourself having to pay for two conveyancers – one acting for yourself and the other acting for the lender. Obviously, it is cheaper and more effective if only one conveyancer handles your purchase, as well as the drawing up and registering of the lender's charge on the Land Register.

The legal process can be broken down into five stages:

- Investigation
- Assessment of Draft Contracts
- Exchange of Contracts
- Completion
- After Completion

Investigation

The immediate action that your conveyancer will take, once he has received your instructions, is to request from the seller's conveyancer **draft documentation** and answers to **pre-contract inquiries**. He will also send off the **local authority search**.

Draft Documentation

Once finalized between the parties, the **draft contract** will form the contract of sale. If the property is subject to a lease then a copy of this will be requested.

If the title is registered, the **land certificate** applies if there is no mortgage or charge relating to the property. The **charge certificate** applies if there is an existing mortgage or charge; it will provide details of who has placed the charge, and to what effect. Both certificates will provide information on any covenants affecting the property or its land, and will further show a plan of the property clearly indicating the boundaries.

If the title is unregistered, an **abstract of title** will be supplied, containing copies or details of all deeds and documents required to prove the seller's title.

Pre-Contract Inquiries

These are formal inquiries made to the seller's conveyancer, and thereby to the seller himself, asking questions on a selection of topics about which you, or your conveyancer, may be concerned. These questions should be replied to by the seller specifically and not evasively, and should tell you whether there are, or have been, any disputes with neighbours or alterations carried out on the property, etc.

The pre-contract inquiries also ask questions of the seller as to what exactly he will be selling within the property. A separate **fixtures and fittings list** is completed by the seller setting out the items he is selling with the property.

Local Authority Search

This is a search in the **Register of Local Land Charges** maintained by the council. A list of inquiries usually accompanies the search. The search may reveal planning, financial and other charges registered against, or affecting the property. It may also reveal to a limited extent proposed changes to the road system (e.g. if a dual carriageway is to be built close by) and other information that the local authority may have concerning the property, as well as matters affecting the local environment within the council's sphere of operation.

The investigation of the above can take up to four to six weeks, although in practice most councils process searches in two weeks or less. It is worth asking your conveyancer how long your intended local authority is likely to take.

Normally, the local authority search is conducted by post, but it can be done personally either by you or an employee of the conveyancer. It is a simple, if rather time-consuming, process involving a visit to half a dozen local authority departments, the payment of a modest fee, the checking of various records held and the filling out of a straightforward form. The local authority officers are normally very helpful to people doing their own searches. In less than half a day, a personal search can accomplish what could take several weeks if left to the post and the hands of an overburdened or inefficient local authority.

Unfortunately, lending institutions generally require an official search – but if time is of the essence, and you need a mortgage, see if your lender will make an exception and accept a personal search. If they will, it can speed up the buying process significantly.

Assessment of Draft Contracts

An essential part of your conveyancer's work is the assessment of the information that he receives from the seller. Much of this will be of little real interest to you personally and will be dealt with solely by your conveyancer, ensuring that the legalities are correct. If matters such as rights of way, planning proposals or other problems with the property do become apparent, however, then he will advise you accordingly. It is when this occurs that you will need to become involved in further instructing your conveyancer, and the quicker this is done the faster the purchase can either take place or, if appropriate, be abandoned. Remember that right up to exchange of contracts the purchase can be stopped or the price renegotiated.

If the purchase involves a lease, then you must take care to ensure that you fully understand the terms of the lease. Leases differ from one property to another, and you must be certain that you do not agree to conditions that you cannot perform or that are unexpectedly onerous or unfair. Expressly check:

- **Apportionment of expenses of the property.** Normally, if the property is one of a number within a building, then all the leaseholders will be equally responsible for any of the building's expenses. So, for example, if the roof needs repairing, then an equal contribution to the cost would be made by all the leaseholders. Some leases do exist, however, which allot this expense to the top flat alone. There may be some clause that may be very disadvantageous to you.

- **Terms of maintenance.** It is important to know how these are defined. For example, some leases will specify exterior decoration every three years, with the 'common parts' being decorated every five years. You should assess whether this is going to be sufficient, whether you can afford the regular expense and also when the next phase of the works is due to take place. If works are scheduled shortly after your intended purchase, then this may cause you considerable financial hardship.

- **Management of the property.** If the property has a formal managing agent then you should find out the cost of this and the powers that reside in the managing agent, particularly regarding your ability to do building works within your part of the property. Some leases are drafted giving the management excessive powers to prevent works occurring – although there are now statutory protections for tenants, designed to eliminate the problem.

- **Charges.** All potential additional charges should be carefully researched, such as **ground rent**, the **service charge** (if any) and **maintenance**, together with the arrangements allowed for increasing them.

It is also at this time that the conveyancers negotiate the deposit payable on exchange of contracts, the time between exchange and completion and any allowance by the seller for you to have access to the property. Normally, the deposit will be between 5% and 10% of the property price, and completion 28 days after exchange, although both matters can vary. There is, for example, no reason why completion should not take place the same day as exchange, providing that:

- the money is available;
- you and the seller agree;
- your conveyancer has done all his post-contract work in advance;
- you are not locked into a 'chain'.

Occasionally, you may want to have access to the property during the period between exchange and completion, perhaps to do some measurements or building works, or even to store furniture and effects. It may be important if you need to be able to move into the property straight after completion, and the building is in some way uninhabitable. In this case, you can try to negotiate access to the property after exchange, to which you would otherwise not be entitled. Obviously, the seller may not agree, in which case there is nothing that you can do.

If the seller agrees in principle, however, then an agreement can be drawn up by the conveyancers whereby you can have access on the condition that you can only undertake certain clearly defined works (as a rule, these will be minor and non-structural), and on the basis that if completion does not take place, then you have to rectify any damage, or reverse any works done. Often a larger deposit than normal would also be required from you upon exchange, as further protection for the seller.

Exchange of Contracts

Once your conveyancer is entirely content with the results of all the inquiries, negotiations and investigations made concerning the property, he will send you the approved contract for signature, or sign it himself if he has your express authority to do so. You must then make available the agreed deposit to your conveyancer, who will hold it on your behalf. If you are in a chain, you may be able to use your buyer's deposit.

Your conveyancer will then confirm with the seller's conveyancer, normally on the telephone, that he is in possession of your deposit money and the signed contract. The seller's conveyancer will, at the same time, confirm that the seller has also signed his contract of sale. The two conveyancers will then agree that 'exchange' has taken place, and fix a completion date. As soon as this has occurred, there is a formal contract in place that can only be reversed by you, or by the seller, at the risk of becoming liable for a legal action for breach of contract.

The actual physical exchange of contracts, and the delivery of the deposit to the seller, will normally be done by post or by hand to each of the conveyancers, once exchange by telephone has taken place.

Your conveyancer will now send off **bankruptcy searches**, which must remain clear until after the date for completion. This search is to confirm that no bankruptcy notice or order has been registered against the seller or the buyer, and is required by mortgage lenders. **Title searches** will also be made at the Land Registry or the Land Charges Department, depending on whether the title is registered or not.

From the moment of exchange you are responsible for the insurance of the property. It is crucial therefore that you arrange for insurance cover as from the day of exchange. If the property burns down between then and completion you will become liable for the damage. That said, some contracts now provide for the seller to retain the risk until completion, and this is worth speaking to your conveyancer about.

Completion

Completion is the date upon which you obtain all rights to the property. It is marked by the actual transfer of the purchase price (less the deposit already paid) from you to the seller. Until this has physically taken place, and has been specifically confirmed by your conveyancer, you will not normally have access to the property.

The time when completion takes place is therefore quite specific and relies absolutely upon the transfer of money. The transfer may be done in a number of ways, normally by telegraphic transfer, but sometimes by banker's draft or building society cheque.

After Completion

Your conveyancer will advise your lender formally that completion has taken place, arrange for payment of stamp duty and then register your name with the Land Registry, together with the details of any lender with an interest in the property. The title deeds will then be passed on to the institution providing your mortgage.

If the property was bought without a mortgage then you can either keep the deeds yourself, get your conveyancer to place the deeds in his archives or, perhaps, give them to your bank for safekeeping.

The overall time taken to complete the purchase of a property depends on a number of factors some, or all, of which can make the process a drawn-out and harrowing affair. It certainly takes only one party within the transaction, whether it is the lending institution, the seller, the estate agents, either of the conveyancers or yourself, to slow the process down. Often this can be avoided by adequate preparation, the choice of a good conveyancer and your determined effort in being alert to any undue delays.

It is essential that, as the buyer, you know the actual process, particularly the legal part, and keep track of the purchase throughout the various stages. If at any time you have reservations about what is or is not happening, then be prepared to apply direct pressure on your conveyancer, the estate agent handling the sale or the lending institution. You should also not neglect the seller, who will normally be as keen to sell as you are to buy, and may also be concerned at the delays. You and the seller, if you get on, can normally isolate the source of any delays on the part of the professionals, and can together exert sufficient pressure to restore movement to the process.

Of course, buying a property is, more often than not, affected by the operation of a sometimes complicated chain of properties being sold. Delays due to this are difficult to get around, but are really no reason for slowness in getting the legal process up to the point at which exchange can take place. In any event, very little investigation needs to be done to check the condition of the chain, if there is one. This is something that the estate agents should know all about in detail, and you should not be shy about regularly contacting them for information.

Apart from the 'loose cannon' factor within chains of property all awaiting their sales, the purchase of a property should be fairly quick and straightforward. This is particularly the case if you are a first-time buyer, cash buyer or have no property of your own to sell, upon which your purchase relies. In this case, any slowness of the process will almost invariably be the responsibility of one of the professionals involved, the seller personally or the lending institution, if there is one – or perhaps a defect in the title. It only takes one of the parties to be less than competent, or too busy with other matters, to hinder the process, to the intense frustration of all the others. If this is the case, the offending party must be identified and challenged.

It is not unusual for exchange and completion to take place within only a few days of an offer being made and accepted. You may have to pay a premium to your conveyancer to obtain this form of concentrated service but, nonetheless, this speed is possible. It does, however, require good planning, competence and a willingness on the part of yourself and the other parties to move quickly.

SUMMARY

- Prior to purchase, set a realistic budget for the potential new property that includes all the expenses involved in a purchase and a contingency sum for unexpected costs.

- Investigate and prepare any conveyancer and bank or building society before looking for a property so that they are enabled to act quickly if necessary.

- Be proactive about coordinating the purchase – do not leave everything to the estate agent or conveyancer.

- Wherever possible, particularly if the property is old, obtain a full structural survey.

- Check the details of the mortgage offer before accepting it, to ensure that any conditions are not too onerous.

- Understand the legal process of purchase and ensure that your conveyancer acts promptly or has valid reasons for any delays.

- Monitor the purchase process from the offer to completion, and do not be afraid to challenge any of the parties or professionals involved, to establish clearly what they are doing.

2

Selling your Property

SELLING a property is always a traumatic experience, made all the worse because, unlike buying a property, you have very little control over the process.

There are a number of actions that you can take to minimize the problems inherent in any sale, however, not the least of which is to understand the options open to you, and the actual process of sale. This can allow you to speed up a sale, or at least to recognize when a buyer is unlikely to go ahead, or your property has been undervalued.

A sale can be broken down into five stages:

- Preparation
- The Valuation of the Property
- The Estate Agent
- Negotiation with the Purchaser
- The Legal Process

PREPARATION

The Property

Before trying to sell, first attend to the actual property itself, to ensure that it looks as good as possible. This may seem obvious but, surprisingly, it is not always done. Despite the fact that a property's true value has nothing to do with its contents or their arrangement, even professional estate agents will be influenced by the way a property looks and feels.

People looking for a home buy because they 'fall in love' with a place, or because it has a 'warm and welcoming atmosphere'. You must therefore aim, before putting your property up for sale, to create a desirable feel to the property. In effect, the property should be dressed almost like a theatrical set. Never show your property to any valuer or buyer unless it is in the right condition. This can be particularly important when there are children around, who can transform a tidy, harmonious house into a place of chaos.

As an absolute priority, your property must be clean and tidy, with no cluttered work surfaces, unwashed dishes, unmade beds, piles of washing or scattered clothing. Special attention should be paid to sinks, baths and lavatories, so that they both look and smell clean. Carpets should be hoovered, and loose toys and the like stored well away. Furniture, regardless of how old and battered it is, should be dusted and cleared of unnecessary clutter.

In set-dressing the property, aim to make the house look bright and airy, and the rooms appear larger than they actually are. Wherever there are unsightly or odd aspects to the house, whether inside or out, try to conceal them with plants, or make them into an unusual but desirable feature. If the property is too full of furniture and ornaments, this will make it seem smaller. Store these excess pieces elsewhere, or remove them altogether. Simple cleaning of windows and net curtains can make a tremendous difference to the lightness of the property.

The property should be warm, although not insufferably so, and if there is an open fire, then this should be lit. It is something that most people find attractive and appealing. It is also worth going to some expense in buying plants and indoor shrubs, which tend to give an impression of care and natural brightness – so long as they are well maintained. Avoid having the television on, and in place of it choose quiet, unimposing music.

If the property has a garden, this should be reasonably well maintained; bare, weeded beds are far preferable to untended areas of overgrown, neglected plants and decaying seeded flowers. The lawn should be cut and edged neatly, and washing should not be left out to dry.

In effect, emphasize the good points of the property, while steering a buyer away from eyesores. Wherever you can, opt for blandness in any choice of colours or decoration, so as not to impose your taste on someone else. At worst, any buyer should leave the property thinking that it offers lots of 'possibilities', rather than endless work to make the property reasonably habitable.

Try to make sure that, at least superficially, the fabric of the property looks sound. Touch up the exterior decoration if it looks tired, even if this just means putting an extra coat on existing paintwork. Internally, it really does make a difference when knocked, bare patches of woodwork are painted, and doors, skirtings and architraves are at least washed down. A sugar soap is effective, and can restore grimy woodwork to its former self. More importantly, the effect throughout the house should be a feeling of cleanliness and brightness and an impression that the property has been cared for.

Go through the house making minor repairs, such as ensuring that loose door knobs are secure, that doors to cupboards open and close properly, taps are not dripping, and collapsing shelves are repaired. All these may be small details, but they will contribute to the overall impression of the property.

Conveyancers and your Lender

If possible, advise the conveyancer who originally did the conveyancing when you bought your property that it is about to be placed on the market. This enables him to have any previous records which he may have kept, relating to the property, brought out of the archives ready for draft documentation to be prepared, should a sale go ahead speedily. If a different conveyancer is being instructed, then he will have to request that the documentation be sent to him. At this stage, obtain a quote from your conveyancer for the cost of the fees and disbursements involved in the sale (a rough average cost of the conveyance for a £60,000 property, would be around £350).

Importantly, if your conveyancer uses the **Trans Action Protocol (the protocol)** then he will send a **seller's property and information form** for you to complete and return to him. The protocol is a streamlining process, designed by the Law Society, that most conveyancers now operate. It allows your conveyancer, when an offer has been made and accepted, quickly to deliver a single core package of documentation regarding your property to the buyer's conveyancer. This, in effect, kick-starts the legal process, and avoids much of the old inefficient procedure of exchanging information in dribs and drabs. The buyer's conveyancer can, in turn, assess the property straight away, raising only particular rather than general inquiries.

Contact your lender or financial adviser to obtain a rough estimate of a redemption figure for your outstanding mortgage. This will tell you how much money you may have left once the property has been sold, and any other financial implications that may be caused by the sale.

General

Collate and place into a neatly paginated ring file copies of any documentation relevant to the property and give it to your estate agent, so that he can show it to any buyer. Keep the originals for your own reference.

Useful documentation includes such things as:

- damp-proof and woodworm warranties,
- certificates of completion from the Local Authority Building Control (see Chapter 14: Building Regulations and Building Control),
- specifications and completion certificates from any engineers who may have supervised work on the property,
- receipted invoices for new roofing,
- warranties for new boilers, and
- receipted bills for decorating etc.

In a separate part of the file have bills for the costs of services such as gas, electricity, water, sewage and council tax. Any buyer is bound to want to know the running costs of the property.

Take decisions as to what to do with some of the fittings, such as carpets and curtains. If you intend to sell these with the property, they should also be listed.

Finally, make a note of any matters to which you would personally have to attend, should the property be sold. These are things like advising the Post Office of your change of address and terminating contracts with all the utility services and the telephone company. Explore the costs of removals companies, and find out how much notice they require.

THE VALUATION OF THE PROPERTY

An accurate valuation of your property is essential and should be done as soon as you start to think about selling.

Often, it is only once a precise value has been ascertained, that you can plan what you can afford in the future, and thus make a decision about any proposed move. Indeed, the valuation may well persuade you not to sell for some time. This may be the case if you have negative equity in the property, in which event you may choose to wait for your property to go up in price before putting it on the market.

As the price for which the property is to be sold is so important, ensure that you obtain valuations from two or three estate agents. This will not cost anything; valuations are normally free as part of an estate agency's marketing function. The various valuations should be close, but if there are variations, then take the average value, unless the agent providing the highest estimate can amply justify his reasons.

Estate agents normally pride themselves on their ability to be precise about their valuations. On properties under £100,000, they will probably be accurate to within a couple of thousand pounds of the true sale price. Their valuations tend to be produced by a combination of gut feeling and knowledge of the local market, backed up by the prices fetched by comparable properties recently sold. Estate agents are really the only people around who know the true price for which properties have been selling – as opposed to the advertised price of properties placed on the market.

There are two areas of controversy with regard to valuations, and they concern the value that an owner believes his property is worth as opposed to the reality, and the potential for an agent to value a property too low in order to obtain a quick sale. Almost invariably, people tend to value their property higher than its true market price. This is partly instinctive, and partly because their only guidelines are the advertised prices of other properties – which may well have sold for less than the prices shown. Agents rarely underprice properties, as they are aware that the seller will generally get more than one opinion and is unlikely to place a property with an agent who has provided a low valuation.

There is only one thing that will prove the accuracy of the valuation, given the reality of the existing market, and this is the number of people who come to view the property within the first couple of weeks of its being placed on the market.

If very few people come, unless your property has some particular peculiarity such as a bad location, or unique features that may appeal to only very individual buyers, then this is an indicator that it has probably been priced too high. Obviously, if several offers to buy are put forward in the first few weeks of the property being on the market, then this may indicate that the property has been priced too low. It may also indicate, however, that it has been priced correctly – so take care not to assume automatically that the price is wrong.

Except in Scotland (see Appendix 1: Buying and Selling Property in

Scotland), you can keep changing your acceptance of any offers, right up until exchange of contracts.

This is certainly an immoral way of getting the highest price for your property, but at the moment is still legal – and to a degree it protects you against an undervaluation.

THE ESTATE AGENT

Estate agents tend to have as bad a reputation amongst the general population as builders. There are the same accusations made about overcharging for the amount of work that they do, and their handling of contracts is often alleged to be erratic and inconsistent. Worse still, many people doubt their integrity, in view of the inevitable conflict of interest that occurs when an agent is selling their property, while trying to close business with the buyer with regard to financial services. This may leave sellers unsure of whose interest the agent is actually promoting.

Exercise care in your dealings with estate agents, to ensure that you get the best service. To do this you must be proactive. That said, any seller should appreciate that the work of an estate agent is often thankless – and can be extremely stressful.

Before you choose a specific estate agent, you should be aware of the general modes of operation and legal duties of all agents.

Types of Agreement for the Sale of a Property

There is a choice of three main agreements for estate agents to sell a property. All of them, by law, should be in written form, and signed by both parties. However, these agreements can be varied, and you can insert clauses to ensure that the agent is expressly bound to comply with any requirements that you want (so long as he also agrees).

Sole Selling Rights

This agreement provides for the estate agents to charge a commission on the sale of a property, regardless of whether or not they have been responsible for introducing the person who subsequently buys your house. So, for example, once this agreement is made, it would be binding even if your sister, living in Hong Kong, decided she wanted to buy your property – notwithstanding that she had no idea the property was with estate agents. This form of agreement is now rarely used – for obvious reasons.

Sole Agency

This is an agreement signed between you and the agent giving the agent sole rights to sell the property for a defined period of time, normally 12 weeks. During this period you can decide not to sell your property, and thereby remove it from the agent. You cannot, however, without the express leave of the agent, then decide to sell and place the revitalized sale in the hands of another agent within the duration of the original agreement. The commission varies, but is normally about 2% (plus VAT) of the sale price.

Multiple Agency

This is an agreement made between you and the agent which allows you to place the sale in the hands of other agents at the same time. Whichever agent succeeds in selling the property will receive the full commission payment, leaving the other agents unpaid, regardless of the work they have done.

The commission is normally higher than that of sole agency, and is around 2.5% or 3% (plus VAT) of the purchase price.

Duties of an Estate Agent

By law all estate agents must:

- advise you in writing of the details of their fees and any other charges;
- specify the terms of business, i.e. whether the agreement is for sole agency, multiple agency, etc;
- detail to you any services that they, or connected people can offer to buyers, such as financial services, removals, etc.;
- advise you, promptly and in writing, of all offers made on your property, regardless of the progress of other negotiations;
- inform you when they are involved in any way in providing any services to the buyer, i.e. mortgages, insurance, etc.;
- avoid any bias between buyers, particularly those not using the agent's financial services;
- not mislead either a buyer or seller as to offers made or the status or existence of other buyers; and
- pay interest on any deposit made over £500 where the interest exceeds £10.

If your estate agent is in breach of any of the above then you should report him to the Director General of Fair Trading or to your Local Authority Trading Standards Department. At worst, the agent can be prohibited from practising.

Choosing your Estate Agent

As a general rule a good agent will be one that is busy and gives every appearance of being successful. So, look around your area, and find out which company has the most 'For Sale' boards on display. This will normally indicate the size of market that an estate agent has, in comparison with his competitors. The location of the office should also be assessed, both to indicate the relative success of the agent and to see how much passing traffic, preferably pedestrian, it attracts. It is a good sign if the agent's office is located near, or by, other agents. This means that people will be attracted to the location for its facility to offer a large number of properties for sale between the various agents.

Unfortunately, in some respects, well-known chains of estate agents do have a distinct advantage over single-branch operations. Their branches will often quite comprehensively cover a large area, and the branches themselves will sponsor leads that a smaller agency would not obtain. Indeed, a chain of agents is rather like having a multiple-agency deal from the outset. The staff of a large chain are also subject to considerable pressure to meet their sales targets, and a great deal of time and effort is taken in their training and organized bonus systems. The larger chains also have the advantage that they are normally better funded and are therefore able to afford constant mailing of details and can obtain good advertising rates, allowing them to advertise more than smaller operations. Potential buyers can also feel more comfortable and secure when they are dealing with a recognized corporate name. This can also be important when the financing of any purchase is required; the bigger chains tend to have a very slick and organized operation offering financial services.

This is not to say that smaller agents are unable to offer a better personal service, which clearly does have a value. The key aspect to trying to sell a property, however, is letting the maximum possible number of people, over the widest possible area, know that your property is for sale, and at the right price.

Working with the Agent for Mutual Benefit

It is essential that the agent you choose tries enthusiastically and conscientiously to sell your particular property, and that it does not just become one of many on the agency's books. It is also vital that you and the agent agree, right from the start, how the property is going to be marketed, and that the terms of this individual agreement are placed in writing.

Obtain a specific written agreement as to how the property is to be marketed. The core features of any marketing of a property are:

- The size and positioning of the property details to be displayed in the agent's shop front, and the length of time they will remain. This is a critical part of the marketing, and you must make sure that your property is displayed well for an agreed period of time.

- The type, extent and frequency of newspaper advertising and the specifics of which newspaper(s) will be used.

- The number of times the property will be included in mailing lists, and their regularity (some agents will send out a mailing list weekly).

- The arrangement for a negotiator to attend a property with a prospective buyer. Will this always occur, or only when you are not at the house? A professional salesperson should be able to sell a property better than you.

- The number and location of other branches that will be selling the property. The more branches that have the details, and are involved in the sale, the better.

- The name of the negotiator who will be primarily responsible for the relationship between you and the agents.

- The facility of the agent to obtain financing for any potential buyer. You should know whether there is a finance consultant within the office and, if not, what arrangements the agent has to ensure this facility is easily available.

- The incentive commission payable to the negotiator.

The best way that you can ensure individual attention to your property – provided this is acceptable to the manager of the agency – is to offer a sum of money to the negotiator who actually sells the property. This should be above and beyond what is paid by you to the agency, as part of the sale agreement. So, in effect, the individual negotiator would receive a bonus directly from you. If you choose to do this then you must do it openly – and through the manager of the agency. This ensures that all the staff of the office and other branches are aware of the bonus, which would be paid legitimately, through the employee's pay packet. It is in your interest that the opportunity of earning the bonus is available to all the negotiators.

The normal bonus on top of salary that a negotiator would expect to earn in selling a property for the agency would be around 2% to 5% of the agency's fee of, say, 2% of the selling price. In other words, a negotiator would receive about £40–100 on top of his salary for selling a £100,000 house.

It is not hard to see the incentive to a negotiator of an added bonus of a couple of hundred pounds or more. This will ensure much greater attention to your property, and possibly greater competitiveness amongst the agency staff. If you do offer a negotiator's fee it is worth agreeing it on the basis of the property being sold at or above a stated price. So, you may have had valuations setting the price of your property at £100,000. You could agree that the negotiator's fee would be 5% of any sum obtained over, say, £95,000. The negotiator would then receive £250 if the property sold for £100,000 – a significant bonus.

As with most aspects of life, agents tend to respond to people they like, and with whom they get on. If he likes you, a negotiator may attend to your property more than another. So it may well be worth showing appreciation for the efforts being made by a negotiator or the office manager, perhaps even bringing into the office a bottle of wine, or flowers, before a sale has been agreed. This small gesture could just make a difference to the effort, or priority, that is given to selling your property. Anything legitimate that will give you an edge is well worth pursuing.

Agency Commission

While you may be understandably reluctant to pay the full agents' commission, be cautious about trying to agree a reduction which may lessen the incentive of the office manager and staff to sell the property. At the end of the day they will have financial targets to achieve, and they will always try to sell the property that will produce the greatest profit. However small the drop in commission, it may be sufficient for a negotiator to press harder to sell a property where the full commission is payable.

Furthermore, any branch that sells the property of another branch will generally only be credited with half of the total commission chargeable. So, if the commission is 2%, then the other branch of the agency will only be able to claim 1% as a contribution to their financial targets. If the 2% is negotiated down to, say, 1.5% or less, then the percentage profit is barely worth any effort on the part of the staff of the other branch.

Checking Up on the Agent

Check up on the agent to see that the property is being marketed according to the agreement made. This checking is something that agents, with some justification, hate. If it is not done, however, then you will be relying on trust alone, which is not necessarily sufficient, when as much is at stake as the selling of your property – possibly the biggest financial deal you will personally ever do.

You must check that the property is advertised in the way agreed, and that the details are displayed in the window of the office. Also check that the property is being promoted in the mailing lists, and by the negotiators.

Make sure that, on occasions, friends go into the agency to ask for details on properties matching roughly the description of yours. A couple of friends should also go on the mailing list of the agency, and perhaps one of the branches, to see that the property is being promoted frequently and well. If it is not, then immediately draw this to the attention of the branch manager first, and then, if still unsatisfied, the area director of the agency.

If the agency is clearly in breach of the agreement made to market the property, then terminate the contract with the agency and find another to sell the property. You must, however, be certain that the breach is sufficiently serious to justify this action.

NEGOTIATION WITH THE PURCHASER

Between 40% and 50% of all offers for property made by a buyer and accepted by a seller break down before the actual sale is completed.

This makes the work of an estate agent stressful, heart-breaking and difficult, with the negotiation period being a time of great concern for all. While obviously for you the collapse of a sale is devastating, it is also very bad news for the agent, as it usually represents the loss of all earnings from the sale. Accordingly, once agents have a chance to negotiate a sale they automatically do everything possible to make sure that it goes ahead. It is at this time that an experienced, motivated negotiator, with perhaps a competent financial consultancy back-up, comes into his own in finding ways of keeping the sale alive.

The biggest problems that negotiators have, revolve around the financing of the deal, and any obstructive chain of properties that may have built up around the sale. They also have to deal with people who are invariably highly emotionally charged. Frequently sales fall through because the buyer or seller is unable to take the stress involved in the transaction.

Financing the Purchase

Generally, the financing of the purchase is not something with which you as the seller can get involved, apart from finding out, when an offer is put to you, as much as you can about the current financial status of the buyer. This is always important, and any offer must be carefully looked at with this in mind.

If an offer is made, and the buyer has not yet sold his own property, then, unless he has finance above and beyond his existing property, the offer is unlikely to be of great value. If, on the other hand, he is a 'cash buyer', then this could present the best and quickest sale that you are likely to obtain, and may be one for which a reduction in price is worthwhile.

Most sales, however, are reliant on the buyer obtaining some external financing, normally a mortgage, which can take time to arrange and is, of course, dependent on the buyer's earnings and credit status and on the value of the property itself. These offers are normally a fairly good risk, so long as the buyer has not been too optimistic about the finance that he will be able to raise. This is something your agent may be able to find out.

It is in the area of finance that the estate agent's greatest potential conflict of interest is likely to take place. The agent may well find that in his eagerness to ensure that the agency gets a return on any financing deal arranged for the buyer, he will lose sight of the fact that you are his primary client. Alternatively, the buyer who arranges finance through the agency may well be given preference over another potential purchaser with a mortgage arranged elsewhere. It is in this area that your conveyancer needs to be proactive, establishing the exact situation and the likely delay before the finance is raised.

Agents do have a very real interest in the money that is made in financing property deals, both in terms of the mortgage and other ancillary matters, such as insurance and even pensions. Indeed, if sellers look behind the big chains of estate agents, they will find that most are either owned by, or linked to, large financial institutions. These institutions are interested in estate agency chiefly because it gives them the opportunity to exploit the financial possibilities that open up once people are in the process of buying and selling property. The agents are a vital link in this process and most agents are under intense pressure from the financial institutions to which they are connected, to deliver potential clients – particularly, of course, first-time buyers.

Property Chains

The biggest single problem continually encountered in the selling and buying of properties is the property chain. These are constant obstacles to the progress of property transactions, and the despair of agents, buyers, conveyancers and sellers alike. They can create considerable delays that are unresolvable until the one sale that is the prime obstacle within the chain finally goes ahead.

Property chains develop when a buyer is unable to exchange contracts until he has sold his own property. He may be unable to complete the sale of his own property because his buyer is, in turn, awaiting a buyer to complete on his own sale. Without the actual sale of their own property, most buyers cannot raise the necessary finance to exchange contracts on their intended purchase, notwithstanding that they may be absolutely ready to exchange contracts in every other regard – with their mortgage offer in place and all necessary legal contracts drawn up.

Property chains can be as short as one property, or of considerable length, extending to half a dozen properties or more, perhaps descending in value to the first-time purchase of a small flat. The complications are obvious, difficult to resolve and can result in the collapse of a complete chain, should any one buyer pull out of a sale. It is not unknown for one buyer, if he has the funds, to buy the property that is holding up the chain, simply to ensure that the rest of the chain can complete their sales – thereby allowing his own sale to proceed.

Sale by Tender

Sometimes there may be several potential buyers for a single property, each one placing a higher offer than the last. In this case an agent may suggest that the property become subject to a formal tender, so that a final conclusion will be reached as to which offer is to be accepted. This can be a useful and decisive way of bringing the negotiation period to a close.

If it is decided that your property is to be sold in this way, then all the potential buyers will be required to notify you of their final best offer in a sealed envelope, to be opened at a specific time and date. A deposit cheque for an agreed sum may also have to be enclosed with the offer. The opening of the sealed bids will normally be done in your solicitor's office, to ensure absolute integrity.

The offer accepted will normally be the highest bid; the deposit cheques of the other bidders will be returned to them. While your acceptance is not legally binding upon you until exchange of contracts, it is probably the fairest way of dealing with a potential 'gazumping' situation.

If the negotiations on a sale appear to be bogged down, or you are unable to satisfy yourself about the position with the agent or your conveyancer, then do not shy away from contacting the buyer directly. This is not something that either the agent or the conveyancer will like, but it can frequently help to get the negotiations back on track again.

Sometimes a buyer will simply not understand the process, and will perhaps not be pushing his own conveyancer or lender hard enough, or a misunderstanding may have occurred that neither you nor the buyer intended. It may be something that you can sort out directly between yourselves. You must be careful, however, not to affect adversely your agent's negotiations.

THE LEGAL PROCESS
(except Scotland; see Appendix 1)

For the most part, the work of your conveyancer is reactive rather than proactive. After the initial work of receiving your instructions and the sending of documentation to the buyer's conveyancer, there is little that he can effectively do to speed up the sale. Most of his early work will be ensuring that he is aware of any financing problems that the buyer may have, being aware of any chain building up, and generally being efficient in his responses to any queries. This latter point is vital; a lot of time can be wasted if your conveyancer does not respond speedily to the buyer's conveyancer – or if unnecessary delays occur in relaying inquiries from the buyer to you, and back again.

If the sale concerns a simple freehold transaction, then the work of the conveyancer should be reasonably easy and straightforward. If the sale concerns a complicated lease, however, then your conveyancer could find there is rather more work to do.

The legal process, in outline, can be broken down into five stages – although the 'protocol', if used, effectively removes the second stage:

- Production of Draft Documentation
- Answering of Pre-Contract Inquiries
- Approval of Draft Contract
- Exchange of Contracts
- Completion

Production of Draft Documentation

Advise your conveyancer, as soon as possible, of the details of the offer made by the buyer, i.e. the price agreed, the details of the buyer's conveyancers and any other relevant details. Your conveyancer will then produce a draft contract. Although this is usually a pre-printed form, there may be additions and amendments to take into account the wishes of both you and the buyer. At the same time, your conveyancer will enclose any draft documentation available, such as a copy of the lease or the title deeds, if he has them at this stage. If the protocol is used then the information forms will already have been completed and will be sent out at this stage.

If he has not already done so, your conveyancer will apply to your lender for the title deeds and other papers relating to the property, such as a charge certificate (showing the bank/building society's interest in the property) or the land certificate. He will also advise the lender of your intention to sell your property.

Answering of Pre-Contract Inquiries

Pre-contract inquiries sent by the buyer's conveyancer will be replied to directly by your conveyancer, except where there are specific questions that only you can answer. These questions will relate to any information you may have that could affect a buyer's enjoyment of the property, and they must be answered comprehensively. So, for example, if you are aware that the property has been moving due to subsidence, you are obliged by law to advise the buyer. If it can be proved at a later stage, once the property has been sold, that you knew about the movement but did not tell the buyer, then the latter would be able to take legal action against you for damages.

If the protocol is being used, this stage will already have been completed.

Approval of Draft Contract

Both conveyancers will assess the contract and agree any variations or amendments to suit you and your buyer, and ensure the contract is legally sound.

Exchange of Contracts

Once agreement has been reached concerning the contract, the amount of the deposit and the time until completion, then the two conveyancers will agree upon exchange, at which point the contract for sale becomes legally enforceable, and the deposit is paid.

Your conveyancer will now also apply to your lender for a redemption statement, which will show the amount still owed by you to the institution.

Completion

The final process of sale will take place at the moment when your conveyancer receives the remainder of the sale price, on the day and time set for completion.

Once completion has taken place, you have no further right of access to the property.

Your conveyancer will normally send you the remaining money from the sale of the property, less his own fees and disbursements, the money owed to your lender – which will have been sent to them directly – and your estate agent's commission.

You will have been invoiced by your estate agent once exchange took place, but the agent is generally not paid until completion. Normally, with your authority, your conveyancer will deduct the agent's fee from the sale money and send this to him directly.

SUMMARY

- Be proactive throughout the process of sale and understand the functions of all those involved.

- Set-dress the property to make it enticing to any buyer.

- Be realistic about the value of the property in the light of the existing property market, which estate agents will know best.

- Research the estate agents in the area to find out the ones who will be able to market the property to the largest number of people over the widest area.

- Draw up a specific agreement with the agents, itemizing the actual marketing to be undertaken.

- Be prepared to pay a commission to the individual negotiator who sells the property – but make sure this is done officially through the manager of the estate agency.

- Check that the agents are actively marketing the property.

- Ensure that the agents and conveyancer give accurate, up-to-date advice about the negotiations and the status of the buyer and any chain.

- Follow the legal process through step by step. Try to use a conveyancer who will use the protocol and be prepared to pay more for a conveyance you want done very speedily.

- Do not be afraid to speak to the buyer directly if negotiations appear unclear or are bogged down.

- Help your conveyancer to be efficient by answering queries quickly.

3

Auctions

A N auction can be a very efficient means of both buying and selling property.

Auctions tend to suit cash buyers, however, and they can also be used by sellers to off-load onto the market substandard property that would be difficult to sell conventionally. That said, bargains can be picked up, and it is certainly at auctions that developers, and those collecting portfolios of properties, do much of their buying. It is by no means always the case that properties for sale by auction are defective, although the private or inexperienced buyer must exercise some caution.

Property auctions are as price-sensitive as private treaty sales, and prices and demand depend greatly on the current state of the economy. As activity in the property market increases, so also do the prices reached in auctions. The resurgence in the property market in 1996 was reflected directly in auctions where sales were buoyant and properties were selling beyond their 'last marketed price'. Even professional buyers were finding that they were having to pay over the odds for the property they wanted. This was particularly true in London, although by the end of the year prices and demand were also increasing outside the capital.

There tend to be several reasons why a property is sold by auction, rather than by private treaty:

- When a quick sale is required: Depending on the overall state of the economy, most properties placed at auction do sell, so long as not too high a reserve price has been placed on the particular property. Indeed, some auction houses will regularly sell, on an auction day, between 90% and 100% of the properties offered for sale. This is therefore an efficient way of disposing of property – rather than suffering the tortuous negotiations and delays involved in trying to sell by private treaty.

- When a property is difficult to value: Some properties can be inherently difficult to value. They may have unique features, or be one-offs within a local area or of such a nature that an estate agent cannot accurately value them. This is often the case with tracts of land, particularly those being sold as potential building plots.

An auction can effectively concentrate a lot of interest in the saleroom which will, at the end of the day, produce an unarguable market value on a property by the mere fact that it will sell for the highest bid. Sometimes exceptional prices can be obtained.

- When a property may create exceptional interest: On occasions a property, by the very nature of its uniqueness, may excite considerable interest in the market. In this case, estate agents can take the view that the best way of concentrating and controlling the interest is to sell by auction, bringing the buyers together at one time to bid for the property. This can be an effective way of pushing the price up.

- When a property has structural faults or is unmortgageable: If a property is in a very run-down state or has significant structural faults, then it will often be difficult to sell on the private treaty market. Mortgage companies may not regard it as a sure enough security for a loan to an individual. Developers, however, are less likely to be put off by the state of the property, having the knowledge and resources to develop it – subject to buying it at a low enough price. In effect, this is a way of selling the property to a niche market.

- When a property has been repossessed: Banks and building societies are under a duty to sell a property for its best possible price, once a repossession has taken place. The nature of auctions allows them to prove to a court that the property fetched the 'best price on the day' at a fair and open sale. They can further prove to a court that there was a higher degree of advertising and a greater circulation of the property details than most estate agents could ever afford. This prevents protests from a mortgagee that an institution has sold his property at a price that only guarantees a return on their loaned money.
    An added benefit for institutions is that they know they will normally sell on a defined date, rather than having to wait for completion of a private treaty sale.

- When trustees or executors are placed under a duty to sell by auction: Trusts and wills often specify that properties are to be sold by auction, to ensure that properties in an estate or trust are sold promptly and with obvious fairness. This should prevent arguments among the beneficiaries about the way in which a particular property is sold and the price it fetches.

- When a property has not sold under private treaty: If a property has not attracted any interest on the private treaty market and the seller is reluctant to reduce the price further then he may decide to sell the property by auction.

SALE BY AUCTION

If you are considering selling your property by auction you are likely to pay more than if it was sold by private treaty by an estate agent. The auction commission payable is normally around 2.5% (plus VAT) plus a non-returnable marketing fee (**entry fee**) of some £300 (plus VAT).

The entry fee covers the marketing of the property, which will be featured, alongside others for sale, in a glossy catalogue that will be sent out to potential buyers. A good auctioneer will spend all the entry fee on marketing to produce the maximum possible interest in the auction.

Although there is nothing, in theory, to prevent you from selling a property by auction yourself, this is not always either practical or realistic. One of the major problems is marketing the property sufficiently well to attract enough interest. Auctions, obviously, rely on several interested people bidding to push a price up.

In practice, most people will place their property with an auction house that specializes in property sales, or with estate agents who have a dedicated auctioneering department. These organizations have considerable experience in selling properties at auction, and often have auctions running every six weeks or so. They also have the benefit of huge mailing lists of potential buyers, who are circulated each time an auction is due to take place. One auction house spoken to by the writer regularly mails 15,000 to 20,000 people each time an auction is due to be held.

The auction house handling the sale will also extensively advertise the auction through national, regional, local and trade papers. This is vastly greater coverage than property sold by most estate agents would ever obtain.

The process of selling by auction is as follows:

Choosing the Estate Agent

First check that the estate agent you choose to handle your sale has a dedicated auctioneering department. This department will then handle the sale of the property, taking it out of the hands of the local branch. The branch will only remain responsible for showing buyers around the property and liaising with the auctioneers should any pre-auction bids be made.

The auction department will be responsible for producing details of your property, which will be much less detailed than for a private treaty sale. There will be a very basic description of the property, the tenure, details of your conveyancer, the viewing agents and, in some cases, a **guide price**. Any further details can be obtained from the local agents.

Agreement with the Auctioneers

As the seller you will sign a specific sole agency agreement which will provide for the property to be sold at auction to the highest bidder (subject to a reserve price). The agreement will also state the commission payable, normally 2.5%, and specify a non-refundable and mandatory entry fee to cover the costs of advertising the property for sale.

The agreement will require you to state a guide price for the property. This is generally the lowest price you might accept prior to the actual auction. Effectively it is a floor-level figure that the auctioneer hopes to better during bidding on the day of the auction. It is different from the reserve price – the figure below which the property will not be sold – which is normally decided a week before the auction and remains confidential between you and the auctioneer.

You should check the **general conditions of sale**. These are applicable to all the property at the auction and define how the auction will be run. The most important term for you, as the seller, is the time stipulated for completion. This is either 20 working days or 28 calendar days (depending upon the auction house) from a successful bid – which gives you little time to vacate the property if you are still living in it.

The general conditions of sale should not be confused with the **special conditions of sale**. The latter relate only to your individual property, while the former govern the rules of the auction as a whole.

Finally, you will be obliged to supply the auction house with a **legal package** which can be shown to potential buyers, together with the details of your conveyancer.

The Legal Package

The legal package, produced by your conveyancer, effectively provides a buyer with all the relevant information on your property. There are three components:

Special Conditions of Sale

These conditions will form part of the contract of sale. They will be expressly drawn up by your conveyancer and will relate purely to your particular property.

Search on the Property

Your conveyancer must conduct a local search of your property. The costs involved in the preparation of the local search are recoverable from any buyer of your property, who will be expected to pay for this on top of the agreed purchase price. The cost is normally around £100–150 depending on how the search is carried out.

Legal Information

This will comprise the deeds to your property showing to a buyer the **root of title** – that is, the history of the previous ownership of the property – and any existing charges on your property. Any other pertinent legal information will also be revealed.

Access Prior to the Auction

You must allow access to your property by interested buyers who may need to see it physically. Surveys may also be required, and buyers using a bank or building society for their finance will need access to allow for the preparation of a valuation report. This access can either be arranged through a local branch of the estate agent's department selling the property, or by your stating a defined time and day when you will be available to let people into your property.

The Legal Process

The critical difference in the process between a sale by auction and that made by private treaty is the stage at which exchange of contracts occurs (i.e. when the contract of sale becomes enforceable). In a sale by auction, the actual sale of the property occurs at the moment when the auctioneer accepts the highest price of the property equal to or above the reserve).

In effect, the moment the auctioneer's hammer drops, the contract to buy is made and the deposit for the property becomes payable. Actual completion of the sale, when the buyer gains full access and possession of your property, does not occur until either 20 working days or 28 calendar days later, depending on the conditions of sale.

The implications of this are twofold. Firstly, you must ensure that your conveyancer has produced the legal package well before the auction, to allow buyers properly to inspect the legal aspects of your property. In effect, the normal negotiation and assessment phase of a private treaty sale is concertinaed into this package of the formal documentation of the property.

Secondly, the actual exchange of contracts occurs on a predefined date, at a defined time – so long as a bid is placed at or over the reserve price. Instead of having to negotiate with the buyer as to the date for exchange, this is fixed and definite. Likewise, the date for completion will have been predetermined. The deposit payable is also detailed in the general conditions of sale – although this can be amended in the special conditions. Normally the deposit would be 10% of the purchase price or £1,000, whichever is the higher, and must be paid as soon as the bid is accepted.

Your conveyancer's work is therefore relatively straightforward and mainly comprises the collating of the legal information, the accurate drafting of the special conditions of sale and the settling of any charge, such as your mortgage. Your conveyancer also needs to be available should any buyers raise queries on the legalities of the property.

The Auction

The auction will take place at a properly publicized time and date, thus allowing buyers to know how long they have to assess your property.

Before the auction, buyers can file bids for the property, with the auction house. These bids must, by law, be referred to the seller by the auctioneers, and you can choose to accept one of these bids. In this case, the bid will be accepted on the basis of an immediate exchange – as if the property had been auctioned

– or on condition that contracts are exchanged at least 24 hours or so before the auction. In the meantime, the property will still be actively marketed by the auctioneers. You will still have to pay the agreed auction commission and will be unable to reclaim the marketing fee that you have already paid. Nonetheless, this can save you the stress of waiting until the auction to sell – when you will have no real idea beforehand of what price the property may actually fetch.

It is not necessary for any potential buyer to attend an auction in person. Bids made by telephone, post or fax are acceptable, so long as the bidder has an agent at the auction who can provide the deposit price on the day, and sign the **memorandum of sale**. Frequently, this will be undertaken by the auction house itself acting under written instructions from a buyer. In this event a member of the auction house staff will bid for the property up to the bidder's specified maximum amount. If this bid is successful then a memorandum of sale will be signed on behalf of the buyer and the previously lodged deposit paid to you.

If your property does not sell at the auction then buyers can approach the auctioneer or his staff to place a **conditional offer**. In this case the auctioneers would get the interested buyer to sign the formal memorandum of sale and pay a 10% deposit. This gives you the option to accept the offer and for it then to be binding. If you do not accept the conditional offer then the auctioneers will return the deposit to the unlucky bidder. Once again, by law, the auction house has to advise you of any offers made.

A distinct advantage of auctions over private treaty sales is therefore that the process of sale, while identical legally to that of a private treaty sale, is done very quickly. There are no tortuous negotiations or delays caused by complex chains of property. A buyer is provided with the details of the property and the date of the sale (the auction). He is either ready and able to buy – or not. There are no delaying tactics that he can employ to prevent the sale taking place. This is obviously of great value to you.

If the property does not sell at the auction then you lose your non-refundable deposit to the auction house but you do not, obviously, have to pay any commission to the agents. You will be left having to pay your conveyancer's costs, but as the work done would have to be undertaken in any sale process, this is not money completely wasted.

PURCHASE BY AUCTION

There are three main problems in buying property at auction:

- Paying more for a property than you can afford: This can occur when you get carried away during the bidding and lose sight of how much you can actually afford to spend.

    It is absolutely critical that, prior to the auction, you set a figure above which you cannot buy. This must be a clearly defined sum and one that you are not tempted to exceed.

- Potential waste of money: This will occur when a desired property is sold to another, higher bidder.

  This is particularly the case when you have to rely on some form of financing, such as a mortgage, to buy the property. If you fail to buy a given property you can find that you have expended quite a lot of money to no avail – the costs of a valuation survey, possibly a full structural survey, and conveyancer's costs. There is also the wasted time. You will doubtless have attended the property a couple of times and had a number of meetings with your lender and conveyancer.

- Time shortage: You must be prepared to act, and make a decision, quickly – so as to be ready for the auction. There really is not a great deal of time between the receipt of an auction catalogue and the auction itself – perhaps six weeks. This is ample for a professional developer or an experienced auction buyer, but does mean that you have to act promptly, particularly if a mortgage is needed for the purchase.

  As a buyer you must ensure that you know all about the property that you intend to buy. Once the auctioneer's hammer drops you cannot cancel your bid because of some factor that you find out subsequently.

If you have not bought at an auction before, then do a dry run. Place yourself on the mailing lists of some auction houses so that they advise you of auction dates and send the appropriate auction catalogues. You should then attend at least one of these auctions to familiarize yourself with the process.

At least one major auction house (Hambro Countrywide Property Auctions) holds seminars for inexperienced people. These seminars are specifically designed to explain the auction process and are well worth attending. Some auction houses will also send out free guides to auctions – which are also of considerable help.

Assess carefully the sales made at the auctions that you attend. This can be of some value, although many of the auctions will be selling properties of all sorts, from different areas, none of which may quite equate with the type and location you want. Nonetheless, you should be able to obtain a fairly good idea of pricing, availability and the standard of property being placed on the market.

Once you have made a decision to purchase by auction then go through the normal purchase preparation of finding a conveyancer. If you need financing then you must also find a lender and establish what they will lend to you in principle. Ensure that any institution prepared to fund a purchase understands that you will be buying at an auction and that therefore any valuation survey and mortgage offer needs to be undertaken quickly.

It is absolutely essential that your lender specifically makes you a mortgage offer on the particular property that you want, prior to the auction. You must then make certain that the offer and your own finances do not exceed the amount for which you bid at the auction.

If you do find a property that you want, look carefully at the catalogue details and then apply for any further information that the auction house may have. The sooner you obtain the legal pack on the house the better, so that you can pass this on to your conveyancer to establish whether or not there are any apparent legal defects or anomalies.

It is astonishing how many people do not obtain the legal package for assessment by their conveyancer prior to the auction. This is critical, as only a practised professional has the expertise required to check the documentation properly. You must never take for granted the title and tenure of a property, nor assume that there are no restrictions or covenants affecting the building.

Be aware that the property may be sold before auction. It is therefore advisable to register your interest in the property with the auctioneers as soon as possible. They should then contact you if their clients decide to accept an offer prior to the auction – if only to ensure that they are obtaining the highest offer possible.

Generally, it is well worth obtaining a full structural survey on any property that you want to buy. It should not be forgotten that auctions really are, with exceptions, the places used to offload problem properties. With this in mind, take great care to check whether there are any innate problems. Also try to find out why the property is being sold at auction, even if this means talking to some neighbours who may know the truth. It may well be that the property suffers from structural defects, or there may be particular problems associated with the local area, perhaps a notorious pub, for example, that make the property difficult to sell.

It is always wise to inspect the property you are interested in on the day of the auction or the day before, to check that as far as possible it is in the same condition as when you previously inspected it. Specifically check that it is still vacant and has not been squatted in. If you do find any alteration to the condition, or if the property is suddenly no longer vacant, contact the auctioneers immediately.

On the day of the auction be prepared for the fact that if you bid for the property then this is completely committing. If your bid is successful you will have to pay the deposit and sign a memorandum of sale as soon as your bid has been accepted. The remaining money must then be found by the time of completion – normally 20 working days or possibly 28 calendar days.

During the bidding ensure that you are noticed by the auctioneer. Generally, this is not a problem, but make sure that your gestures or signs to the auctioneer are reasonably obvious or, if it is to be done secretively, that your signs are made known to the auctioneer prior to the bidding. Often the best way of drawing the auctioneer's attention is to make your first bid as soon as the sale starts.

If for some reason you do not want to, or cannot, attend the auction then you can bid by proxy. In this case you must sign an authorization to the auction house to bid for you either by telephone or by proxy. The authorization will instruct the auction house to bid up to a certain defined amount (if by proxy) and, whether by telephone or proxy, will authorize the auctioneer to sign the binding memorandum of sale, should your bid be successful.

You will have to send to the auctioneers, prior to the auction, £1,000 or

10% of your maximum purchase price – whichever is the greater. This will form the deposit on any successful bid.

Bidding by proxy can be a useful way of bidding. It avoids the potentially wasted time of attending an unsuccessful sale, and can be used as a discipline to prevent yourself getting carried away and bidding for more than you can afford.

At the time the bid is accepted you become liable for insuring the property, so prior to the auction it is important to arrange insurance at least in principle. Be aware, however, that many domestic insurance companies will not insure you when the property concerned is unoccupied or has vacant possession on the auction date. Their concern will be with the potential for vandalism, squatting, etc. prior to completion. Most auction houses will be able to provide short-term insurance policies on the day of the auction and this is something that is worth exploring beforehand.

If, for some reason, you do not complete on the property then you will be liable for breach of contract and can be sued by the seller. He will be able to claim against you for the difference between your bid and the amount that he subsequently obtained in selling the property. You would also be liable for all the seller's additional expenses.

SUMMARY

- Auctions can be an efficient way of disposing of property quickly and can yield real bargains.

- Property sold at auctions is as price-sensitive as that sold by private treaty. If the market is active and rising, the price of property may actually exceed that of a private treaty sale.

- If the property is sold at auction the seller has, normally, only 20 working days or 28 calendar days to vacate the property.

- Caution should be exercised when buying at auction, as there is normally a specific reason why a property is being auctioned, and this may be due to an inherent fault of some kind.

- A thorough survey and check of all the available details should be undertaken prior to bidding for a property.

- Any financing, such as a mortgage, must be in place for the day of the auction.

- Ensure that any budget is not exceeded during the excitement of bidding.

- Remember that the deposit, normally 10%, is payable on the day of the auction.

- The contract of sale is enforceable the moment the highest bid is accepted.

4

Mortgages

BUYING a property represents the single biggest financial decision you are likely to make, and invariably requires the frightening prospect of borrowing substantial amounts of money – to be paid off over a long period.

Effectively, you can end up with a commitment that will take you most of your working life to settle. It is therefore critical that you make the right choices when arranging this finance, to ensure that you are getting the best possible deal – and one that suits you as an individual.

Up until the past ten years or so, financing the purchase of your property was a relatively simple and clear process. There were few real options available. The market for mortgages and loans on property has expanded massively, however (particularly the market for remortgaging), allowing you the opportunity to shop around for what suits you best. Up to a point, you can now design the package that you want, and negotiate with a lending institution to provide this.

The area of home finance is a minefield of different companies and individuals, all making money out of your borrowing requirements. It is vital that you are careful, and set aside time to research your mortgage options properly. It is all too easy to react in a panic, during the stress of buying a property, and accept the first mortgage made available to you. Often this will be from a potentially biased source, such as your bank, or perhaps a broker within your estate agents, linked to one particular lending institution. In this case, you are unlikely to receive impartial advice about all the options available to you on the market. Subsequently you can find yourself locked into a deal that has not necessarily benefited you, but may be all too profitable for the lender or the broker that advised you. This can leave a sour taste in the mouth, to say the least.

WHAT IS A MORTGAGE?

A mortgage is essentially a long-term loan of money, upon which interest is charged, using a property as security.

The interest charged on the loan is worked out by lending institutions in accordance with the Bank of England's interest rate – which varies up and down, depending on the economy. The basic rate of interest you will be charged is normally around 1.25% above the Bank of England's rate. So, if the

Bank of England has set interest rates at 6%, you are likely to pay interest of approximately 7.25% on a standard variable-rate mortgage.

The actual structure of mortgages varies considerably in almost every respect, and it is essential that you choose the right structure for your needs. There are tax implications in taking out a mortgage, and the payments that you make can be vastly different, depending upon the type of mortgage you have. You may also find that you have been advised to take any number of 'tie-ins', that you may not need or want, from your particular lender – such as indemnity policies, mortgage protection insurances, buildings and contents insurance and so on.

Mortgages are now provided by a number of institutions including banks, building societies, insurance companies and centralized lenders. As a rule, you no longer have to have had any prior relationship, such as an account, with any of these lenders. The mortgage will be sold as a distinct financial package, dependent on your income and financial means.

PREPARATION

Before deciding on a mortgage, or seeing a building society, bank or registered broker, assess exactly what you need, what you can afford and what your aims are for the future. The latter point is of particular importance as most people, especially when young, are very mobile. There is nothing unusual about moving house every five years or so – and for some, much more often. If you think you are likely to move frequently, then a medium- or long-term fixed-rate mortgage, for example, would be entirely inappropriate and could actually cost you money through **redemption penalties**. (These are charges made by a lender in the event of your changing your mortgage once it has been formalized.)

There are a number of factors that you must consider.

Financial Implications

- How much capital do you have available to put down towards the property? Remember, it is unwise to put all your capital into a property. You are bound to need some money for alterations to the property, the buying process (solicitor's and surveyor's fees etc.) and a contingency amount to cover unexpected expenses. You will generally be expected to put down some form of deposit yourself (normally a minimum of 5%) before the lender will loan you money. That said, 100% mortgages are available, particularly for first-time buyers – so long as their income is sufficient for the repayments.

- What disposable income do you have currently? You can obviously deduct any rent that you are paying as this can be put towards a mortgage.

- What increased costs do you estimate you will have if you own a property, as opposed to your current situation? Don't forget to include items like buildings and contents insurance (approximately £300 for a £75,000 house, depending on the area), council tax (you should be able to gain a rough idea, given the price band you are looking at) and all the bills for services.

- If you are looking at a property further away from your work, do not neglect to work out travelling costs. These can be a significant fixed expense.

- Be aware of the long-term discipline necessary when obtaining a mortgage – you will be making set payments, normally monthly, for a long time into the future!

Long-Term Strategy

- Try to assess your long-term aims. How long do you intend to live in the property that you are about to buy? Is this a first home? Are you married? Do you anticipate having children (or additional children)? Is it likely that you will move jobs to another geographical area? Are you retiring and looking for a home to last?

Income

- How stable or dynamic is your income? Are you salaried, with a secure job that offers good future prospects, or are you self-employed in a new and uncertain business?

- What is your income? Can you prove what you earn? If self-employed, do you have three years' accounts to show what funds are available to you? If you do not have accounts, be prepared for the fact that you may need to find a lender who will accept 'self-certification' of your income.

Investment

- Is the purchase primarily for investment purposes? Do you intend to rent the property out, or perhaps just let one or two rooms? In this case, you may be able to offset the expenses of your property against rental income, for tax purposes.

The Economy and Interest Rates

- This requires some thought – although even for professionals it often seems like guesswork – to project what is going to happen in the future. It can, however, be an important factor in deciding the way you pay off interest on your mortgage.

Once you have assessed all the above, you should be able to calculate, fairly accurately:

- The amount you have to spare to put towards a mortgage on a monthly basis.

- The amount, if any, that you have available for a deposit on your property.

- The approximate time that you will be requiring the mortgage on your particular property. A five-year fixed term of mortgage, for example, could be inappropriate if you are thinking of moving within a couple of years or so. Although some lenders are now quite flexible, and may negotiate with you favourably on redemption penalties, you should by no means take this for granted.

- Your potential long-term ability to pay the mortgage. You may be in a volatile industry, in which case you could be out of work for some time. You may decide that you need a redundancy insurance – some lenders make this compulsory, depending on your circumstances.

- Whether you want to base your monthly payments on the fluctuations of interest rates, or fix them at a set rate for a set period of time.

- If you have children or other dependants, whether you should have mortgage insurance protection, or level term insurance – this will pay off your mortgage in the event of your death.

- Whether or not you need, or want, to have a joint mortgage, allowing you greater potential for borrowing.

- Whether you are going to need to sublet or rent out part, or all, of your property.

By assessing all the above factors, you should be able to work out a basic package to suit you. If you can do this before you see a lender or financial adviser, so much the better. It will save time, and can help to prevent you feeling pressurized into accepting a package that you may not actually want, or that does not suit your particular needs. In any event these are the types of questions that your broker or a lender will (or should) ask you, before advising you on a package. It is extremely helpful to write these factors down and give a copy to your lender or broker. That way, if you do find that you have been advised improperly, then you have proof of the facts you presented.

Before finally choosing a method of financing your property, make sure that you have specifically understood and assessed the following, discussed in detail below:

- Vehicles for Repayment of your Mortgage
- Mortgage Options
- Alterations to your Agreed Means of Mortgage Payments
- 'Add-Ons' to Mortgages
- 'Hidden' Costs in the Mortgage Agreement
- Conditions Imposed Prior to Provision of a Mortgage
- Tax Relief

Vehicles for Repayment of your Mortgage

There is a range of ways to repay your mortgage. These can considerably affect your monthly outgoings, and the efficiency of redeeming your mortgage at the end of its term. There are certainly some risks attached to choosing some of the options available. You should be particularly careful when looking at mortgages that will be redeemed from an investment fund. The value of these funds, over time, can go down as well as up.

The most common vehicles for repayment are as follows:

Capital Repayment Mortgage

Over the term of the mortgage you pay the interest and the capital off the loan at the same time. You would have to take out an insurance policy that would pay off the loan in the event of your death. This insurance would be either a decreasing-term or level-term insurance policy.

- A **decreasing-term** insurance policy would pay off the amount of the loan outstanding at the time of your death.

- A **level-term** insurance policy has marginally higher premiums but would pay off the total sum borrowed at the start of the mortgage term, regardless of the amount outstanding at the time of your death.

Endowment Mortgage

Throughout the lending term, you repay only the interest on any capital sum borrowed. At the end of the lending term, the capital borrowed is settled from the proceeds of a separate life assurance policy, that you will have been paying into as a condition of the mortgage. This life assurance policy produces a lump sum on maturity (to coincide with the end of the term of the mortgage) and should be sufficient to repay all the capital borrowed. Like any investment, however, there is no guarantee that the policy, when it matures, will be able to repay the capital borrowed.

Death cover is included in an endowment mortgage, so, if you die during the term of the mortgage, the outstanding loan will be paid off.

There are two types of assurance policy:

- **With profits endowment:** This is where the assurance policy depends on the performance of the insurance company concerned for the annual and end of term payments. If the insurance company performs well, then the value of your policy will increase – and could prove to be an investment that produces a net profit on the capital you have borrowed. If the insurance company does poorly, however, then you may find that the policy, when it matures, does not cover the capital.

- **Unit-linked endowment:** This assurance policy depends upon the movement of the stock market, with which it is linked, for annual and end of term payments. As in a with profits endowment, the value of the policy can increase or decrease.

PEP (Personal Equity Plan) Mortgage

Like an endowment mortgage, you repay only the interest on the capital sum that you have borrowed over a fixed term. The capital, however is repaid from an accrued sum invested in a Personal Equity Plan – within the annual tax exemption limits. All the income and gains within the investment fund are free from personal taxation. Again, at the end of the term repayment of the capital borrowed is effected from the value accumulated in your PEP fund. There is a risk that the investment may not have been good and at the end of the term be insufficient to repay the capital. Equally, if the PEP works well you may be able to repay your mortgage early.

Unit Trust Mortgage

This is the same as a PEP mortgage but without the tax efficiencies. The advantage is that you can choose from a wide range of unit trusts. With the right choice, you may find that the unit trust performs better than an equivalent PEP, even given the lack of tax-efficiency.

Pension Mortgage

You repay only the interest on the capital borrowed for the term of the mortgage. You make payments into a pension fund, however, which upon maturity should pay off the capital borrowed from the tax-free, lump sum element of the fund. In addition, the remainder of the fund will provide you with a pension for the rest of your life. This can be an attractive mortgage for tax purposes as all your contributions into the pension fund get tax relief at your highest personal rate of tax. That said, the adequacy of any pension will depend on the success of the pension fund. If the fund does poorly you may find the amount left for your pension is not sufficient for your needs.

Flexible Mortgage

This type of mortgage is comparatively new, and comes with a chequebook. In effect, it acts rather like an overdraft facility. You are able to borrow up to an agreed amount and then make monthly payments that cover both the interest and the capital borrowed. You only get charged on what you actually borrow, however, so if you do not borrow up to your maximum you will only be charged on the basis of the capital you use. If you have not borrowed up to your maximum, then this can be a useful facility, should you need a loan for other purposes. So, if you need £10,000 to do some improvements on your house, then you can withdraw this amount easily (so long as it does not exceed your maximum allowance). You will be borrowing the money on the interest rates agreed for the original borrowing, and your monthly payments will be altered accordingly.

Foreign Currency Mortgage

This is a mortgage for the sophisticated. Effectively, it gambles on the movement of exchange rates for the repayment of the capital sum.

Home Income Plan Mortgage

This is normally for elderly people, who wish to make use of the income potentially available, due to having a high equity holding within their property. Money is borrowed from a lender on the basis that it will be invested in an income-producing investment. The lender places a charge on the property for security. The money borrowed, and the interest, is then repaid when the property is sold – either on the death of the individual or, perhaps, if it is sold in order to buy a smaller and cheaper property.

Mortgage Options

There are a number of options available, when you come to choose the way in which you will be making the interest payments on your mortgage. The particular option you decide upon can have quite serious implications for your monthly repayments. For example, if interest rates seem set to rise for a sustained period, you may be wise in agreeing with your lender a fixed rate of interest. This may result in your payments remaining lower than if you were paying on the basis of a rate that varies with interest rates. If you have a fixed rate when the interest rates are dropping, however, you may find yourself paying more than necessary.

Unfortunately, deciding on the best way to base your interest payments is a very real gamble. Unless you are particularly knowledgeable about the economy (global as well as national), you will be really out of your depth in trying to predict the movements of interest rates over a period of years. Even the professionals have considerable difficulty with this, and their advice and predictions should only be taken with great care.

The choice, for the layman, is normally made on the basis of security. If you want the comfort of knowing that the payments you are going to make will not vary over a period of time, then you are likely to choose some form of fixed rate. This will allow you to budget ahead, on the basis that your payments will remain the same for the fixed term, regardless of interest rate movements. The main trouble with this approach is that once you have agreed a fixed rate for a set period, any change will incur financial penalties from a lender. So, if you have agreed a fixed rate for five years, and then decide to redeem your mortgage (because you wish to move, for example), or wish to change your payments to a variable rate, then the lender will charge you for this change.

The financial penalty can be quite severe – sometimes as much as three months' total payments. So, always check, when taking out a fixed rate, what penalties attach to any change.

Variable Rate

This is the most common way of making interest payments. The interest you will be paying on your loan will fluctuate with interest rates. The rate will normally be about 1.25% above the interest rate set by the Bank of England, depending upon your lender. Adjustments by your lender will be done periodically, to follow the Bank of England's interest rates, up or down. Some lenders will only adjust the rate on your interest payments once a year, others will alter it more frequently. You should establish how your lender operates, and how often they will adjust the rate.

Fixed Rate

The interest rate for your payments can be fixed at a defined rate by your lender for a set period of time. This is usually done for a period of between one and ten years. If your interest rate is fixed for, say, three years, then the payments that you make will not alter from one month to the next, until the end of the set period. At this time, you can renegotiate with your lender for another fixed period, although the rate offered is likely to be different – reflecting the lender's long-term view of interest rate movements. Beware the penalties attached to any fixed-rate deals, as discussed above. Agreeing a fixed rate can be quite a commitment.

Discounted Rate

This is an option available that will discount the rate of interest you will have to pay over a set period. The discounted rate is a variable rate that follows a lender's interest rates – but at a set lower amount. So, if your lender's interest rate varies over a twelve-month period between 6.5% and 7% the interest rate that you will be charged during the same period may be between 6% and 6.5% (depending on the agreement with your lender). The discounted rate is normally offered for quite a short period, such as one year, particularly to help those with a new mortgage.

Cap and Collar Rates

The interest rate is agreed at the outset of the mortgage to be restricted between an upper (**cap**) and lower (**collar**) level. So, if interest rates rise above the level of the cap, the rate that you will pay will not go beyond the cap – likewise, if interest rates drop substantially, you will still have to pay the collar rate.

The advantages and disadvantages are obvious. If interest rates drop significantly below the collar level, you will be paying more than people on a normal variable rate. If interest rates rise above the cap, however, then you will be paying less than everyone else. This can be quite a useful way of hedging your bets.

Alterations to your Agreed Means of Mortgage Payments

It is important to check with your lender precisely what your rights are, as regards varying the payments that you make once the mortgage is operational. You may, for example, inherit some money and wish to pay off some or all of your mortgage. In this case, you must know whether or not there are financial penalties if you do so. Check:

Additional Lump Sum Payments

Establish whether you can make additional lump sum payments, during the course of the mortgage, to reduce your loan. Find out what will happen when you do this. Is it allowed by the lender? Will there be any financial penalty? Check whether the timing of the payment is important with regard to any interest rebate calculation.

If you do make a lump sum payment, make sure that you advise your lender that it is to be credited against the mortgage – as distinct from an early repayment of your normal monthly contribution.

Be aware that if your mortgage is fixed or discounted then the option to redeem it all or in part will not be available without financial penalties that can be quite severe.

Voluntary Increase of your Monthly Contributions

You may find in the future, perhaps because of a job promotion, that you are in the position to pay off the mortgage faster than originally planned. Check to see if you would be able to increase your standard monthly contributions. This can make a huge difference to the speed at which you reduce your mortgage. On some mortgages this may not be possible, however, or advisable. On endowment mortgages the term for repayment is normally fixed to the maturity date of the policy, and can be difficult to reduce. Paying more than you need to in your contributions may, in fact, be a poor use of your money.

'Add-Ons' to Mortgages

There is a whole range of packages that can be added on to mortgages. Some of these may be compulsory, depending on the lender; others are optional. Either way, they can significantly increase the overall amount that you will be paying to the lender and, of course, the cost of buying your property. This is a critical area where a lender may hope to make considerable further profit from you.

It is vital that you are able to decide for yourself whether you really need these add-ons. You also need to know whether or not you have to buy these from your lending institution, which may be more expensive than other institutions providing comparable services. A good example is buildings and contents insurance. Your lender will invariably make buildings insurance compulsory, and will define the amount for which you must insure the building. Obviously this protects them in case your property, their security, is in some way destroyed. There is usually nothing to stop you from obtaining the necessary insurance package from elsewhere, which might be considerably cheaper. The lender may charge £25 as an administrative fee, however, and you will have to prove to their satisfaction that the insurance is bona fide.

Some of the more common add-ons are:

Mortgage Indemnity Policy (MIP)

This is often made compulsory for borrowers when the loan required is high in comparison with the equity held in a property. Typically, if you want a mortgage that is 75% or more of the value of your property then you will have to take out a MIP as a condition of the loan.

This allows the lender to buy insurance cover, when it feels that lending the money to you exposes it to a risk. While you may consider the MIP of no benefit whatsoever to you as a borrower, nonetheless, unless you agree to this add-on, you may find that your lender will not loan the money you require.

Level-Term/Decreasing-Term Insurance

These two forms of insurance protect you, or rather your dependants, if you should die during the term of the mortgage. In that case the mortgage will be paid off by the insurance policy. (See under Capital Repayment Mortgage, on p.45 above, for the distinction between level-term and decreasing-term policies.)

Accident, Sickness and Redundancy Insurance

These policies will protect you if you should be unable to make your repayments. Be sure to check very carefully upon what conditions these insurances will act, for how long payments to your mortgage will be met, and what they will cover. Be especially careful to check the small print if you are self-employed or have your own business.

Buildings and Contents Insurance

These are two separate insurances, although they are normally linked together. Buildings insurance covers the actual fabric of your property and will protect you (and the lender) against damage to the property, such as fire, subsidence, collapse, etc. Your lender will insist that you have insurance to cover the cost of rebuilding your property from new. This is not necessarily the sale value of the property, although that is a rough guide. Normally, the lender's valuation report will give a rebuild cost.

Contents insurance covers the fixtures, fittings and your personal belongings: the carpets, beds, clothes, furniture, etc. that you have in the property (and sometimes outside). Quite often, you may find that a lender will overestimate the insurance needed – thus increasing the premium payable. That said, the cost of replacing possessions is surprisingly high, so take care to assess – and update – the contents insurance on an annual basis. Also make sure you check that the policy is for replacement of items on a 'new for old' basis.

It is absolutely essential to check carefully, prior to accepting either building or contents insurance, the small print. Find out exactly what you are covered for, and what are the specified **excess** sums. The latter are limits below which you will have to pay yourself. So, if you have cover that will insure you against the theft of a bicycle, there may be an excess of £50. If the bicycle is stolen, then you will have to contribute the first £50 to any new purchase.

'Hidden' Costs in the Mortgage Agreement

Check the following before finally coming to a conclusion as to your proposed mortgage. You may find these matters are tucked away in your lender's detailed agreement, or are things about which you can negotiate prior to accepting the mortgage.

Arrangement Fees

Sometimes a lender may charge you an administrative fee for arranging the mortgage. These fees can quite often be as much as £300.

Valuation Fees

A valuation report is always commissioned by the lender on your intended property, regardless of your own wishes or any report you may have had prepared. Establish how much this will cost on the type of property you are considering buying. (See Chapter 1: Buying your Property).

Some lenders will do a free valuation, or rebate the valuation fee if you arrange a mortgage through them. It is always worth checking what offers lenders are providing to entice you as a customer.

Legal Fees

Check that your lender will allow your own solicitor to act for them (he must be on the 'panel'). If not, then check the fees the lender will charge for any legal work – such as registering their charge on your property at the Land Registry.

Redemption Penalties

Find out what penalties, if any, will be applied by your lender if you decide to change your mortgage in any way, or to change it altogether to another lender. These penalties can be very considerable, particularly with regard to fixed and discounted mortgages. Make sure you find out exactly what the penalty would be and make a note of any negotiated agreement made that improves upon what the lender would normally do.

Closure Fees

Check to see what will happen at the end of your mortgage term. You may be charged an administrative fee that covers the lender's costs in removing their charge from the Land Registry and closing down your account.

Conditions Imposed Prior to Provision of a Mortgage

Conditions can be imposed by your lender prior to agreeing to provide you with a mortgage, or the full amount of the mortgage sum. The most common conditions relate to the condition and use of your property.

Mortgage Conditional upon Certain Works to Property

Frequently, after the lender has had a valuation report done on the property you intend to buy, they will make their offer of a mortgage conditional upon your doing certain works to the property, within a set time period. (This is discussed in further detail in Chapter 1, p.10.) The implication of this is that you must not stretch yourself financially too tightly, at least at first. You might otherwise find yourself unable even to start paying off the mortgage.

Subletting/Renting of your Property

Most standard mortgage agreements forbid you to sublet, rent out or change the use of your property (e.g. to a shop or office), without the lender's prior approval. This may be of crucial importance should you be relying on paying off the mortgage with the help of, say, some rental income. Check to see whether the lender will allow this and, if so, under what conditions and at what expense. The lender may charge you for their legal costs in assessing, for example, any letting agreement that you intend to use. They may refuse you permission to make the change that you need. If you do change the use, or rent out your property, without their express agreement, then you will be in breach of contract. At worst, you may find that your lender will terminate their agreement with you, and claim the money loaned back – which could necessitate the sale of your property. In practice, a blind eye is normally turned when there is merely the renting of some rooms on a casual basis.

Tax Relief

The most common form of tax relief available to anyone with a mortgage, regardless of income, is **MIRAS (Mortgage Interest Relief At Source)**. This is a scheme originally set up by the government to encourage people to own their own property. It allows tax relief on the interest charged of up to a maximum of £30,000 of your mortgage used for house purchase for owner occupation. So if you have a £40,000 mortgage then you will get tax relief on the interest charged on £30,000 of the mortgage.

Frequently, when people can afford to pay off their mortgages completely they will still retain a mortgage of £30,000 to obtain the tax relief available. It is likely that MIRAS will be phased out altogether within the next few years and its benefit is increasingly becoming marginal.

OBTAINING YOUR MORTGAGE

There tend to be only a couple of ways of obtaining a mortgage. Either you will make an appointment with a building society or bank, to meet one of their mortgage advisers, or you will get in contact with an independent financial adviser or registered mortgage broker, who will be able to provide you with different mortgage options. Whichever route you take, you will find yourself in the hands of a **financial adviser**.

The problem that you, as an individual, will face is the difficulty of finding someone who can advise you impartially. You must recognize, from the start, the considerable amounts at stake when mortgages are being arranged. For the lending institution, whether a bank, building society or centralized lender, the prospects of having you as a client are wonderful. In theory, they can close a deal with you upon which they will be making money for a very long time – maybe thirty years on a long-term mortgage. Better still, for the lender, are the prospects of all the potential add-ons to your mortgage, such as insurances for a miscellany of purposes. With a bit of luck they may be able to obtain your private pension plan as well. All these payments to them are likely to last for many years, particularly as, after a while, you will have quite forgotten for what you are paying. The direct debit system is ideal for not prompting people into reassessing their payments.

In trying to take out a mortgage, you are therefore entering an area where your business is very desirable, and where there will be immense pressure to expand on it. The financial institutions are enormous, and many have grown to their present size and profitability by making money from people, like yourself, trying to finance the purchase of their property. A lender's staff, as a consequence, are under considerable pressure to sell you the lender's products, and thereby to fulfil tough monthly sales targets.

Caution also has to be exercised when dealing with independent financial advisers – not least, because not all of them are truly independent. Even if they are not tied to a financial institution, they are naturally going to try to sell you a package that will be as profitable as possible for themselves. With hundreds of different combinations of mortgages and packages to recommend, they will only tend to advise you on a select few. That said, a good independent financial adviser, of integrity, can be your best route to negotiating a mortgage with ancillary packages appropriate for you.

If you do choose to go through an independent financial adviser, you must check that he has the status and qualifications to advise you properly. He should be registered within the terms of the Consumer Credit Act, before he advises or sells you a mortgage or loan of any kind. Establish exactly how independent he is, whether he is linked in any way with a financial institution, and how he earns his money on selling you any loan package. Be wary if your adviser is a one-man operation – he may not be in business for very long. Sometimes the best advisers are found within reputable organizations that specialize in giving independent financial advice.

Strict legislation has been enacted over the selling of financial services (the Financial Services Acts), but you must still be very wary. The key is for you to know what type of basic package you want, to fit in with your particular needs. Make sure that you can specify, at least in outline, what you need and what you can afford. If you have the slightest doubt about the integrity of a financial adviser or broker then be sure to leave him straight away and find someone else.

Allow time, once a financial plan or package has been presented to you, to go and approach several other brokers or institutions for their individual assessments (without disclosing the presentations you already have). Only when you have researched all the various options, should you commit yourself to one lender. Even then, try to get your adviser to give you a breakdown in writing of the key queries you have raised. For example, if it is important to you that you can sublet your property, and the adviser states that this is all right under the package he is suggesting, make sure he confirms this in writing. Often mortgage or financial services agreements are quite dense, and can be difficult for you, as a layman, to understand fully. Place the onus of clarification firmly on your adviser – and make sure that the clarification is always in writing, and in clear terms, not legalese.

PROBLEMS WITH ADVICE PROVIDED

Investment (Endowment, Pension, PEP and Unit Trust Mortgages) or Insurance Advice

If you find you have been poorly advised, or that your adviser has breached the rules, then you must take action as soon as you realize there is a problem. As with all problems, the first line of attack should be with the company or person who sold you the service. They must be given the opportunity to rectify any errors made, and you must advise them of the problem in writing. It is often wise to send this letter to the highest-ranking partner or official that you can reach within the organization.

If you are still unsatisfied, however, then write to the Personal Investment Authority (**PIA**), who are responsible for the regulation of both institutional lenders and individuals involved in either advising or selling investments and insurances. If you still find no satisfaction, then there is an **Ombudsman for the PIA**, who has powers over any firm or person registered with the PIA.

If you still feel aggrieved, then you can go a further step and, depending on the problem, contact either the **Insurance Ombudsman** or the **Investment**

Ombudsman. Both are capable of investigating complaints made by individual consumers in their particular areas. They are appointed by the government and completely independent of the financial institutions.

Mortgage Advice

You may find that you have been given the wrong advice, and have landed up with entirely the wrong type of mortgage. If this happens, then again your first step should always be to the institution with whom you have the mortgage. If you have little joy with the office or branch dealing with your mortgage, then contact their head office complaints department.

If your lender does not give you satisfaction, then you will have little alternative other than to contact either the **Banking Ombudsman** or the **Ombudsman for Building Societies**, as appropriate.

PROBLEMS WITH PAYING YOUR MORTGAGE

There may well come a time when you are unable to pay your mortgage. You might have lost your job, or perhaps the interest rate has gone up so much that you are unable to sustain your monthly payments. The latter (combined with a massive national loss of jobs) occurred during the recession of the early 1990s, when interest rates reached an alarming 15.4%. Problems with the economy seem to be roughly cyclical, every ten years or so, so the likelihood of similar problems recurring is, sadly, reasonably great. Almost invariably the value and saleability of properties also drops, albeit temporarily. The overall effect of this can be to cause **negative equity**, which means that you owe more on your property, because of the size of your mortgage, than it could be sold for. This is a potentially disastrous position to be in (see below pp.57–8).

If you find, for whatever reason, that you are unable to continue paying your mortgage, you must react reasonably fast, to prevent the situation getting out of control:

- Contact your lender as soon as possible, and warn him that you may have a problem. This should be done before you fail to make any of your payments, and certainly before you start being threatened with legal action. If this has happened already, then it is still well worth making sure that you have a face-to-face meeting. Try to avoid any court action continuing, as this is likely to impede direct communication between you and your lender.

- At any meeting with your lender, it is best to be completely open about your situation, the problems you face and your future plans and prospects. Only then is your lender able to assess what to do, and how best to help you. Most lenders will try hard to prevent any repossession. It is not in their long-term interest to lose your business – if they do repossess your property, they know you will never return to them.

  Lenders have, at the end of the day, a variety of options with which to help – and it makes sense to get them on your side as soon as possible.

- The majority of lenders (particularly mutual building societies) will look at your situation on an individual basis, and use a fair degree of subjectivity. They will initially look at their own exposure to loss. This they will do by assessing the **loan to value**. In other words, they will look at the size of the mortgage, in comparison with the value of your property. So, if your property has a mortgage that is 90% to 95% of the value of the house, they will be much more concerned than if the mortgage is considerably less.

  Initially, your lender is likely to advise you to try to find out if Income Support can help to pay your outgoings. They will also want to establish whether you have any further income that can be diverted to the mortgage, or if there is any other way of helping your cash flow that you have not realized. They may advise you to go to a **Citizens' Advice Bureau (CAB)**, so that you can seek some other advice as to your options. It is reasonably likely that they will give you three months in which to try to sort yourself out, before acting further.

- Lenders have some options of their own that they can use, at their absolute discretion, to alleviate your problems. They are likely to try hard to reschedule the loan, if at all possible. They may also choose, for example, to charge you interest only, for a set period of time. Alternatively, they may make a concession on the interest that has started to roll up since your inability to pay. Another provision that they may exercise is to alleviate the debt by using the value of any endowment policy that you may have built up. You may even find that the lender will extend the period of your mortgage. Any of these could be of considerable assistance, and may help to tide you over until you are sufficiently ready to start making your full payments. None of this will be done, however, unless you are seen to act in good faith with your lender.

  Interestingly, this is one area in which smaller **mutual societies** (building societies that have not altered their status to become public companies) can come into their own. They do not have to chase profits for their shareholders, and can afford to take a longer view on the lending that they do. There is some evidence to suggest that you would be better, long-term, given the vagaries of life, to consider taking a mortgage out with a small mutual society, rather than one of the huge centralized lenders. However hard the latter try, it is difficult for them to offer the same level of personal service. You may not receive quite the same cost advantage from the small operation, but this may be compensated for at a later date, when you need an understanding ear from someone who knows you. Some of the very small societies, perhaps with only one or two branches, have very deep roots in the local community, and can give a particularly attentive service.

If you do not respond to your lender, as you cease to make payments, then the following sequence of events is likely to take place, although the timings and procedure may differ somewhat from one lender to another:

- After the first missed repayment, you are likely to receive a courteous letter prompting you to pay.
- By the second missed repayment, you can expect a reasonably strong letter asking for a meeting. This will probably be accompanied by additional charges for the letters and statements that have been sent to you.
- By the third missed repayment (normally the third month), you will receive a letter stating that legal proceedings will be started by your lender for repossession of the property within (normally) seven days, unless you settle the outstanding payments.
- The lender will then start legal proceedings, and you will find yourself served with a summons.
- It will take some three months, approximately, for your lender to take proceedings to court and obtain a repossession order. Until they have this order from the court, they cannot take possession of your property.
- In effect, you are likely to have about six months from the date of your first non-payment before your house is repossessed – unless you take prompt action as outlined above.

Repossession

If your property is repossessed, then your lender will sell it to recover the loan that was made to you, together with any expenses incurred by the lender. They are, however (contrary to popular belief), under a duty to sell it for the best market price which they can reasonably obtain. Normally, your lender will therefore sell your property by auction (see Chapter 3: Auctions). By doing this, they are able to prove conclusively to a court, if there is a dispute, that your property sold for the best possible price. If, however, the lending institution has many repossession matters on its books (such as during a recession), it will be anxious to reduce its exposure, and may try to sell your house quickly to a cash buyer.

If, in selling the property, your lender has still not recovered all the money owed, then they can pursue you for the money outstanding. Your credit rating for future borrowing may be adversely affected.

NEGATIVE EQUITY

This is the situation in which the mortgage on your property is greater than the current value of the property itself. If you have a mortgage of £50,000 and your property is now worth only £45,000, then the amount of your negative equity is £5,000. Negative equity commonly occurs when you have borrowed a high percentage (perhaps even 100%) of the sale value of your property, and the property market, for some reason, has since dropped. Sadly, the greatest sufferers are likely to be first-time buyers, whose grip on the property ladder is often initially rather tenuous.

Although historically property does increase in value over time, temporary dips or slumps in the market can last for some years. The past 20 years have seen two major recessions – the last quite spectacular – after two booms. Until the first of these booms, properties increased in value only slowly. Once the booms occurred, however, for a few years properties leapt up in price quite unrealistically.

The problem for you in this situation is the time it can take for an upturn in the market to increase the value of your property sufficiently to erase your negative equity. If you wait long enough it is bound to happen. The trouble is that as time passes, so your needs change. A small flat may have been adequate while you had no family, but may be impossible when you have young children. In that case, waiting for an upturn can be unrealistic.

Fortunately, as a result of the trauma of the early nineties, lenders have now found a way of helping people with negative equity by allowing them to take their mortgages with them to a new property. The extra amount required to buy the new property is then added on to the existing mortgage. Sometimes lenders will go so far as to allow the new purchase even though an element of their loan is actually unsecured.

For example, you may have bought your original property for £50,000 with a mortgage of £45,000. The property might have dropped in value to £40,000, leaving you with a negative equity of £5,000. Your lender may then allow you to buy another property for £60,000 by transferring the original mortgage of £45,000 to the new property and giving you another loan of £15,000. You will have a 100% mortgage, but you will at least have been able to move to a more suitable property, rather than being trapped until the market rises. Some lenders will allow you to borrow as much as 120% of the value of a new property to allow you to repay your negative equity. Your lender is likely to be very careful to check your intended new property, however, to see that it is a reasonably secure investment.

GENERAL MORTGAGE OVERVIEW

In principle, a well chosen mortgage is a very good way of borrowing money at reasonably cheap interest rates, over a long period of time. The key, however, is to make sure that you make any decision about your mortgage carefully, after thought and investigation. If you do not extend your borrowing too much, and the mortgage is a sound package, then you should have little cause for concern.

If, however, you rush into a mortgage without understanding the implications and packages on offer, then you could find yourself paying well over the odds. You must choose a mortgage with the same care you would exercise in buying your property. Take time over it, and be sceptical about what the person selling says, until you are quite sure of the truth. Do not be afraid to ask any questions, however stupid they may seem, of your lender or financial adviser. If they cannot be answered simply and clearly, then walk away – and find someone who can fully explain what they are selling, to your complete satisfaction.

LOANS AND GRANTS

At some stage you may need further finance, perhaps to do work on your property. If this is the case, then you have five main options:

Grants

Grants can be obtained from both central government and local authorities for certain defined works to a property. Over the past few years these grants have been reduced, however, and now the criteria for obtaining grants tend to be very narrow. Individual local authorities differ greatly as to what grants they will provide, with the bottom line often being whether they are a rich or poor authority.

In broad terms you are unlikely to obtain grants unless you are over 60 or living on state benefit, and your conditions are very poor indeed. Even then, you may find that you will not obtain the grant unless you can prove that you have lived in the property for three years or more. If you are disabled there is rather more help available, although you should initially apply to Social Services to help you process any claim.

It is always worth contacting your local authority housing officer to see if there are grants available, but you would be unwise to buy a property on the assumption that grants will be available, without first checking on what basis they are provided.

Loans

Loans are available from many sources, whether banks, building societies, credit card companies or other institutions offering various forms of credit. They are normally charged out at a higher rate than mortgages, and are for much shorter periods – generally not longer than five years.

When considering taking out a loan, you must look with great care at the conditions of the loan. Check the **annual percentage rate** (**APR**) that is being charged. This can vary enormously, and may be very high. As with all loans and forms of credit, check the other options available to you on the market before signing any agreement. One of the cheapest forms of finance is a mortgage, and it may well be that by extending your mortgage you can obtain the additional money that you need at a much better rate than by taking out a separate loan from elsewhere. If you do take out a loan make sure, obviously, that you can maintain the increased staged payments and that the amounts to be paid are clearly set out in any agreement.

The **Consumer Credit Act** does afford some protection to you when taking out loans, and you should be aware of your basic rights (see Appendix 4: Consumer Protection) concerning extortionate credit agreements, and the **cooling-off periods** allowable, in certain circumstances, after you have signed an agreement.

Extension to an Existing Mortgage

One of the most cost-effective ways of obtaining a loan is to extend your existing mortgage. In this way, you can potentially borrow money on fairly low interest rates – those already agreed on your existing mortgage – and pay the additional money off over the period of the mortgage. Most lenders will consider this option, so long as you have existing equity in the property. If this is marginal, or the amount of the loan will take you up to within a small percentage of the overall value of your house, then your lender may refuse. In fact, of course, you would be unwise to borrow money to do works on the property unless the overall value of the property is likely to be increased. Take care to assess the increased mortgage payments as these may, with the additional loan, amount to more than you can sustain.

The procedure for extending your mortgage is reasonably simple, and can sometimes be put in place without a meeting. You will have to state your reasons for requiring the loan, and may have to allow the lender to inspect the property later, to ensure that the money loaned has been spent on the project stated.

Readvance on an Existing Mortgage

Should you be in the fortunate position of having paid off say, £5,000 from your original mortgage, then there is the option to reborrow that sum or any amount up to it with the minimum of problems. Obviously, you will have to agree repayment terms with your lender but this should not be difficult – they like good borrowers. This can be an efficient and easy way to obtain a loan.

Second Mortgage

If your existing lender does not allow you to extend your mortgage, then you can go to an alternative lender and attempt to get an additional mortgage from them. However, the lender will want to secure their loan on your property, so you will have to demonstrate to their satisfaction that there is sufficient equity left in your property. You will have to go through the same procedure for ensuring that you obtain a sound package as described above.

This can be an expensive way of obtaining a loan, not least because of the legal fees involved in registering the second lender's charge on your property at the Land Registry.

SUMMARY

- Do not rush into obtaining a mortgage. Carefully study your own situation, both from a financial and from a long-term personal standpoint.

- Understand the basic mortgage options available, the add-ons and related conditions and expenses.

- Allow sufficient time to research several lenders and financial advisers before you agree to any single package.

- Give the lender or adviser a factsheet setting out your personal circumstances and financial means.

- Do not be rushed into agreeing to a mortgage until you are certain of the implications.

- Make sure that your lender or adviser gives you, in writing and in clear English, advice on any matter about which you are uncertain.

- If you find that you have the wrong package then ring first to complain. If you do not obtain satisfaction then write to the head of the branch organization of your lender before taking the matter, by stages, to the appropriate Ombudsman – or take legal advice.

- Do not overextend yourself; remember the maxim 'Every mortgage is a potential arrears case.' Avoid taking risks on future interest rates – the professionals have enough trouble getting this right.

- If you fall into arrears, or are heading that way, get in contact with your lender straight away, so that rescheduling of the loan can be considered.

- If you need to raise further money, do this cautiously and remember that your property can go down in value as well as up.

PART TWO

Small Works Construction

5

The Builder

BEFORE employing a builder, it is helpful to understand something of the small works construction industry: how it tends to work, and the potential problems and inherent pitfalls. This information will help in choosing a builder and managing the project overall, and will allow the quality of work and its related costings to be monitored.

For the purposes of this book the term 'builder' has been given a very broad definition. It covers everyone involved in working on buildings, be it brickwork, plumbing, joinery, semi-skilled labouring, other trades, or the actual running of a construction company.

The small works construction industry is unlike any other industry in the country and is hard to define. There is a bewildering array of activities, performed by a kaleidoscope of different people, qualified or unqualified, working in a range of organizations. There are formalized companies, small informal partnerships and people operating on their own.

Many of the problems experienced by the industry are due to the low level of entry, and the fact that there is nothing to prevent anyone from setting themselves up as a builder. In addition, there is little effective self-regulation. As in any profession, the work performed can vary from the very highest standard to the appallingly poor. Equally, the costs charged for similar work can vary greatly for reasons which are not always obvious, so that fine work can be had for a reasonable price, while poor-quality work can be expensive. Furthermore – and this is where the industry does differ from so many others – many contracts are unique, and a builder may find himself tackling projects, aspects of which fall outside his speciality or previous experience.

The sheer variety that the builder encounters, combined with the ineptitude of many clients in defining their needs, leads to much avoidable distress. This may help to explain why the industry has one of the worst reputations of any profession or trade. While this is extremely unfair to the many people working in the industry who do consistent good work with pride, on time and to budget, it is also cause for concern. By following the advice found on the following pages, you will be able to:

- distinguish between 'good' and 'bad' builders;
- achieve quality and value in work performed; and
- avoid potential stress by understanding the building process.

QUALITY OF WORK

What we have a right to expect, above all, is that the completed work should be of a good standard. Unfortunately one of the reasons for the poor reputation of builders is poor-quality work. As well as the many excellent, well qualified builders in the industry, there are also those working in the trade who have never had any training in building. The past few years of economic recession have seen many people with a little DIY knowledge take up building as a profession. To you, they may be indistinguishable from a tradesman with years of experience and a five-year apprenticeship.

This is not to say that they may not be capable of excellent work. It is possible for the workmanship of an ex-DIY person to match the quality of a time-served professional. Conversely, a professional builder who has spent most of his working life doing banal site joinery, for example, may be simply bored with his work, and lack the motivation to maintain a high standard.

The apparently impressive training of a person who has, say, a City and Guilds Certificate in decorating and has done a full apprenticeship – as opposed to a short government retraining course – is no *real* guarantee that he has ever worked to a particularly high standard in his trade. A tradesman who has spent his apprenticeship and working life doing 'tosh' work for councils may not be prepared for hanging an expensive wallpaper in your furnished house.

A problem that is central to the difficulties associated with the small works construction industry is that a builder often has to be master of several skills if a contract is not to be uneconomic. To call in a different specialist each time one is required is simply not viable. This is particularly true of renovation work, where a builder refurbishing a house may find that in order to go ahead with his main job of, say, joinery, he may have to do some plumbing, electrics and plastering. He will often perform all of these functions himself, probably to an acceptable standard, but few builders can possibly do everything really well – so immediately there is potential for poor quality.

To stay in business, builders often have to bid for, and carry out, work outside their main profession. This may be fine on a basic building project, but is less desirable, and can be disastrous, where a high-quality finish is required.

If a builder has quoted on an area of work with which he is unfamiliar, he may find himself working to tight and perhaps even unmanageable margins. There is a possibility that he may not have quoted accurately on the work, either out of inexperience, or to be sure of obtaining the contract. Once a builder finds out that he is definitely losing money on a contract – and this may not be until half-way through the job – he may try to save on materials and labour. Instead of using expensive waterproof board on a bathroom floor, for example, he may use a cheap chipboard. This will look the same to you, but may cause problems in due course.

ORGANIZATION

Generally, quality of work on site, however large or tiny the building company, is dependent upon good management of the site, combined with very real integrity on behalf of the site manager, backed by enthusiastic, skilled manpower – whether formally trained or not.

One of the perennial complaints about builders is that they are erratic and disorganized. There are a number of reasons for this, some of which go to the heart of the problems associated with small works. Many businesses engaged in this area are very small indeed. There may be only one or two partners, with perhaps one of their wives doing the paperwork and accounts. The partners will often be physically working 'on the tools'. They may have a few full-time employees, but it is also possible that they will respond to any work by bringing in labour as and when they need it.

The problem that readily arises is that the people who need to manage the business are actually involved in the day-to-day site work. At the very least, they will supervise it daily. Most of the work is physically demanding, and the hours long – most small works builders work a basic day on site of between 9 and 10 hours.

The result of this is that the administration and organization of the business is often performed in the evenings and at weekends. Even in the best-run businesses this can make it difficult for the builder to plan ahead, with the result that he is constantly moving his staff around to cover one problem or another.

The best solution is for the builder to employ effective foremen to supervise the sites. This is rarely feasible, however, if for no better reason than that effective, motivated foremen/project managers are difficult to find, let alone keep. As a rule, anyone who is sufficiently motivated is likely to become self-employed, so that the pool of good managers for a builder to call upon is extremely limited. This means that a builder either has to be 'on the tools' himself or, if he is employing others, he has to be on site for a substantial part of every day. Commonly, the first time that a builder in small works really starts to have trouble with his business (and clients) is when he does not attend to the daily detail of every site himself.

Alongside the obvious problems of trying to run the technical side of the business, frequently problematic in itself, are the traditional ones of any small business. As elsewhere, the actual business side of the concern requires sufficient time and ability to administer it efficiently. This can be a problem, particularly as many builders leave formal education early, to study a trade. They then work 'on the tools' for some years, before starting their own business. While they are therefore skilled in their particular trade, they may have little management experience or specific knowledge of how to run a business. This can result in a number of problems, from poor management of staff, right through to inadequate attention to accounts and the assessment of the viability of contracts. Marketing is almost completely ignored and general administration may be badly in arrears.

These problems are common to a number of small businesses in any industry, but are somewhat compounded in building, due to the nature of the daily work. Not only are the people running a small works building company often on site every day, but in many cases they may find themselves moving from one site to another very frequently. For example, a plumber may find himself conducting two or three jobs simultaneously on different sites, which makes it almost impossible to take time out for the running of his business. Even if he has a job which keeps him on one site (emergency call-outs notwithstanding) for perhaps a couple of weeks, he will inevitably be working on a dirty, cold site, scattered with equipment, materials and other men – making it impossible to do any paperwork.

The result of all this is that small works construction businesses are often only just in control of their destiny – with all that implies as regards financial stability, client relations and, most importantly, quality of overall work. It is of some sadness to encounter, time and again, excellent craftsmen or tradesmen whose work has deteriorated because they have started to run a business that they cannot manage.

One of the most common problems for small works builders is the difficulty of employing competent tradesmen on site, while retaining a sufficient margin to make the contract profitable. In fact, it is hard to find good, energetic and reliable tradesmen to work for any length of time within a business; naturally enough, if they do have these qualities, then they will know their value on a self-employed basis. The self-employed rate that they will require from the builder may, however, leave him with little or no profit margin. The result of this is that a builder will, all too frequently, be forced to employ too few good tradesmen on site. Much of the work will therefore be done by using a combination of semi-skilled and unskilled labour to help increase the profitability of the job.

For quite understandable reasons, semi-skilled and unskilled labour is inclined to be unreliable. Quite often the unskilled labourer will be working for derisory money, while performing some of the hardest and most tedious work on site – and all this while employed, probably for cash, only on a day-to-day basis. He has no security of tenure and can be sacked at any time, for any reason. Accordingly, while he may well be unusually conscientious, so as to retain his chance of a continued job, he may equally well be completely uncaring, as he knows that he will not be with the builder for long. As the builder is usually unable to be on site the whole time for the necessary supervision, poor work can be the result.

One of the most frustrating aspects of the small works construction industry from the client's point of view is the timetable. In normal commercial life, in theory at least, there are fixed weekday working hours, and contracts are commenced and finished within reasonably clear deadlines. This approach is not always feasible in the building industry, and builders are frequently criticized for starting projects late, for working erratic hours and for delaying the final completion of a contract beyond a client's patience.

Part of the reason for these criticisms stems from the unpredictable circumstances in which many builders find themselves operating. They suffer from a real difficulty in trying to obtain work far enough ahead, in order to plan future workload. Almost invariably clients want their chosen area of work to be commenced, if not straight away, then at least within a few weeks. It is rare to find someone who is prepared to wait much longer. More often than not, if a builder cannot start within a short period, his tender will be dismissed in favour of someone else. This is quite understandable; if someone has just purchased a house, he will want to move his family in as soon as possible.

For the builder, however, it presents the problem that he will generally only have a few weeks', or months' work booked at any given time. He is therefore left with the option of either losing the work, or starting the new project before the completion of an existing one. Naturally enough, the builder will be anxious to obtain the contract. Having done so, however, he will not necessarily be able to start on the given date. If he does, then it may be a rather half-hearted operation until he has finished the other project – which may in turn be prejudiced by the sudden disappearance of personnel.

The work of plumbers and electricians tends to be even more precarious. Their response times have to take into account emergency call-outs, and the often extremely small, short-lived contracts that make up a significant part of their income.

Often the lead times for plumbers and electricians are so short that they are unable to plan ahead for more than a week at a time, while awaiting confirmation that builders for whom they work are at the right stage. To complicate their lives further they often have to do a few days' work on a site to 'first fit' electrics or plumbing, and then wait while other construction and decorating works take place, before the 'second fit'. Naturally enough the 'second fit', when requested by a builder, sometimes cannot be done for some time – thus placing a further strain upon the efficiency of the site. A number of small works construction firms have their own in-house plumbers or electricians (they may indeed be running the business), but generally they are brought in on a subcontract basis.

SUBCONTRACTING

There is widespread subcontracting in the small works industry. On the whole, this is a healthy situation; in fact, problems arise all too frequently when builders do not subcontract work to a specialist, and attempt to do it themselves.

Virtually every possible trade and activity can be subcontracted. The only real danger to the client is that if too much of the core contract is subcontracted by the builder, then you can end up with someone apart from your chosen builder, effectively running the project.

It is always important that a builder knows something about the trade to which he is subcontracting, and that he is able to regulate effectively the works being performed. Normally, the latter is not too great a problem, as an experienced builder will generally have worked with his subcontractors. He will also probably, have some real knowledge of the trade concerned – although he may not be able personally to do the work to a high standard. One of the benefits of the cross-fertilization that tends to occur throughout the industry is that builders can often have an impressive working knowledge of a multitude of activities – but you should obviously be wary of one who claims to have mastered them all.

Extensive contracting out, however, requires good organization on behalf of a builder, who has to ensure that the progress of the project does not become erratic. There can be considerable difficulties with matching effectively the interfaces of the different skills, all often needed at reasonably precise times. The quality of the contractors' work can also be variable, and they may have little regard for the work to follow. It is not unusual for the last people to work on the project, the decorators, to find that they have an almost impossible job to do in rectifying areas of poor initial construction.

PRICING

Builders essentially make their living from charging out their own time at a basic day rate. This will differ from one part of the country to another and will depend, to some extent, on the type of work in which they are involved. Not surprisingly, a builder doing very basic-quality work for the local authority in a provincial town will charge a quite different day rate from a builder undertaking a high-standard renovation in the centre of London. Nonetheless, the principle is much the same. It is normally quite easy to establish a rough day rate below which a builder will not work, and one that is the approximate average for a given type of work, to a common standard, in your area. This can be done by asking friends who have had building done or, better still, some local architects, surveyors or structural engineers.

The basic set rate will generally indicate what the builder himself will charge as his minimum. He will then raise, or retain, that figure to take into account variables which he considers pertinent to the work and the client. The builder will set rates for his in-house manpower according to their level of skills, and then add on an appropriate profit margin.

Essentially, small works construction tends to be extremely labour-intensive, whether skilled or unskilled, and for many contracts it is the cost of manpower that defines the cost of the work. Prime examples of this are decorating or plastering, where the material cost can be as low as 10% of the manpower. Obviously there are areas, such as the fitting of a kitchen, where the material cost is greatly more than the manpower, but this tends to be the exception.

While the money that a builder will make on his manpower is obviously the core of his income, he will also try to make something on the general building materials. He will mark up these materials at a profit and, wherever possible, he will try to negotiate cheaper rates from the supplier than, in theory, the non-builder can obtain. Generally speaking, however, there are not many areas where a substantial profit can be made, and often the contribution of general materials to the profit on small works is not great. The quantities purchased do not allow for negotiating substantial discounts – certainly not to the extent available to builders working on major contracts.

A builder will, however, potentially be able to make a reasonable mark-up on substantive items such as kitchens, sanitary ware, lighting, tiled flooring and so on. These items are often available, to the builder with good contacts within the trade, at reasonably heavy discounts, and can represent a significant profit.

Subcontracting is not always profitable. On occasions a builder will find it necessary to use a subcontractor in order to be able to complete the project as a whole. In this case, he may employ the subcontractor at cost, recognizing that any profit made will come from elsewhere. For example, a builder may have a project that requires the supply and fitting of a new boiler, together with the extending of a room, with joinery and decoration involved. If margins on the project are tight, he may rely on the actual building works for his profit, knowing that marking up the work on the boiler could lose him the contract. In this event, as a client, you could probably not better the price for the boiler installation, and you have the benefit of the builder being responsible for its fitting and the coordination of the collateral works.

Normally, however, subcontracting is looked upon as a real and important source of profit. Indeed, some small works organizations are sometimes little more than project managers, with all functions on a project being subcontracted to a whole number of separate trades. In this event, a builder may well only perform the functions of coordinating the work and liaising with his client, while perhaps supplying some basic labour. This can work well. It normally means that the builder will be using only contractors who specialize in the types of work required.

Generally, subcontracting in small works construction will involve only a small part of the overall project. It may be that the builder subcontracts only the flat roofing of an extension he has built, or the construction of some french windows. Ideally, in this event, he will then mark up this work to the maximum possible – though this will vary considerably, depending on market conditions – while still retaining the overall contract. Certainly, as a general rule, a mark-up of less than 20% is rarely worth the builder having any involvement in the work.

Extras

There is one further area in which builders make their money, although it is almost as controversial for the builder as it is for the client. The term **extra** covers any additional cost that was not specified in the original quotation – that is, the performance of work that was not envisaged at the start of the project. For some builders the extras on a contract will amount to a significant contribution to their overall profit. Indeed, on occasions, a project may even be undertaken with the specific aim of trying to find opportunities for profitable extras. You should therefore always insist on a **schedule of rates** for the various aspects of the work, so that you have a fixed agreement should extras become a part of the contract.

Every builder knows that once he has commenced a project it is difficult for the client to refuse his recommendation to rectify an obvious problem. Because of this, he may be tempted to charge a premium for the work, knowing that it is difficult for you to seek quotes from other builders – particularly if the overall progress of a site depends on the additional works being carried out as soon as possible. You would also be placed in the awkward position of showing that you did not trust the builder, if you tried to bring someone else on site to carry out the works. Apart from this, other builders would be reluctant to start work while the first is still engaged on the site. You might therefore feel obliged to accept the extras.

For most builders, extras are a somewhat inevitable part of their work, but not their main way of making a profit. Of course, sometimes additions are welcomed, as they help to extend a contract when work elsewhere is scarce. But if the extra work, whether absolutely necessary or just a whim of the client, does extend the time of a project, it can prevent the builders from commencing their next scheduled project on time. This can upset their next client – before they have even started work.

The Day Rate

Apart from providing a quoted price, builders will often work on a fixed day rate for their work. This can have some clear benefits, in that there will be no question of extras. Also, you will not be paying a premium on a quote – quoting a price in advance is inevitably risky and attracts a premium. Employing a builder on a day rate is also a good way of ensuring excellent quality work. A tradesman knows that he can spend time undertaking work that otherwise he might have to rush, just to stay within his budget.

The problems with builders working on a day rate are obvious. Firstly, you will have no fixed end cost for the work and, secondly, monitoring the builders' real time and energy input is difficult. Over sustained periods you might find that the builder did not put the same amount of urgency into the work as he would have done, had he been working to his own price.

For builders, working on a day rate can be very welcome, particularly when they are working on an area of a project that is effectively unique or requires very high quality. In fact, there are occasions when even experienced tradesmen may not previously have encountered some aspect of the work involved in a project. This is especially true of new designs, or of the restoration or recreation of old designs. In such cases, tradesmen often find that they cannot quote effectively, and will only undertake the work by way of a set day rate.

INHERENT VALUE OF THE BUSINESS

One of the attractions for builders in starting up in small works construction is that the overheads of their businesses will generally be very low. Indeed, many experienced builders possess little more than a vehicle (not always even a van), a telephone, a lock-up of some sort and some hand tools. Particularly in metropolitan areas, builders will often not have a yard or workshop, and will effectively conduct all their work on site, hiring capital equipment as and when it is needed. Materials are generally bought specifically for a given contract, and delivered to site when required, straight from a builders' merchant's.

Furthermore, for builders involved in small works, the extra expense of a formal office is rarely necessary. Meetings with a client, or with architects and engineers, are invariably on site. A builder does not even need to look particularly good, or even to drive a new vehicle filled with gleaming tools. All of these quickly degrade under the hardships of day-to-day building – and, in reality, tell you little about the business.

One of the consistent factors throughout small works is that the business of the builder will probably have little inherent value – apart from the intangible nature of 'goodwill'. Investment in a small works business is rarely necessary, apart from the immediate tooling required for the builder's main trade. Even then, the equipment is difficult to sell for more than a fraction of its original value. As a generality, small works builders do not make very much money – contrary to common myth – and suing them can be a waste of both time and money.

LEGAL/ILLEGAL

Small works construction is notorious for its 'black market' element. These are builders who are working for cash, and are running businesses outside legitimate industry. This does not mean that their work will necessarily be poor. Indeed, there are some quite excellent builders working this way. They are likely to be uninsured, however, and it can be difficult to bring them back onto a project to correct problems once they have been paid.

There are several reasons why builders working in small works construction might be tempted to work only, or partly, on the black market. One reason, ironically, is due to government policy, and concerns **Value Added Tax (VAT)**, which must be charged by anyone with a turnover in excess of £48,000 per annum (as at September 1997). A small builder can of course stay below this sum, particularly if he is involved in relatively small contracts during the course of a year. If he is not liable to be VAT-registered, he will, quite legitimately, not charge VAT on his work.

Other small builders, however, with a turnover in excess of this modest limit, must charge VAT – and they may be competing against non-VAT-registered rivals for vital contracts. So a VAT-registered builder, bidding competitively against one who is not registered, is often tempted to resort to a cash deal, if he is not to lose the opportunity to obtain a new contract. Many clients unwisely encourage this by offering the builder at least a proportion of the bill in cash, in order to obtain a reduction.

CHOOSING A BUILDER

The perennial problem of how to choose a builder is as hard to resolve as anything in construction, with no really steadfast guidelines available. The very nature of small works construction makes it difficult to identify who will, or will not, perform a contract properly, effectively and at a realistic price – while acting throughout with some integrity.

Certainly appearances are of little help; a builder who drives a rusty old van and is somewhat scruffy may well be a superb, time-served tradesman, who will provide an excellent personal service, even if he has delivered his quote on a poorly written piece of letterhead, devoid of indications that he is a member of one trade organization or another.

Personal Recommendation

Obviously, the ideal way to find a good builder is to obtain one through recommendation from a friend who has recently had satisfactory work performed. Even then, it is well worth speaking in detail to the person concerned, to establish how the contract actually progressed and whether or not the work done was comparable to your project. Wherever possible, go and see the work, and assess whether the quality is to the standard you require, whether it was performed by subcontractors and, if so, what element of it. Establish who actually managed the site during the conduct of the works. The latter is important when the builder has other partners or site managers who may be of lesser ability than the one who completed the original work. Finally, the costs of the project should be investigated, to establish at least a rough idea of the prices charged, with particular attention to the all-important day rates.

Unfortunately it is not always possible to obtain a builder through recommendation from a friend or acquaintance, in which case it is well worth visiting a few local builders' merchants. Although they are generally not allowed to suggest a tradesman, they may be prepared to hint at someone who does have a sound reputation. A more reliable way of obtaining a recommendation can be by contacting some structural engineers in your local area. These professionals work closely with builders, and are often the people most involved in their daily supervision on site. They will carry lists of builders that they use, and would recommend to their own clients. These builders will have been well tried and proven, to the high standards required by an engineer.

It is also worth keeping an eye out for any builder consistently working in your area. This tends to indicate that he is getting work from rolling recommendations, enabling him to remain constantly working in the area. He is also less likely to do poor work for you, as it could be bad for his local reputation.

Most builders are only too keen to speak with potential clients, and will often show them around the sites on which they are working – although this can be a mixed blessing. You will inevitably only see, at best, a shell of a site, on which it is difficult to judge an end result. Work rarely looks good, or properly finished, until carpets and decorations are in place, at which time most people are reluctant to allow a builder to show his potential clients around. Even if he does have this opportunity, it may not be of the greatest help – no builder is likely to show you any but the best work that he has done.

Trade Organizations

There are lists available of builders working in your area, which are kept by the various trade organizations associated with building. These organizations will only be able to provide a list of builders, however, without advising on their merit, or their suitability for the particular job. Membership of some trade organizations is not necessarily a good guide to a builder's competence.

Many such organizations exist for the trade, not the consumer, and their functions tend, naturally enough, to revolve around providing back-up for the builder in his business. The trade organization will supply the builder with valuable technical information, a useful legal service, connections with other builders and (of increasing importance) competitive insurance deals for public liability, vehicles and tools.

Indeed, with some notable exceptions, some of these organizations are, in reality, little more than businesses themselves, effectively supplying a product to the builder or tradesman. While complaints can be made by an aggrieved client to an organization of which their builder is a member, the only effective enforcement may be to dismiss the builder from the organization. In this event, he is likely to join one of the other trade organizations, of which there have been a growing number over the past few years. It is therefore worth checking with the organization concerned, to establish whether they have an effective complaints procedure.

Warranties

More important is the question of whether or not the builder you choose has an **insurance-backed warranty,** covering the work that he performs. Very few of the trade organizations make this compulsory for their members and, until they do, their relevance to the consumer is always going to be somewhat marginal.

If a builder does claim that his work is backed by a formal warranty, first ensure that the warranty is current, and then check precisely what it covers, and whether or not it is insurance-backed. Unless the warranty is backed by a regular insurance company, it will be little better than a written promise, on behalf of the builder, to return to rectify any problems. If it is insurance-backed, however, then it may provide considerable protection.

Some of the warranty schemes available will cover you should your builder go into liquidation before the works have been completed. They will also guarantee the work for a number of years for faulty workmanship, materials and structural defects. This protection is worth having, and you would be well advised to pay for a more expensive builder to do your work, if he holds a good-quality warranty.

Sadly, on the whole, warranties are comparatively rare in small works construction, apart from those businesses involved in damp, rot and wood-worm treatments. This means that you generally have to rely upon the goodwill of the builder to return to rectify defective works. Alternatively, you have to be prepared to take legal proceedings against the builder, which can be hazardous – and may only establish that he has little on which to levy a court judgement.

Regulatory Organizations

There are some organizations that do have considerable importance within small works (and construction as a whole). The single most common, and perhaps important, is **CORGI (Council of Registered Gas Installers)**. This organization regulates all the functions surrounding work involved with gas, such as the installation of boilers and the related pipework. Any builder not registered with CORGI will be contravening regulations if he does any gas work whatsoever on site.

Working with gas is now almost an integral part of a plumber's work, and you should be wary of employing any plumber who is not registered. Most builders involved in small works, quite properly, subcontract this type of work out to plumbers or central heating engineers who are registered. The CORGI-registered member is tested once a year, and three of his sites are inspected, to ensure that the member is operating to the standards and procedures required.

It is certainly vital to recognize the difference between a trade organization and one that is regulating the work of those in the building industry. The distinction in the case of CORGI is considerable. While the trade organization is primarily aimed at helping the builder, the requirement of membership of CORGI is aimed at protecting you, as a consumer. This protection does not, however, extend to the charging practice of the member, nor his reliability in other respects, but only – and importantly – to his technical competence.

In summary, there is no cast-iron way of finding a good builder, nor of isolating him from his many competitors in small works construction. The industry is enormous, obeys few of the rules of conventional industries, and is one that can seem perplexing even to those operating within it. An understanding of the industry will help, however, and should emphasize the absolute necessity of ensuring that you, alone, properly manage and monitor any small works – from inception to completion.

SUMMARY

- Appreciate the problems inherent in building work and any employment of a builder, *before* starting a project.

- Start the project in the expectation that the quality of work may be a problem.

- Be prepared for your builder to be poorly organized, rushed, and with an inefficient administration.

- Subcontracting by the builder can be beneficial, so long as it is properly supervised and the overall day-to-day control of the project remains firmly in your builder's hands.

- Find out the daily rate charged in your local area by builders, electricians, plumbers, plasterers etc. This will provide you with a point of comparison for any quoted prices you receive.

- Beware of paying money in advance – the inherent value in most small building works businesses is small, so there is often little point in suing them in the hope of obtaining money.

- Do not rely on appearances when choosing a builder. Many excellent builders look untidy and drive scruffy vehicles.

- Always try to choose a builder on the basis of a recommendation, either from a friend or, better still, a construction professional such as a structural engineer, surveyor or architect.

- Wherever possible, go and see the work that your recommended builder has done. Try to speak to his previous client alone, to find out who managed the day-to-day work and the overall conduct of the project.

- Try to ensure that any previous work you inspect is comparable in content and quality to the work you are proposing.

- If possible, try to employ a builder who can provide you with an insurance-backed warranty for any work done.

6

Defining the Scope of Works

WHILE it is true to say that many people have a 'bad builder' story, it is also the case that most builders have a mass of 'terrible client' stories. Indeed, a great many problems stem directly from the property owner. All too often a project starts before a person has prioritized the works required, defined the detailed end result he wants to achieve or even given proper attention to a budget for the works. As a consequence, builders soon find they are performing work in an illogical order, while trying to achieve an aim about which they are unclear. As the project progresses, so the problems and the costs increase, as a builder is constantly asked to do further work or, worse still, variations on what has already been done.

If you are not absolutely clear about what the project is trying to achieve, then problems are guaranteed to occur. Indeed, frequently a perfectly good, organized builder finds himself helplessly bogged down in a project that is being run by someone with little idea of what he actually wants or can afford. If you, by ill-chance or poor planning, have also managed to find a bad builder or tradesman, then these problems will be compounded. The project will inevitably dissolve into a mess, and possibly one that you may not have the funds to rectify.

It is absolutely critical, however small the potential works, that you devote considerable time and effort to the planning of the project. You must respect the complexity of small works construction, with its almost unlimited potential for problems and misunderstandings. The aim of the planning phase must be for you to be able to produce a schedule of works, preferably with plans, that will unambiguously convey your detailed aims to the builder.

You should also check, at this stage, that what you wish to do is viable, given any planning constraints (see Chapter 15), and any potential problems that you may have with building regulations (see Chapter 14). Difficulties in either of these areas may make your project unworkable – either because the works may not be allowable, or because of the cost.

There are three main stages to developing a scope of works:

- Budget and Timetable
- Prioritization
- Defining Detail

BUDGET AND TIMETABLE

Critical to your development of a definition of the works is a realistic attention to your own budget and timetable – well before any works are commenced. It is only once a budget has been decided on that any realistic definition of the work you want to do can be undertaken.

As a general principle, in fixing a budget, you should allow for a contingency sum of not less than 20%. If you have £10,000 to spend, try to make sure that no quotation exceeds £8,000, particularly if the project involves any kind of work on an old property.

Building work is notorious for going over budget and small works construction is not, by any means, immune to this problem. Indeed, in some areas such as the renovation of houses, particularly those built during the Victorian era or earlier, building works are almost guaranteed to exceed the original quotations – and often by a great deal more than 20%. If you have not allowed for a contingency sum you could find that you run out of money before the work is finished, or that you do not have enough to make changes which you consider necessary once you have seen the results of the new work.

This exceeding of the budget is by no means always the fault of either the builder or yourself. Unfortunately, not even experienced builders, let alone surveyors, can accurately predict the state of older buildings. While superficially sound, they can often suffer a multitude of hidden defects, either as a pure consequence of the ravages of age, or the equally destructive actions of previous builders and house owners.

Sometimes, for example, where a property looks as though it has been rewired, it is only the sockets and surface fittings that have been renewed, or maybe just sections of the cabling. Alternatively, there may have been some previously bodged building works concealing a structural fault that will unavoidably need to be remedied. Such problems are often only discovered once building works are started, perhaps on a quite unrelated matter. Once found, however, they then present you with no real choice but to rectify the revealed problem, often regardless of the cost and its impact upon your existing budget.

You must also be self-disciplined during the course of the works themselves and take great care not to increase the costs beyond what you had planned to spend. Doing this during the initial enthusiasm at the start of the project can be particularly dangerous, as you may find too late that a problem arises towards the end of the project when you have already used up your contingency money.

You must be realistic about any timings for the work. Invariably building works take longer than anyone, including the builders themselves, expect. Again, add on at least 20% to the time you believe the project will take – or indeed, to what your builder tells you. You will have to be prepared to be reasonably flexible throughout the project and, at best, expect timings to be correct to within a few days, rather than to the day. This does not mean that you should give your builder the impression that time does not greatly matter

– quite the reverse – but that your expectations should not be too high.

The starting date for a project is equally hard for the builder to predict; expect flexibility of a few days either way, and avoid fixing the expected start date into an unrealistically tight personal schedule. Building is not an exact science, and even when things are going well you must appreciate that any timings provided by a builder are likely to be no more than educated guesstimates.

PRIORITIZATION

Decide on the works that need performing in order of priority. This may not be so important if your financial resources are unlimited, but it is crucial to get it right if you can only afford limited amounts of professional work. Either way, you will not want to have to do work twice or to spoil work that has been completed satisfactorily.

Unfortunately, in prioritizing works, aesthetics have to take a back seat. You really must tackle the unglamorous work first, ensuring that any remedial work to the exterior is dealt with as a priority, so that the property is properly weatherproofed. There is absolutely no point, for example, in starting to decorate inside rooms, when the external pointing or woodwork is allowing damp to penetrate the walls. Likewise, any problems with roofs or defective structures should be dealt with as soon as possible.

Internally, work on the basis of getting all the inherently messy works out of the way before any actual decoration takes place. If possible, try to make sure that similar areas of work are undertaken at the same time. For example, electrical and plumbing/central heating works tend to necessitate the removal of floorboarding, and thereby cause a high degree of disruption throughout a property. Wherever possible, they should be done together, and preferably as early on as possible. The same is true of general construction and plastering, when it is impossible to avoid dust and mess.

Normally, a builder who is given a free hand on a range of works to a property will concentrate on getting any major construction works done first, such as the removal of any walls or ceilings. He will then do the 'first fit' pipe and cable work of any electrics and plumbing, before commencing the major reconstruction works and replastering. Any joinery will then take place, after which the site will be well cleaned prior to any decoration and 'second fitting' of the electrics and plumbing – that is, the installation of baths, sinks, electrical face plates and so on.

While this may be fine in practice, however, your needs may mean that your priorities cannot be quite so logical. For example, if you have young children, or you work from home, then it may be vital to have particular rooms made habitable straight away. This is, of course, possible, but can result in completed work being subsequently damaged, or at the very least covered in layers of dust.

DEFINING DETAIL

Always define your desired end result in detail. In some cases this is really quite simple. If your property has no central heating, then obviously you will be able to define clearly your aim – to heat the house adequately. Even here, you will have to make some subjective decisions, such as the preferred location of the boiler and the positioning of the radiators within the different rooms. You may also be considering extending your house at some time. You should therefore allow for this factor when the piping is being laid, together with the fact that the boiler may need to be larger, to allow for any future extension of the central heating system. Essentially, however, the aim is quite clear and does not, initially, require too much consideration.

The opposite is true when the proposed works involve an element of design, and it is here that many of the problems between a builder and yourself will occur. The problem in part is invariably a misunderstanding of roles.

Generally, builders are enablers. While they obviously have views on what work can look like, and are frequently capable of design, their main function is to convert specific instructions, preferably with plans and drawings, into reality. On the whole they are simply not equipped to deal with people who have an ill-defined idea of what they wish to achieve, and it is rare for a builder ever to obtain payment for his design work. Neither he, nor you, will think of his work as being that of an interior designer or architect. The latter structure their costings around time spent on design, and are practised in drawing out from a client a clear definition of what they want to achieve. For most builders this is anathema, and all they want are straightforward, unambiguous instructions that will allow them to proceed with clearly defined work.

Up to a point, you really have only two choices in trying to assess what you want done clearly enough to develop a schedule of works. If you have sufficient money, the optimum course is to employ a quality interior designer or architect. These people can spend time with you to clarify ideas, and they have the capability and patience to do three-dimensional drawings, showing their ideas off in some detail. They also normally hold a library of pictures and designs of all types, which you can go through to crystallize your own ideas. Once the overall effect has been developed satisfactorily, they can then produce detailed drawings, sufficient for a proper schedule of works to be drawn up.

If you have neither the money, nor the time to employ an architect or designer, you will have to define the works yourself. This is not always as easy as it sounds, particularly if there is a large amount of aesthetic judgement involved in the project. That said, there are many design-related books and magazines on the market, and time spent going through these is rarely wasted, especially, and critically, if you make a well-ordered collection of the pictures that feature the effects or details you want. These are of tremendous help to any builder, who can then clearly assess the details that may be required. If you want a vanity unit constructed, it can be of critical help to the builder if he is shown a picture of the desired result, and preferably one that clearly shows any special finishing details. A mere verbal description is never sufficient – and will always lead to misunderstandings.

This question of quality and detail must be settled early on during your definition of the works. Naturally, everyone wants work of excellent quality, but the difference between the cost of basic and very good-quality work can be enormous. It is therefore important to define clearly to any potential builder, *before* he provides a costing, the level of finish that you require. This is certainly better done with the use of photographs and good drawings than anything else, but still requires some specific decisions.

For example, you may decide you want a wall replastered, as the existing surface is unsound or too bumpy for decoration. On the face of it there should be no possible question of degrees of quality. There is a tremendous difference, however, between patching up unsound plasterwork and then plastering a wall surface to a smooth finish, and the actual squaring of a wall to ensure a perfectly flat, vertical, smooth plastered surface with right-angled corners to all other walls and the ceiling. The first action is reasonably quick and satisfactory in many circumstances, but on high quality work it would be unacceptable.

In essence, you must approach any project on the basis that it will contain major areas of uncertainty, and that the overall aim may be unclear to anyone but yourself. If you are not absolutely sure of what you want done – then no one you employ is likely to be.

One of the gripes of builders operating in small works is that they frequently do the work several times over. This is not because the quality of the work is defective, but because the client is unable to describe adequately what is wanted, until an example is produced by the builder. In effect, the project becomes one of negative design. For example, a builder may construct some wardrobes with doors hung with butt hinges, only to find that the client does not like the way they look. He may then try piano hinges, but end up with the client actually wanting kitchen-type hinges. All may have been equally capable of making the doors swing satisfactorily, but all look rather different, and have different functions – and kitchen hinges would require new doors altogether.

While this is a minor example, it shows how important attention to design detail is, prior to the work being commenced. Certainly, even in this example, it is easy to see how a number of factors quickly conspire to damage the relationship between the builder and yourself, notwithstanding that both of you were acting in good faith. In the example given, there are significant differences in the cost of the materials, in this case hinges, and also in the labour time required to fit them; and this is before the builder has had to do the same work several times over, with a consequent need to charge an 'extra' for the additional work. If these types of things occur frequently during a contract, the project will quickly become fraught, and can end up barely resembling the original specification for the works – let alone maintaining the desired completion date or budget.

SUMMARY

- Set a budget, prioritize the works and then clearly define intentions and aims before writing a specification.

- Anticipate that some of the works will exceed the budget and allow for a contingency of at least 20%.

- Prioritize the works, if possible, on the basis of weatherproofing, structural alterations, electrical and plumbing, and *then* decoration.

- Define clearly the required end result, paying particular attention to anything with an element of design.

- If possible, employ a designer or architect to articulate the desired effect.

- Collect pertinent drawings and pictures that represent what is required, as attachments to any specification.

- Tackle the question of quality head-on, and be prepared to define it clearly in writing, or by way of a drawing or picture, with respect to any part of the project.

- Understand that if you do not know exactly what you want then the builder will have no chance of producing the work required. This is the main reason for contracts going wrong.

7

The Schedule of Works

ONCE you have clearly settled the desired overall scope of works, prepare a schedule, preferably with plans attached. This process in itself will further clarify in your mind's eye exactly what it is that you want to achieve.

In many ways this is the most vital area of the project to get right, and it justifies time, research and expense to ensure that a written schedule of works is produced, which is comprehensive, unambiguous and accurate. This will form the basis for any contract and will, on its own, largely contribute to a smooth and successful project. It must be done regardless of the size of the project, whether it is the decoration of one room or the renovation of a complete apartment.

If you neglect the preparation of a schedule of works, then you do so at your own risk. Failings during a contract can often be traced directly back to a lack of adequate preparation of this document. This aspect of your responsibility to a project cannot be overemphasized, and you should allow in your budget for a professionally drawn schedule and plans wherever possible. (See also Appendix 2: Specimen Professional Schedule of Works.)

There are three ways of preparing a schedule of works:

- Professional Preparation of Schedule
- Personal Preparation of Schedule
- Schedule within a Quotation by a Builder

PROFESSIONAL PREPARATION OF SCHEDULE

Ideally, a schedule of works should be drawn up by a professional, such as a consulting structural engineer, architect or surveyor. These professionals produce schedules and plans as a regular part of their job, and their knowledge of buildings and building work is normally comprehensive. They will also know about any planning restrictions and the way to obtain the necessary permissions or, perhaps, the best way to alter your project so that it can fit within acceptable forms of development. Their schedules and plans will also be drawn up to comply with building regulations.

That said, ensure the professional you turn to is properly qualified in small works construction and your particular type of project and has indemnity insurance. A surveyor dealing in commercial property deals and city rents would obviously be inappropriate, as would an architect normally employed on substantial new building works, if your work involves renovation. Consulting structural engineers are often the best people to employ, as their hands-on knowledge of building works can be unrivalled and, where a building is old or the structure complex, they can often anticipate potential problem areas. On the other hand, where there is design sensitivity, such as in areas of special architectural or historic interest, or perhaps where there are spatial problems, the service of an architect may be advisable.

Ensure when choosing a professional that there is no confusion in your mind as to who is the right person to draw up the schedule of works.

An all-too-common fault is using interior designers to prepare the building works schedule. This is an inappropriate mixing of functions. If you have employed the services of an interior designer, then a structural engineer, architect or surveyor must draw up the schedule of works from the designer's plans. Too often a designer is used to manage the construction phase of the project, when his talents and training really lie in the finishing works or the overall concept.

Any schedule drawn up by a professional should be in great detail, similar to the copy schedule in Appendix 2, and should cover every possible facet of the proposed works, however minor. Wherever possible there should be floor plans or drawings, with details of the actual materials that must be used.

In the example provided in Appendix 2 note that the schedule of works also takes the form of a **tender document**, thus performing two critical functions. On the right-hand side of the page are columns for the builder to enter his prices for each given function, which then allows you to assess the costs individually. This has a number of advantages, including allowing you, on the returned schedules of works, to compare the prices of the different builders who have quoted. You or your professional adviser can assess where the variations are acute between different builders, and where one builder is charging an inordinate amount for a part of the works, compared to others. Equally, it can sometimes help in showing where a builder may have dangerously underquoted, indicating that he may be quoting on works for which he has insufficient experience. You can also easily cut out areas of work that you may feel are not a priority, given the constraints of your budget.

Not surprisingly, a professionally drawn-up schedule of works and plans can be quite expensive, depending on the size and complexity of the proposed project. Invariably, however, this is money extremely well spent. You will effectively recoup the cost during the contract, by not having the builder making constant, probably justified, demands for additional money due to ambiguities in a poor, unprofessionally developed schedule. You also have the advantage of possessing a document that will, with analysis, help to choose not just the cheapest builder, but the one who appears to be the most competent.

The other function that professionals will undertake, in conjunction with the preparation of a schedule of works, is that of preparation of a **specification** (see Appendix 3: Specimen Professional Specification) or pro forma list of practices, with which the builder must comply. This document covers a wide range of activities and will, for example, define the type of timber to be used and the way it should be fixed, or the makes of paint that can be used and the way the paint is applied. This tends to be a deliberately comprehensive document. It is produced by a structural engineer or other professional, and is sent out with the tender document and adjusted as necessary, depending on the type of works. Not all the contents may be relevant to your particular project, but it will bind the builder, together with the schedule of works, to stated basic practices which, if contravened, expressly breach any contract. In effect, this document further removes any latitude that a builder may have for arguing that what he is doing is good practice, when in fact it may not be so.

PERSONAL PREPARATION OF SCHEDULE

If you decide not to use a professional to draw up the schedule of works, for reasons of expense, then you should attempt to copy the professional's approach. The schedule that you draw up should be in writing, as detailed as possible, and preferably drawn up in the format shown in Appendix 2.

Do not be shy about itemizing every possible function, even if it seems blatantly obvious that the work to be done is an integral part of a particular parcel of works. If you want a ceiling and cornice painted, then you should go as far as specifying, for example, that you want the particular crack on the left-hand corner raked out and filled, and the misformed piece of cornice above the door re-formed. If you do not do this, then you are allowing the builder to interpret what he wants and the builder may say, with some justification, that decorating the ceiling and cornice meant just a basic making good, followed by painting. One person's interpretation of making good or decorating is invariably very different from another's.

A schedule of works must specify everything you want done – clearly and unambiguously. There should also be no doubt about the precise locations referred to in the schedule.

No builder will feel patronized or upset if he finds that he is given a detailed schedule of works. On the contrary, most builders will be delighted that they have a clear document from which to quote, and one that relieves them from trying to find out what you actually want. In any event, most builders are used to, and comfortable with, dealing with schedules of works, specifications and plans, and it is rare that a schedule drawn up by a layman will be as detailed as a thorough schedule produced by a good professional.

Obviously, one of the difficulties is that you may lack the relevant knowledge clearly to define areas of work and appropriate materials. In some cases, you may also unknowingly specify works that contravene either planning or building regulations, or things that are not logical or even possible. You must first of all decide whether, in the light of your lack of knowledge, you should attempt to draw up a specification in the first place. This can be a 'chicken-and-egg situation', as you may not recognize potential problem areas until they are pointed out by the builder; but a schedule of some kind is better than none at all.

If you do draw up a schedule of works, anticipate that some, perhaps significant, changes are likely to be needed once the builders have themselves assessed the property. The builders will possibly have a number of suggestions of their own that may be structurally necessary or aesthetically pleasing, or may bear on regulations (see Chapter 14: Building Regulations and Building Control, and Chapter 15: Planning Permission) which stop you from doing what you initially desired. In this event, considerable changes may need to be made to the schedule. They must be marked both on the schedule itself and on any plans, so these can remain the core documents of the contract. Then they should be resubmitted to the builders, to enable them to requote.

SCHEDULE WITHIN A QUOTATION BY A BUILDER

The final, most common and most deeply flawed way to obtain a schedule of works is by allowing builders to produce their own.

In this case, you will show the builders around the relevant area, describe your requirements and show photographs or pictures that will give a clear idea of what you want. In theory, the builders will then send you their quotations, with any relevant drawings attached. These will set out in writing exactly what they intend to do, if their price is acceptable. You can then compare the different quotes that you receive, before choosing the builder with whom you are most impressed.

Unfortunately, this way of forming a schedule of works is a very hit-and-miss affair.

Part of the problem lies in relying on builders to deliver precise written quotations, as opposed to a brief summary of the works or even just a short letter providing little more than a price. Builders in small works construction frequently just do not have the infrastructure or time to produce detailed quotations. You are therefore unlikely to receive anything that would stand as a proper schedule. The danger is that your contract will be started on the basis of price alone, with much of the project vague or dependent on what you or the builder thought you told each other. Even if both the builder and yourself are operating in good faith, there are bound to be misunderstandings, which always lead to trouble – at best, variations in price and a loss of confidence.

Furthermore, if two or three builders quote for the works, it is extremely unlikely that their quotations will be presented in a form that allows for comparison. Also, basing your decision on well-written, extensive quotes tends to exclude builders whose organization does not allow them to produce impressively presented costings. Inadvertently, you may exclude some excellent builders, more than capable of doing the works well and, perhaps, cheaper than a company supporting an administrative structure.

Finally, relying on a builder to draw up a schedule of works does tend to place the builder in the driving seat during the course of the project. If you have failed to develop a schedule of works yourself, then it is quite likely that, having never really put your mind to the detail of the contract, you may never fully know what is happening.

On new building works in particular, a well-prepared schedule of works, good plans and a comprehensive specification should enable a contract to proceed with little or no variation to either the scope of work or the quoted costs. With renovation works, however, even an excellent schedule of works is unlikely to anticipate all changes to the work or costs. Old buildings often have unseen defects which, when revealed, will create additional work and expense. That said, a thorough schedule of works will, in conjunction with a formal contract, significantly reduce your exposure to substantial variations in cost and timing.

SUMMARY

- A comprehensive, unambiguous and accurate schedule of works, accompanied by good plans and a specification, is the absolute key to a successful project, regardless of size.

- If at all possible get the schedule of works drawn up by a professional such as a structural engineer, architect or surveyor.

- Ensure that the schedule of works covers every possible facet and detail of the work, regardless of how minor or blatantly obvious it may seem.

- The format of the schedule of works should allow it to be used as the tender document.

- If possible, obtain from a professional a specification or standard form of practices that covers the type of work you are performing and attach this to the schedule of works.

- If the only effective schedule of works is the written quote of the builder, ensure that it is sufficiently accurate, and leaves no possible areas of ambiguity. If it does, then clarify undefined areas in writing and get the builder to agree to the changes.

8

The Quotation

ONCE a satisfactory schedule of works has been prepared, you can obtain quotes from builders to do the work. All the quotes should be based only on the schedule of works, with the columns of the schedule completed by each builder.

Once again with small works construction, the best theories tend to fall apart. The correct theory is that you should always obtain three quotes for any works that you want doing. While it can be difficult, however, to find one good builder (see Chapter 5: The Builder), who you feel could perform the proposed project, to find three could be even more of a problem. This is compounded by the fact that even if all three attend your property, it is not uncommon to find that one, or perhaps more, never actually provides a quotation.

In this event, you have little choice but to choose a couple of builders 'blind'. There is no reason why one of these builders may not turn out to be very good, and end up being the one that performs the work. At least if they provide a quotation, you will have some idea of the comparative costs of your preferred builder.

It really is important to obtain more than one quote, unless money is no object and you are determined to have one builder in particular. The variation of costs in different quotations can be tremendous. This is particularly true in renovation, where one builder's appreciation of the extent of work that lies behind a schedule can be quite different from another's. Also, particularly if you are producing your own schedule of works, it can be of great help to hear the different perspective that another builder may place on the project. He may have better ideas than a previous builder, or be able to suggest alternatives to the original scope that may significantly reduce costs or be more aesthetically pleasing. He may also pick up where planning controls or building regulations apply, that might have been missed by the other builders.

When a builder does come to assess work on the property, make sure you give him all possible information regarding it. If there is a surveyor's report which contains any information bearing upon the proposed work, then a copy of this should be given to him. Likewise, if you already know of any potential problem areas, then you should advise a builder accordingly. Often no one knows a property better than the person living in it, and a builder rarely has the opportunity to investigate the area of work properly. To do this would require exploratory works that you may not be willing to allow, particularly if you are gathering together quotes to see if you can afford to have the work done in the first place.

Certainly, hiding known flaws can be counterproductive. If a builder commences work and finds flaws about which he could not reasonably have known, he will be well within his rights to consider their rectification outside his scope of agreed work. In this case, you will have to obtain a cost from the builder for the additional works. Of course, this cost will be provided by the builder, anticipating, probably correctly, that you will find it difficult to get other quotes. The price charged for the additional works will, therefore, most probably be higher than if it had been quoted for originally – and competitively.

In some areas of work, such as the construction of a new extension, the builder should be able to assess much of the work accurately. In other areas, the builder, even with the help of a good schedule of works and plans, will end up 'guesstimating' the costs involved. This is particularly true where the builder has to assess works when the property is already inhabited, with furnishings and carpets in place. It is even more difficult if the house is old.

Even the simplest job can be hard to quantify and one builder's assessment can be quite different from another's. For example, you may want a radiator installed in a room. This is normally quite a simple job, with the plumber locating the pipework to the rest of the house system, draining down the system, rolling back a carpet, taking up sufficient floorboards across the room to feed his pipes under the floor, and then fixing the radiator to the wall and connecting the pipework. There are, however, many variables that can completely change a builder's assessment. The previous pipework may not have been performed logically, and therefore be hard to find or adequately connect to; the floorboards below the carpet may be tongued-and-grooved, thus being extremely difficult to take up and possibly hard to replace; and the wall that the radiator must be connected to may be unsound, making even the fitting of the wall brackets a time-consuming undertaking.

It is for reasons like these that quotations can vary so much, and this is why it is in your interest to try and provide the builder with all possible information. Without it, he may deliberately quote high, anticipating problems when there are none, or he may find that he has quoted too little, and be forced to start finding extras to cover his costs. Certainly, when you come to analyse the quotations that you receive, you must bear in mind the potential variables. A builder who has provided the lowest quote may simply not have realized the potential problems inherent in the work, in which case he may find himself in financial difficulty before the completion of the project.

Trade manuals exist to quantify every possible variable of building work, from the cost of brickwork per square metre to the cost of painting several different designs of doors. However, these soon go out of date, and they cannot take account of local market conditions. They are even less applicable when new work is being done on, and around, old property. Invariably the builder will not have a clear run at any of the jobs he is being asked to do and, knowing that, cannot price the same job for the same amount from one property to another. The builder will often, therefore, end up pricing a schedule of works on the basis of experienced guesswork, accepting that on some items he is likely to make more money that expected, and on others less. While this is always frustrating for the builder, it is not too worrying, so long as the project as a whole makes him money.

The difficulty when appraising a quotation is therefore to take a balanced view of it as a whole. If the overall cost of the project is similar to that of a competing builder, variations on separate functions can be largely ignored – unless there is some absurdity which indicates that the builder simply has no idea of what has to be done and how much it should realistically cost.

Of course, at the end of the day there is nothing to stop you from simply employing the builder who has provided the lowest cost for the specified works. Indeed, this is often the way of awarding work when builders tender formally to professionals. In the normal course of events, a professional would have to produce a very good reason to persuade you, as his client, to opt for the builder whose bid was higher. As this is the standard way of operating throughout the industry, you should not necessarily always look to the middle bid as being the appropriate one.

That said, professionals do have some important factors in their favour. They will invariably draw up a proper contract, which domestic clients rarely do. This enables them to hold the builder to completion of the contract for the sum quoted, regardless of the fact that he may have made a mistake in the costings of his quotation, and be losing money on the project. The professional will take the view that completing the contract to standard and time is the builder's problem. Any attempt to obtain extras to make up any monetary deficiency will be strongly resisted. Indeed, it will be very difficult for the builder to obtain additional money during the project as the contract, backed by the precision of the schedule of works, the specification and plans, will preclude most chances of obtaining extras.

The professionals will also be involved in the supervision of the work. Part of their contract with you will involve their checking that the schedule of works and specification are kept to by the builder, and that all the works are completed using the correct materials and an adequate standard of workmanship. They will know the areas in which a builder could attempt to save money by using cheaper materials or perhaps a quicker, but less satisfactory, way of doing the work. Accordingly, they will schedule site inspections at critical points in the project to ensure that the builder is complying with the contract. Often a builder will be specifically forbidden to proceed further on an area of a project until the relevant inspection has been made.

To a lesser extent professionals can also exert pressure on builders through the mere fact that if a project is well run by the builder, he can expect more work from the professional in the future. It may well be in the builder's interest simply to accept that he has made a mistake quoting on a particular contract, and complete it in the hope that he will receive more work from the professional – from which he will make up his loss. As a private client you cannot exert this pressure, which is why you may find it helpful to engage a professional to monitor the work if possible.

A well drawn-up contract will enable you to choose the lowest quote. If you are relying on the integrity and good will of the builder, however, and do not have the expertise to supervise the works, then you may find it better to choose the builder who did not produce the lowest bid, particularly if it is well below the others. This way you may avoid the builder who will quickly run into trouble due to his own misquoting, and who will be doing everything possible to save money, perhaps to the detriment of the project. At worst the builder may just give up on the project and refuse to continue. In this event there really is little you can do, especially if the builder has been paid roughly up to date. Trying to take legal action against a small works builder can be quite hazardous, and is unlikely to force him to complete the project successfully.

Certainly, one of the worst things that can occur is for your builder to refuse to continue with the project, or for you to have to get rid of a builder before completion of the works. Most builders loathe coming onto a site that is half-finished, and will do everything possible to avoid it. Apart from the obvious problems associated with trying to continue with the other builder's work, which may have been done quite differently, they have to face a client who will be more than usually anxious about their performance. Of course, you would first have to find another builder who could take over the project quickly. This is problem enough, let alone trying to negotiate costings from a very vulnerable position.

SUMMARY

- Quotes should be obtained from three different builders wherever possible.

- When they come to assess the property, provide builders with as much information as possible to enable them to prepare accurate quotes.

- Be prepared to amend a schedule of works and reissue it for requoting, to take into account a builder's own recommendations.

- When assessing quotes look at the overall costs first, and then see if any particular areas have gross variations.

- If there is a gross variation, on an individual item, not seen in the other two quotes it will probably indicate that the builder does not know the area of work well.

- If a lowest quote is to be accepted, ensure that it is covered by a precise schedule of works, good plans, a specification and contract, and consider using some of the money saved to employ a professional to monitor the critical stages of the contract.

- If you have to rely to some extent on the good will and integrity of the builder, then choose the middle quote, if there is a large differential between that and the highest price.

9

The Contract

IT is vital that a contract is finalized before any work starts. The sophistication of the contract will depend to a large extent on the size, complexity and value of the work to be done, but even for very minor works there should be some written evidence.

LEGAL CONTRACT

The essence of a contract is that, between the relevant parties, three components are clearly established. There must be:

- an offer (normally the builder's tender or quotation);
- acceptance (unqualified acceptance of the builder's offer by yourself); and
- consideration (the monetary value of the contract).

The three components amount, in legal terms, to a binding agreement (*consensus ad idem*) – complete agreement to the undertaking of a matter, for an agreed sum of money. Unless all three of these components are satisfied, a contract will be defective.

The contract must not concern an illegal action, nor must either party be placed under any duress to agree. Silence cannot be considered acceptance. So, if an assertion is made by one party and not expressly agreed to by the other, either orally or in writing, then it will be unenforceable. This will also be the case if there has been misrepresentation (see Chapter 16: Law and Disputes).

ORAL AND WRITTEN CONTRACTS

In contract law there is no difference whatsoever between a written and an oral contract, so that an oral agreement made on site to plaster a room for £500 would be just as valid as one in writing, signed by all the parties in a solicitor's office.

An oral contract, however, always tends to suffer from a lack of clear evidence to support it. When problems do occur, not surprisingly, everyone's memories of the exact contract terms are different, and it can sometimes be nearly impossible to prove what was actually agreed. This can result in the contract being difficult to enforce, should the matter go to court. There is the further disadvantage of not focusing clearly the mind of the builder or yourself, right from the start of the work. It is therefore important for both you and the contractor to have a written, signed contract clearly setting out the relevant terms. Indeed, you must take the same care over the contract as you do over the schedule of works, and itemize any matters about which you are concerned.

IMPLIED TERMS

Many contracts have terms 'implied' to them by statute or the common law (see Chapter 16). These will be terms which either cannot be excluded, even if all parties involved wish them to be, or which would be read into a contract by a court, in the case of a dispute, if the contract was not in immense detail. The implied terms generally act to protect you (acting as an individual consumer), and enable a contract to be workable.

A contract does not have to specify, in a general sense, standards of service and the quality of material or equipment supplied. If the contract with the builder is made by yourself, as an individual, as opposed to acting as a corporate body, then the contract is covered by existing legislation. These implied terms, however, will only provide for the work being done in an adequate manner, which may not be sufficient if you require top-quality work. The normal express term a court would expect in a building contract, unless otherwise stated, is that: 'Works would be completed in a good and workmanlike manner with materials and workmanship of proper quality.'

EXPRESS CONDITIONS

The express conditions of any small works contract will vary, but there tend to be a number of constants that are vital to even the most minor of works, as discussed below:

- The Cost of the Works
- The Terms of Payment
- Specifying the Schedule of Works
- The Start and Finish Dates of the Project
- Agreeing Variations or Additions to the Schedule of Works
- Public Liability Insurance Cover

Further terms can be written into the contract, depending on your wishes. You may want to specify the times during which work cannot take place, such as during the weekends or after 6.00pm, or you may wish to make it a term of the contract that the builder clears all his rubbish daily. There is no limit to the terms that can be placed in a contract but, for small works, the terms listed above are the absolute minimum, and should be stated as express conditions (see Chapter 16).

Devote time to considering what areas of the project may require specific written clarification – although these terms should relate to the conduct of the contract rather than to the actual nature of the building works. In effect, while the contract as a whole will, of course, comprise the schedule of works, specification, plans and quotation (preferably within the schedule of works) it is helpful for the sake of clarity to have a separate document itemizing the terms of the contract. This can be set out by a solicitor, as a formal document, in the form of a letter or even, at worst, in writing on a clear area of the schedule of works. Obviously, the clearer the documentation, the easier it will be to refer to, should any misunderstandings or problems occur.

Ensure that there is only one overall document that stands as the contract. Avoid having a miscellany of terms that you and the builder might have put forward in an array of documents. Both you and the builder must be certain when final agreement has been reached, and this must be easy to prove conclusively.

In many areas of small works, contracts are never formalized, beyond simply advising the builder that his written quotation has been accepted. While this is often quite sufficient if a project progresses in a trouble free manner, it is of little help should anything go wrong – and the starting point, when planning a project, is that something is bound to go wrong.

The Cost of the Works

This is a common area for disagreements.

In some areas of small works, particularly anything to do with renovation, the exact cost of a project may not be defined by a builder in his quotation: it may be impossible to calculate the price until the works are under way, or sufficient exploratory work has been done. In this event, a contract may have a number of areas where only **provisional costs** are provided by the builder. Alternatively – and this is very common – the project may, in any event, incur additional work, for which the builder can justifiably charge extras.

Once you have a builder working on site, you will, in practice, find it hard not to accept his costings for additional works. It is therefore necessary, before the work starts, to define what the potential charges will be for additional works, and on what basis the builder will work out his charges. This should become an express part of the contract.

Commonly, in this instance, you and the builder may specifically agree hourly or daily rates, if additional work is necessary, for a combination of trades such as labourers, joiners, electricians, plasterers, plumbers, etc. You must also agree upon a method for the charging of any extra materials. The materials are normally charged at cost to yourself, with a profit charge accruing to the builder. It is in this situation also that the value of the schedule of rates, referred to earlier, becomes apparent.

Provisional costs should always be of some concern, as the true cost may be far greater than indicated. Indeed, wherever possible you should try to persuade a builder to give a firm quotation. However, in fairness to the builder, this is not always possible, in which case you are in an unavoidably exposed position. Contractually, your only real option is to set a limit on the provisional cost, above which the builder cannot charge without express written agreement.

The Terms of Payment

An essential part of a contract is the terms of payment. On minor contracts this can be quite uncontentious, with payment expected by the builder within seven days of completing the work. However, on larger contracts, or where expensive materials or equipment are required, particularly at the outset of the project, the builder may expect an up-front payment. This will then be followed by stage payments throughout the contract.

In major construction works, or where an architect is involved, builders are normally paid in arrears of either 14 or 30 days, with a retention sum of 5% of the contract price outstanding for six months or more.

This is not always feasible in small works contracts, where a builder may simply be unable to fund a project if he is paid in arrears. Also, it has to be said that builders may have the same scepticism towards their clients, as you to them. Builders who have experienced problems in obtaining money from their private clients will be anxious to be paid in advance, or at least as soon as possible. This is something that you will need to settle from the outset, although you should be prepared for a certain amount of negotiation. Some builders will simply turn down work, rather than be exposed too heavily on costs.

Wherever possible, avoid giving a builder money on account. If you do, then try to make sure that any money you provide is only for goods or materials already delivered. If your builder asks for money to pay for kitchen units, for example, which may need to be ordered well in advance of any work, then only pay him once the units have been delivered to your address – and do not pay for the fitting until this has been completed. Most builders will be able to buy materials on account, with a monthly payment term. If the materials cannot be delivered in advance, because of a lack of storage space on your property, for example, then go with the builder and pay for the goods personally. This way there can be no argument as to the ownership of the goods, and the builder will not feel vulnerable, as he will have had to make no outlay himself.

Whatever terms are negotiated, they must be clearly set out in the contract and the stages of payment must be easy to understand. For example, the stages may be payable either on completion of a part of the works, or at specific times. In the latter case, the builder may be due for payment every two weeks or so, regardless of his progress.

Probably the safest method, and the easiest to monitor, is to pay for completed stages of the work – although even this cannot be a hard and fast rule. In some works, such as the renovation of a property, it is sometimes hard to finish any part of the works satisfactorily until nearly the end of the contract, thus making stages of completion difficult to define. Also, while construction, rather than finishing, work is in full operation, the inevitable mess and activity can make it quite hard to assess real progress – let alone whether or not the quality of the work is up to standard.

On substantial small works operations it is wise to ensure that there is a retention clause in the contract allowing you to hold back up to 5% of the contract sum until six months have elapsed. This percentage is normally sufficient to ensure that a builder will return to sort out any problems, failing which he will not be paid the remainder of his money. This clause provides well needed leverage to bring a builder back to sort out any defects. If the contract concerns some complex machinery, perhaps a large boiler or new lift, then it is worth trying to insert a retention period of 12 months into the contract.

Specifying the Schedule of Works

There should be an express reference within the contract document to the schedule of works, specification and plans (if any), as being the actual works to be performed. This is important, particularly when there have been a number of different schedules of works that may have been altered and discarded during the negotiations for the contract.

The Start and Finish Dates of the Project

It is vital to have a clear idea of the start and finish dates for projects and the overall duration of the work. In some cases this can be of primary importance, such as when you wish to move into a new property. You must therefore ensure that the dates and timings are clearly itemized in writing, and are not left as some sort of vague conversational commitment. If the date for starting and finishing the contract is of vital importance, then you must use the term **time is of the essence** after the dates specified. This is a recognized legal term that will emphasize the importance to the contract of the time periods stated.

It may be advisable to insert **damages clauses** (often incorrectly called 'penalty' clauses) in some contracts, to provide for financial compensation if your builder does not complete the work on the appointed date. There are two factors, however, that can negate their value: builders will either not agree to a strict time schedule when there are damages clauses, or only agree if the time is in excess of what is really required.

Be warned that any variation made by you during the course of the contract will, if it entails more work, negate a damages clause. You must therefore ensure, when agreeing to a variation, that a specific increase or reduction in the contract time is expressly stated and agreed to by the builder – at the time of the variation. (See below.)

Agreeing Variations or Additions to the Schedule of Works

It is critical that there should be an agreed method of varying the contract. This is imperative in small works where variations can, on occasions, amount to a significant part of the total finished contract price. It is also an area that causes constant upset.

In contracts supervised by a professional, such as an architect or structural engineer, a builder will be provided with a detailed written instruction concerning a necessary variation. The builder will then provide, in writing, a price for the varied works. If this is accepted, he will be able to perform the variation and charge for it accordingly. If this procedure is not followed, then the builder's claim for any payment may be rejected.

A condition of any contract must expressly state that variations to the contract must be in writing, and agreed to by both you and your builder, before any addition or change to the works is performed.

While it is not essential on minor variations to go to the lengths of typing out formal letters, it is still necessary to have written agreement, even if it is just a question of both of you signing a docket with carbon paper in between, specifying the exact variation, the cost differential and the time the works will take.

Public Liability Insurance Cover

This must be an express condition of any contract and should specify a minimum insurance cover. Normally, this will be £1,000,000 but it may have to be greatly more, depending on the environment in which your builder will be working.

You must always insist on actually seeing the builder's current insurance certificate to ensure that it is up to date.

LARGE OR COMPLEX WORKS

If the works are of a significant size or complexity, though still within the definition of small works, then it really is necessary to ensure that an extensive, formalized contract is drawn up. This will deal in great detail with the problems inherent in building works. There are accepted formats for building works contracts, used throughout the industry, which have been developed specifically for small building works – but few people are aware of them and they are generally unnecessary on very minor works.

These documents tend to be similar in content and format, and deal formally with conditions such as:

- the determination of any contract;
- responsibility for planning and building regulations approvals;
- extensions of a contract period;
- damages clauses;
- retention periods;
- warranties;
- removal of equipment and rubbish from site; and
- dispute resolution.

The builder may also be expressly bound to do the work in a 'good and workmanlike manner' while using materials that are of 'merchantable quality'.

Make sure that any contract for works of high value or complexity is properly drawn up, specifically deals with building works and is as rigorous as possible. As a general rule, any contract for a value of over £5,000 or so should be based on a standard form of contract.

Fortunately, it is easy to obtain standard forms for small works building contracts that are designed for easy use. These can be obtained from a number of sources (see Appendix 6) and are cheap, easy to use and understand, and will cover most eventualities. They also save you having to go to a lawyer, or draft out a contract personally. A further advantage is that most builders will be familiar with the format and content, thus reducing any contention over the document.

Always make sure that you understand the contract, however, and the terms set out. Do not allow your builder to make variations 'because that's the way it's always done'. If you are in any doubt about variations to a contract, or you feel uneasy about a contract provided by your builder – do not sign it. Take advice on the matter.

The most common standard contracts are those published by the **JCT** (**Joint Contracts Tribunal**). **JCT MW80** is the contract that most professionals will use to bind a builder on any small works project. The courts are also familiar with the JCT contract, which they accept as being the construction industry's standard form of contract. The cost of buying one of these is small, the effort to fill them out minimal, but the protection afforded is considerable.

You should never feel concerned about getting a builder to sign a formal contract. In all works where a professional such as a structural engineer, architect or surveyor is involved, a builder will be made to sign a formal JCT contract, or its equivalent, before undertaking any works. Most builders, except when doing works for private clients (who, unwisely, rarely go to the trouble), are therefore used to being bound by formal, written contracts and accept them as a part of their commercial life.

SUMMARY

- A contract is only valid if there is total agreement between the parties as to the work to be done and the money to be received for it.

- Theoretically, there is no difference in strength between an oral and a written agreement – but the former will be difficult to prove in cases of dispute.

- Always look at the worst-case scenario and make sure there is a proper, clear, enforceable contract in place before work commences.

- Ensure that any contract made is in the form of a written document signed by both parties.

- The contract should always clearly set out the vital terms of: price, terms of payment, methods of agreement for variations of contract, the start and finish dates of the project and the requirement for public liability insurance.

- The schedule of works, specification and plans, if any, should be clearly defined and expressly referred to as a part of the contract.

- If the works are of reasonable size or complexity a formal, standard small works contract, such as that produced by the Joint Contracts Tribunal (JCT), should be obtained and signed by you and your builder.

10

The Works

IDEALLY, all small works should be monitored by a professional (even if the monitoring only amounts to a couple of short inspections), unless they are so straightforward that you can quite clearly see if there are any potential problems. As a non-professional, you must be careful not to overrate your ability to manage a project successfully.

If you do find that there are areas of which you are uncertain, or where you suspect something may not be quite right, then you must bring a professional on site as soon as possible. That said, there are a number of things that you can do yourself to ensure a project proceeds satisfactorily, so long as you have an appreciation of some of the more common problem areas (see Chapter 12: Checklist of Typical Problem Areas). If you are going to manage a project without professional help, then you must be proactive as soon as the works start.

RELATIONSHIP WITH THE BUILDER

You must consider your relationship with the builder very carefully. On the one hand you must make sure he is aware that you will be supervising the works on the site and constantly checking that they match the schedule and specification. On the other hand, this does not mean that you have any right whatsoever to interfere in the builder's actual work, or that of his men, until something has clearly gone wrong.

The builder, having had his bid accepted, has a right (within reasonable parameters) to approach his work as he sees fit, and you must afford him considerable latitude in the way that he performs it. Few things are more galling than a person who criticizes work before it is finished, or who is constantly fussing about the works or pestering the builder. A blatant lack of faith, when not justified, can be very demoralizing for a builder and therefore counterproductive.

It is normally helpful to make a formal arrangement with the builder, before work is started, whereby meetings on site are set for either once or twice a week. This enables the builder to put time aside formally for meeting with you, to discuss any problems or to clarify any areas of work that may be troubling you. It is at these meetings that the overall progress of the project can be discussed, with attention given to the achieving of targets and time schedules. At the same time, you should make a tour of the site with the builder in attendance, to check the work against the schedule of works. At this stage, any variations and their specific costings can be attended to, and paperwork brought up to date.

Although there is nothing wrong with looking round the site during the working day, it can be quite disruptive if you needlessly interfere while work is being carried out, particularly if the builder in charge of the site is also working 'on the tools'. If you do see something that you feel is not correct, however, you should mention this to the builder as soon as possible, so that it can be rectified before other works, which may make any alteration difficult, are performed.

Some people have a tendency not to point out a change until some time after they have seen it, thus giving the builder the impression that it has been approved. If, for example, you have been round the site and clearly seen some shelving that has been put up rather differently than originally planned, the builder will assume that you are content with the alteration unless you say otherwise. He may then commence the time-consuming act of painting them. If you subsequently mention that you are not happy, then the builder will, with justification, feel aggrieved.

For much of the time you may be out at work, and you will not necessarily see your builder every day, so you should agree on a place on site where you can leave notes. Notes are a good, clear form of communication and generally more effective than phone calls. It is also possible to keep a copy of them, in case a record is subsequently necessary.

For the most part builders respond well to people who take an interest in their work, and who treat them with care and courtesy. In fact, you should try to develop a good relationship with the builder, and his men on the site, straight away. All too frequently people treat builders without consideration: they seem to think that because the builder dresses scruffily and is dishevelled for much of the day, then he must also be rather stupid and a lout. It is easy to forget that site work is almost invariably dusty and dirty, and physically demanding.

In fact, of course, builders are like everyone else, and the better you treat them, the more care they will take over the work, and the greater the likelihood that they will do additional works free, or at a nominal cost. Fairness and generosity on the part of a client will often reap real rewards. You may even find the builder performing the work to a higher standard than originally intended.

Wherever possible, take an interest in the work, and if an element has clearly been well done then praise it freely. Most tradesmen take great pride in their workmanship, and are only too pleased to explain what they are doing and the particular skill involved in their specific function. It can make a considerable difference to their overall attention to the job, if they know that you have the ability to recognize quality work, and are willing to comment on it appreciatively. Of course, they are being paid to do good work, and should do so, but nonetheless do not disregard the value of praise throughout the course of the project. The only caveat to this is that you must not be too gushing, or make the mistake of being pleased when the work is not well done.

The latter particularly can be counterproductive; it gives the builder the impression that you have no idea of quality, and may encourage him to try and get away with substandard work. It is a tricky balance, but worth getting right.

Small things can also make a difference to a builder, such as the occasional mug of tea or coffee if the work happens to be within your house, or the delivery of biscuits or sandwiches to the site. If you are enthusiastic, this quality will transmit itself to your builders, and may lead them to take a greater interest in the work. Your aim should be to make the project a pleasure for the builder to work on, and one that is quite different from the norm.

PREPARATION OF THE SITE – MESS AND DUST

One area which constantly provides trouble, and which requires the attention of both client and builder prior to the start of the works, is that of the dust and mess involved.

Small works are, by their very nature, often undertaken either within a house or very close to it. Most people have no idea how much mess is involved in even the simplest building work – whether it is the decoration of a small room, minor plumbing repairs or the undertaking of a complete extension. They are therefore horrified to find that almost from the start of the works every room is filled with fine dust, and soft furnishings and furniture are in danger of being damaged. The garden is often quickly covered in mud, and treasured plants and shrubs are at risk.

The truth is that almost all building works are inherently messy and to underestimate this, and the potential for collateral damage, is a mistake. You must adequately prepare your property prior to any building works. All possessions should be moved from the area of work and stored out of the way. If a builder is going to do any work at all, he must be able to do so in a completely cleared area, preferably with the carpeting (if any) removed.

Accept that for all practical purposes you will be unable to use the relevant area until completion. Ensure that the builder has free access to his area of work, a safe place in which to store his tools and materials, and also somewhere that can be used as a temporary dumping ground for rubbish.

Few places are harder for the builder to work than an inhabited, fully furnished property with little or no garden or storage area. Before any work starts, you must realize the real difficulty for a builder who is trying to operate in a cluttered environment. Some works can be nearly impossible to undertake efficiently, because of a total lack of appreciation of the clear space that is needed. A consequence of this is that a builder will take longer to complete the works, become quickly demoralized and spend an inordinate amount of time vainly trying to protect a householder's treasured possessions.

It is extremely difficult to protect a property adequately while works are in progress. Dustsheeting, even if it involves a combination of plastic and cloth, rarely completely prevents the penetration of dust, and if there is a spillage of water or wet plaster it will inevitably occur where the sheeting has been displaced or torn. Furthermore, at some stage the daily cleaning of the site will have to be done and the dustsheeting removed, which creates dust on its own account.

Before the builder arrives to start work, consider the worst possible scenario with regard to collateral damage, and then act to prevent it. While the schedule of works or specification may well stipulate that the builder is to protect your property adequately, the reality is that he has to rely on you to pay at least equal attention to the problems.

ASSESSING THE WORK

There is no doubt that it is quite hard to identify whether a builder is doing a sound job until the finishing works are being completed – at which time defects suddenly become apparent. It is often only at this stage that you will notice that joinery or brickwork is not straight, or that pipes have not been properly concealed, or that a socket or light switch is missing. Equally, plastering that looked smooth when damp may look lumpy and scratched when dry and painted, or central heating that has been installed can turn out to be inadequate. Many of these problems stem from poor foundation work – i.e. work done during the beginning and middle of a contract as opposed to the end.

A frequent complaint of the decorators – normally the last tradesmen left on site – is that their job becomes virtually impossible because the work done by others before them is defective. They may end up trying to repair cracking in plasterboard which simply did not have enough nails to secure it to the joists properly, or to make good some bodged joinery which, with the best will in the world, will always look bad.

While many aspects of the project will be beyond your technical expertise there are, nonetheless, a number of things you can do during the project to avoid finding out, too late, that the builder has not done a sound job. Once again you must be proactive, and look for potential problem areas (See Chapter 12) before they become actual problems.

You must visit or check the site frequently; the optimum times are during the evenings or weekends. Even without turning to specific areas, you can generally get quite a good idea of the builder's overall competence, just by looking at the way that the site is run. A well run site is almost invariably tidy, if not clean, with tools neatly sorted out and materials and rubbish in defined areas. At the end of a day's work, most builders will sort out a site and clean it, given the confines of the task in hand. There is normally a fairly logical process of work, although this may not necessarily follow the format of the schedule of works. If the conduct of the work on site looks chaotic, then there is a reasonable chance that the result will be the same. If cabling or pipework looks jumbled and disorganized, then this could be a pointer to a future problem.

During an inspection of the site take a camera with flash, to record as many stages of the work as possible. This has two purposes. Photographs form a first-class record of the detail of the work, should problems later emerge; they are also useful for showing to anyone who subsequently wants to buy the property. You should always have a long spirit level and a tape measure, preferably new and of good quality. Wherever possible, double-check that any new work is straight and level, and matches the dimensions and layout laid down in the schedule or plans.

PROBLEMS WITH THE WORK

If there are indications that the project is not proceeding properly, then you must react quickly before the situation gets worse. Sometimes you may be unable to specify precisely what it is that is not right. In this case, you must bring a professional on site to investigate.

Your first approach, of course, should be made to the builder, who must be advised of any areas with which you are not happy and given every opportunity to rectify the fault. You may find that it is a problem of which the builder is aware, or perhaps the builder has a plausible reason for doing work in a different way from that expected. In the vast majority of cases, if there is a genuine problem, then the builder will remedy it straight away – having double-checked the schedule of works, plans and specification.

CALLING IN PROFESSIONAL HELP

If you have any real doubts about the builder's competence, or are not persuaded by his reasons, seek a second opinion immediately. Needless to say, you should not make any further stage payments until the situation has been resolved, regardless of what pressure the builder may bring to bear. This may seem obvious, but time and again, a second opinion is sought too late, when the builder has been paid up to date, or with too little owing to allow for remedial works to be performed by someone else.

Ideally, any investigation of the site should be accomplished while the builder is not present, to give the professional, who should be a qualified consulting structural engineer, architect or surveyor, a chance to look carefully at the work on his own. This also makes it much easier for you if the professional confirms that the contract is, in fact, proceeding satisfactorily with no apparent problems. In this case, no damage is done to the builder's honour, and the project will proceed with no break in your relationship.

If the professional does find that there are significant problems with the work, then a meeting with the builder must be arranged, preferably with the professional in attendance. Ideally, the professional should come to this meeting with a written schedule of the problems. This would be presented to your builder, who would have to explain his reasons satisfactorily, or agree to remedy the defects. Naturally, this is an undesirable situation and, up to a point, it can be rather like crossing the Rubicon. Once problems have got to this stage, it is quite likely that you will then need the professional to continue to monitor the project until its completion.

Even if this happens, depending on the complexity and type of work, the professional may not have to make many visits to site. He will normally be able to advise you and your builder of the specific stages at which he will need to check the work. This will be at particular, clearly defined junctures of the project. For example, a critical stage may be the completion of all the timbers on a new roof, prior to fitting the covering. He may then wish to inspect again, once the roof covering has been completed and the flashing fitted.

This inspection of the different stages of a given job is critical. Often, once an area of work has been completed, even an experienced professional cannot tell whether or not it has been carried out correctly, without further exploration. The degree of exploration required to check some works can be considerable and could even destroy the integrity of the work itself. On a flat roof, for example, checking whether three layers of felt, or two, had been fitted could require the removal of all the roofing felt.

It is astonishing how reluctant people are to arrange for spot checks by a professional. The money involved is normally very small in relation to the cost of the works. If you were to purchase a second-hand car, of even modest value, you would obtain a report from one of the motoring organizations or, at least, take a mechanic along to check that the vehicle was in good order. This is precisely what should be done when building works are carried out.

Even if you think that all is well, try to get a professional to make at least one monitoring visit – and perhaps more, if the works are extensive.

Ideally, you should arrange for someone to inspect a project well before completion – and certainly before you have paid the builder more than a small proportion of the contract money. Obviously, the time at which an independent inspection is made depends upon the type of work that is being performed. For example, if the contract is only for the supply and fitting of central heating and a new boiler, the appropriate time for an inspection would be once all the radiators have been hung and the boiler connected. While this is almost at the end of the works, the independent adviser would nonetheless be able to check that there was sufficient heating capacity for the property, and that the boiler was correctly fitted, before you made your final payments to the builder.

Alternatively, an independent inspection can sometimes be best performed early on in the course of the works, and may not be required again. If a new staircase is being supplied and fitted to a property, with the other works being mainly composed of simple decoration, then the inspection should take place towards the end of the fitting of the staircase. This is likely to be an expensive and crucial part of the works, and it is vital that this is approved before they proceed too far. Otherwise, by the time the staircase has been found to be defective, you may find that you have already effectively paid for it.

Do not pay too much money to a builder before you are certain that the works done are satisfactory. If there is any area of doubt, where the work goes beyond your direct knowledge or experience, always have it inspected by a professional first. Never pay all the money owed until you are completely satisfied.

Obviously, the best person to call on to inspect the works is the professional who developed the schedule of works and the specification in the first place – if a professional was used. If not, then you will have to find an architect, surveyor or consulting structural engineer who specializes in small works construction. Failing that, you can contact a tradesman who specializes in the relevant area, and get him to look at the work. For a relatively small fee, tradesmen or other builders will sometimes come and inspect other work, and they can be useful in pointing out flaws or omissions, or in commenting upon the integrity of the work. However, there is generally some reluctance to criticize colleagues, and, of course, they do not have the recognized qualifications of, say, a consulting structural engineer. The latter's presence alone, apart from his higher qualifications, will carry considerable authority if it is necessary to confront the builder. This also applies to any written report which, if it comes from another builder or tradesman, may have little force. Nonetheless, using a tradesman or another builder is cheap and may, if nothing else, confirm your suspicions.

THE BUILDING CONTROL OFFICER

A number of areas of small works construction are subject to mandatory inspection by the Building Control Officer (BCO). This can be of very considerable help – so long as he is advised that his presence is necessary. The BCO (see Chapter 14: Building Regulations and Building Control) is responsible for the implementation of the building regulations, and must attend a site to ensure that certain works itemized in the building regulations are carried out to a minimum standard. A good example of this is where a material alteration is made to a property, such as the removal of a wall to make two rooms into one. In this case the work may involve the insertion of a structural steel joist to maintain the integral strength of the property. The function of the BCO is to ensure that the works are carried out correctly and safely, and his visits will be made during various stages of the work until completion, at which time, if satisfied, he will issue a **completion certificate**. The involvement of the BCO, if the works do involve an area covered by building regulations, occurs regardless of the presence on site of a consulting structural engineer, architect, surveyor or experienced builder.

Some builders and their clients try to avoid using the BCO, either because of a fear that he will increase the cost of the work through insistence on regulations, or because his inspection visits can slow the work down. It also has to be said that some builders are unaware of all of the areas in which a BCO should be involved This is despite the fact that it is the builder's duty, in law, to abide by the building regulations, and to ensure that the BCO is present when works requiring his supervision are being undertaken. This is the case regardless of your wishes. In fact, almost invariably the presence of the BCO is of considerable help in ensuring that basic minimum standards are met when certain building works are being performed. You would be foolish in the extreme to try to persuade your builder not to comply with building regulations or not to call in the BCO when required.

THE SNAGGING LIST

As a project progresses towards completion, concentrate on the finishing work being performed by the builder. It is at this time that you need to consider drawing up a preliminary **snagging list**. The snagging list will be an itemization of anything with which you are not happy, however minor it may appear. It may be that there is some paintwork remaining on a window, or perhaps a new socket is missing a screw to the faceplate, or a newly hung door has started to stick. A good snagging list will perform almost the reverse job to that of the schedule of works, in enumerating every possible area of work where you are not satisfied – and you should be as nit-picking as possible.

Present the preliminary snagging list to a builder, in writing, some time before he is actually scheduled to finish the contract. Depending on the size of the contract, this may be some one or two weeks before possible completion. Certainly, a long and comprehensive snagging list given to the builder the day before he is due to finish is both inefficient and unfair.

Most builders will not resent being provided with a fair, clear and well written snagging list. They may actually consider it to be of some help. Quite often, if a builder has been working on a site throughout the project, he may honestly overlook problem areas that are glaringly obvious to you, or he may well have misinterpreted a part of the schedule of works. In either event, the snagging list will help him to focus on areas that require further works, and will allow him to reappraise his completion date as appropriate.

It may well be that disagreements occur over some of the points on the snagging list, which may or may not be outside the original schedule of works or specification. In this case, it is important for you and the builder to sort these out well before the last days of the project. This enables the builder to make best use of the time left, and gives him an opportunity to get back on site specialist tradesmen and materials that might have been removed. If it is agreed that some of the snagging points are outside the original schedule of works, it allows you and the builder to come to an agreement on any variations, with a good chance of getting them done before the scheduled finish date.

The final snagging of the work should then be done almost at the end of the project, once the builder has satisfied himself that the schedule of works has been completed. Take great care, when going around the site with the builder, to make this the definitive snagging meeting. The builder will certainly not wish to return to site, or accept further snags, after this meeting, unless they are defects clearly not apparent at the time. Inevitably, some snags will be picked up, particularly if there have been considerable works done during the project. If this is the case, do not pay the final amount owed on the contract until they are corrected.

If there is a retention clause in the contract, do not be tempted to dispense with this just because the works done appear satisfactory at the end of the contract. Always wait for the time stated in the contract to elapse before settling the final sum. At the end of the day, the most effective way of getting a builder to return to sort out a problem is by retaining a reasonable sum of money – he will not want to write it off.

SUMMARY

- Ideally, a professional should always monitor a project, unless it is of the most basic content.

- The builder should realize from the outset that you intend to be proactive and will be inspecting the works throughout the project.

- Formal weekly site meetings, with a full progress inspection, should be arranged at the start of the works.

- Keep a complete written record of any alterations to the schedule of works.

- Check the site frequently and draw the attention of the builder immediately to anything you may be unhappy about, however minor.

- During casual inspections of the site, take photographs of the work and make detailed checks using a good spirit level and tape measure.

- If anything appears to be badly wrong or out of place, immediately employ a professional to inspect the potential problem area. Retain him to monitor the rest of the work if there are any doubts as to the integrity of the builder.

- Prepare and give to the builder a snagging list well before completion of the works.

- Ensure that the final snagging list at the end of the works is definitive.

- On no account pay all the money owed on the project until you are completely satisfied with the works.

- Do not pay any retention money until the end of the stated period.

11

Cost-Cutting

WHILE you may employ a builder or tradesman effectively to do all the work on a given project, there are occasions when you may want to do some of the work yourself, either for pleasure or as necessitated by your budget. In either case, quite significant savings can be made if you do not mind suffering the physical hardship of the work, or if you have some management skill and the spare time to devote to the project.

In seeking to cut costs, you have to take great care that your direct participation does not become a negative influence on the works. You must decide whether the project is going to be essentially a DIY job, with intermittent professional help, or a professionally run job with you doing some of the more basic functions. There are important distinctions here which you must address, together with assessing the real benefit that your direct input will produce.

There are four main ways that you can cut costs. These stages should not be considered to be too rigid; it is possible to combine elements of all of them:

- Basic Enabling Works
- DIY with Trades
- Direct Management of the Project
- Purchase of Materials

BASIC ENABLING WORKS

One of the simplest and most effective ways of reducing costs is to undertake the basic enabling works yourself. These can take a number of different forms, from simply clearing a site before any work is started, to acting as a quasi-labourer for skilled tradesmen such as electricians and plumbers.

By performing the unskilled work yourself, you can save labour costs. Ironically, much of the time worked by skilled men is taken up with unskilled work. An electrician working to rewire a house will spend much more time trying to route his cables around the property, and forming holes for the back boxes of sockets and switch plates, than performing any complex wiring. Often he will hire a labourer, but much of the wiring is simple and repetitive, and can be undertaken by a conscientious person, if his work is then checked by an experienced tradesman.

Equally, there are areas of plumbing that you can deal with, which would make any employment of a plumber, in theory, much more efficient. Again, in properties that are being replumbed, or having a new central heating system, an inordinate amount of time and effort is expended by the plumber just taking up floorboards and cutting holes through walls to route his pipework – and then replacing, and frequently renewing, flooring that has been broken.

It is also worth taking on enabling works which depend more on strength than skill. This is the case with taking down ceilings, cutting back defective plaster, removing surplus doors and door frames, disposing of rubbish and so on.

Look at the project as a whole, and isolate all the areas of work that you can reasonably do yourself. In this way, you can ensure that any builder or tradesman, in principle, will only be working on constructive skilled work. Of course, you can also directly employ labourers, which will be cheaper than having to pay the builder to do the same.

You must ensure that the builder or tradesman knows about this reduction in the overall work prior to delivering his quote, so that he can allow for this in his costings.

You can make significant savings by avoiding having to pay the labour costs associated with basic site work, together with the mark-ups that would be charged on rubbish removal and supply of basic materials. The saving can be quite considerable, not least because the builder supervising the works will be charging at his normal skilled day rate for his own time, and if he hires labourers, his charge-out rate will, of course, include a profit figure for himself.

DIY WITH TRADES

Clearly, you can save an enormous amount of money on almost all small works by doing the majority of the work yourself. This is quite possible if you are naturally capable at DIY activities, and have the patience to go through the proliferation of excellent books on the market which will take you step by step through almost every possible activity. The savings made will justify the purchase of good tools, and the time taken to master basic building skills. Of course, time itself is the major factor here; if you are going to undertake all the works yourself, you do have to accept that the project could take a considerable amount of time. Even simple functions within a trade, such as the wiring up of electrical sockets, can take the layman a frustratingly long time. Also, the quality of your work may be poorer than that of a professional doing the job as his day-to-day trade.

You must also be wary of employing unskilled labourers. While on the face of it they represent good value for money, their actual work output might turn out to be derisory or the quality unacceptable. Unskilled labour can be of such poor quality that the overall cost ends up being more than that of employing a good semiskilled or skilled man. A skilled man will know exactly what to do, the time it should take to do the work and, most importantly, the technique required to perform the work quickly and to a high standard. He will not need the constant supervision required by someone unskilled, and will be able to anticipate the possible interface problems between the work that he is doing and that of the next trade.

The natural extension to working alone is to employ tradesmen only as and when you need them on site, either on day work or on quotes. The quotes need to be very carefully delineated, however, so that the tradesmen know exactly where their responsibilities in the work lie. You would, in extreme cases, be acting as both client and foreman of the works.

You may only need the professional builder or tradesman to do some specific work, such as wiring up a fuseboard or installing a boiler, and then checking the system that you have installed. Alternatively, you can work alongside a tradesman, doing as much work as your time and ability allow. This can work well, but does require some degree of organization: you must be shown by the tradesman the directions (or 'runs') of the pipework or cabling, the depth to which walls or floors must be chased, and the size of holes needed for access to any area. This he can sometimes do by chalking lines across a site. He can advise you of how many floorboards, for example, to take up for access, and you can then start to feed the cabling or piping around the property. Once the tradesman's work has been completed, you can then be responsible for the remedial works. These can be very time-consuming, with flooring having to be replaced and holes, sometimes quite large, needing to be filled or bricked up.

The problems with working this way are reasonably obvious. First, you have to obtain costs from the tradesman for his particular work, whether in the form of a fixed quoted price or a day rate, which will adequately reflect your input. If the tradesman is employed on the basis of a quotation, then you are unlikely to see much of a return on his work. The tradesman will probably load his costs onto the skilled areas of the work, thus providing you with a relatively small discount on the overall project.

This, on the part of the tradesman, is quite wise. Almost inevitably there will be some problems with your direct involvement with the work. Typically, the tradesman will probably still end up having to do some of the enabling works himself, as they may not have been done adequately. For example, while doing the work, the tradesman may find the chasing is not deep enough, or the angle of a hole incorrect. It will be quicker and better for him to sort out the problem himself, so that he can continue with his quoted work.

Secondly, the interface between you and the tradesman can become an area of contention, and needs to be clarified quite clearly, in writing, before the commencement of any works. This also applies to the charges made by the tradesman for visiting the site, to advise you what precise enabling works are required, and to check, before starting work, whether or not the enabling works are adequate.

The best solution is to agree with the tradesman on a day rate for his work. This way, any problems with the interface will not adversely effect either the tradesman or yourself. Furthermore, when you run into problems, you can get the tradesman to help you out, without concern that the original quotation will quickly become distorted with extras. The day rate will also probably enable you to use the tradesman's equipment such as long ladders or, if he is trusting, power tools, without which some enabling works are very difficult and slow.

DIRECT MANAGEMENT OF THE PROJECT

You can employ a builder to do most of the basic construction works, but then, yourself, directly employ any subcontractors required. For example, if the work involves the renovation of a property, you may want the builder to be responsible only for his actual trade. Any other trades required on the project will be your responsibility to arrange, manage and pay for.

There may be some plumbing and electrics required or perhaps some skilled joinery, all of which a builder can normally take care of if he has quoted for, and undertaken to complete, the project as a whole. He will, of course, be making money out of any trades that he has subcontracted (see Chapter 5). You can cut costs by bringing in the trades yourself, thus avoiding paying the builder's mark-up.

If you do take responsibility for the direct employment of other trades, while having a builder on site, then you must ensure that you manage the interaction between the trades carefully. This can cause problems even on a professionally run site, but for a person with little experience of construction it can turn out to be very difficult. Unless the trades are well organized and the delineations between their work clearly set out, disputes can occur as to whose responsibility it is to perform some of the functions and, as a result, some aspects of the work can be neglected.

A classic example of what can occur is when a new bath is being fitted. This may require the presence of three trades: a plumber to do the pipework; an electrician to extend or renew the supplementary earthing to the bath; and a builder to repair some flooring and construct the bath surround. Unless this comparatively simple operation is carried out efficiently, and managed well, you can end up with a bodged job and unhappy tradesmen – some of whom may be looking to charge extras for additional work. The builder may not have repaired the flooring in time, or the plumber may not have turned up on the right day, thus requiring, perhaps, another visit to site by the builder to construct the bath surround. Furthermore, at the end of the work, it may be found that the bath was not set level or that one of the pipe joints has started to leak – with all the tradesmen blaming each other.

If you are going to employ trades separately on a site, you must try to minimize the possibilities for friction between them. Ensure that before any actual work starts, each tradesman visits the site first to agree the condition and the extent of his area of work.

If a roofer, for example, is going to be employed to hot-asphalt a flat roof, he must first physically check that the roof surface and timbers put up by your builder are adequate for the job. You must then establish at what exact points his work starts and stops. This will save the roofer coming on site to find that the roof timbers and surface are not adequately completed. He may then asphalt the roof, but, due to pressure of time, leave some flashing for your builder to undertake, for which the latter had never costed. Of course, in the future, when problems do occur, the roofer will state that the builder had not built the roof properly, while the builder will maintain that the roofer should have specified what was needed for the particular roof covering used. While legally any contractor working on another contractor's work or surface has by implication accepted the suitability of that work, in reality this may be of little help to you.

While savings can be made by separating a builder from the profit he can make from his subcontracted trades, great care must be taken to manage the work effectively. On a site where there is a lot of work, this amounts to a full-time job. In reality, most builders earn their money when subcontracting work, by getting the trades on site at exactly the right time, monitoring quality, and identifying and resolving any interface problems. If you take charge of employing trades on site, you lose the benefit of being able to deal with just one party if something does go wrong. Trying to sort out who is to blame, when several trades have been working, can be a real nightmare.

PURCHASE OF MATERIALS

You can also save money through the direct purchase of materials and fittings, particularly items such as boilers, kitchen equipment, and sanitary ware. On these items, a builder would generally expect to make a reasonable margin of profit. He would usually obtain a discount from the supplier, and be able to charge for handling, collecting and delivering the items to site.

Purchasing all the necessary materials for the project offers much less scope for saving. In most situations it is in your interest to allow the builder or tradesman to supply all his own general building materials. Apart from the fact that his mark-up is reasonably modest, you are unlikely to satisfy all the requirements of the professional builder. For many of the building products used on site, there are a number of different manufacturers, and builders often have preferences based on years of experience.

While a list of materials can be made up by the builder for you to purchase, it is unlikely to be comprehensive, and it is all too easy to misunderstand something and order the wrong materials. This deficiency will probably not come to light until the material is actually required, causing your builder a delay which is not his fault, and which is ultimately chargeable to you. Needless to say, the cost of paying your builder for a lost day will generally be greater than the saving made on the purchase of materials. If you are concerned about being overcharged for the general building materials, you can open an account with a couple of good builders' merchants, allowing the builder or tradesmen to use the account for the project. Alternatively, get the builder to give you copies of all the receipts for goods bought.

If you do choose to purchase materials, then you must not attempt to cut costs by buying poor quality, as these will invariably either be useless to a tradesman, or will significantly extend the time a job takes to complete. A good example of this is cheap, poorly prepared timber, that may be warped and wet.

If the timber is intended for internal work, it will be virtually unusable; it is likely to bend out of shape once it dries, however well it is fixed by a joiner. Equally, there are paints on the market that are very cheap, but when used, tend to be so watery that countless coats are required to produce an acceptable depth of colour and finish. If possible, buy only from a source recommended by the tradesman, or from quality builders' merchants.

In some areas, it is very much in your interest for the builder to supply materials. This is particularly the case where a specialist material is being ordered, that may depend on the skill of the builder to specify exactly what is required. For example, a piece of structural steel may be needed, and have to be supplied to precise dimensions. It is much better if the builder supplies the measurements, and is entirely responsible for this item. If there are any problems with the steel, it is then up to the builder to sort these out. The last thing that you want is to become embroiled in a dispute about misunderstood measurements, sizes or timings for delivery.

However, it is almost always worth doing the negotiation and purchase of items that have a high integral cost, or where there is a large quantity being ordered. Kitchens and sanitary ware are good examples of high-cost items, but you should not neglect 'second-fit' items such as quality lighting, brass electrical faceplates, tiles and so on. Also, you should buy any one-off item yourself. The builder will have to mark up the item, sometimes very highly, just to cover the cost of locating and collecting it, when you could have done this free and probably enjoyed the research.

Furthermore, on most one-off items the builder is unlikely to obtain a bigger discount than you, unless he has a very good relationship with the supplier. Even with kitchens, unless the builder or tradesman is buying a lot from a supplier during the course of the year, he is unlikely to get a much better discount than a hard-bargaining individual. This is partly because a small builder will simply not do business regularly enough with a supplier to obtain serious discounts, and partly because trade suppliers have opened up to the retail trade.

Even when cutting costs, you must still address all the basics of small works contracts. Ensure that the manpower used on site is well chosen, and subject to a specification, plans and contract, if only of the most basic kind. You will open yourself to abuse the moment these elements are disregarded. The old cliché of 'paying peanuts and getting monkeys' is as true in small works as in any other walk of life.

Take care, when cost-cutting, not to fall into the temptation of trying to find the cheapest possible builder to do the work. This does not make sense, either in the short or long term. There are rates below which competent builders simply will not work, and cowboy builders thrive on those who are not prepared to pay the basic market rate.

If you simply do not have the money to do all the works you want, then you must accept that you will have to wait until you have, or go ahead with only a small section – but properly. The key to good works is always the quality of manpower employed and materials used.

SUMMARY

- Strip, clear and prepare site prior to the builder starting work.

- Perform all unskilled work such as pulling down ceilings and chopping out defective plaster.

- Prepare all the pipe and cable routes for electricians or plumbers, either working alongside them or under their instructions before they start work.

- Negotiate and purchase directly all one-off or high-cost items such as boilers, sanitary ware, kitchen units etc.

- Employ subcontractors directly to avoid the builder making a mark-up on their work, but recognize that good management will be required to prevent problems occurring between the builder and subcontractor.

- Take care to make absolutely clear the work interface between the different tradesmen and between the tradesmen and client.

- Do not neglect the necessity for clear specifications and contracts even if the work to be done is minor.

- Avoid supplying general building materials.

- Do not compromise on the quality of the tradesmen or the materials.

12

Checklist of Typical Problem Areas

THE array of potential problems in small works construction is infinite, but there are definable areas where poor work tends to occur repeatedly; many of these can be picked up by the observant layman. While the following listing of potential problems is not comprehensive, poor work in the areas described will reflect badly on your builder, and should act as a warning light. The areas touched on encompass many of the works that you are likely to perform on your property; they can be used in drawing up a schedule of works, and as pointers to problem areas when inspecting work.

It cannot be stressed too highly that if for any reason at all you feel that any part of your project is not proceeding to standard, then you must immediately seek a second opinion from a professional. It will always pay to get a professional to inspect work before it is completed, even if, to all intents and purposes, the work is proceeding well. A couple of hundred pounds or so for a professional's fees really is very little extra in your budget, given the overall expense of even minor works.

STRAIGHT, LEVEL AND SOLID

All work done by a builder should meet these criteria and any variation will indicate that the builder has not paid sufficient attention to the work, or has used the wrong materials. Reasons given by the builder may be that the walls of a property are bowed, or move off at an angle, or are out of plumb. This is not a valid reason for work not being made level, even if the work concerned is awkward and made worse by, for example, decaying plaster.

Invariably, if the work done is not straight and level, at some point in the future it will look obviously out of true. This may not become apparent until curtain rails are fitted, shelving is put up, a door is hung, or a room is wallpapered. Check new work with a spirit level to ensure that it is true to within a small tolerance. In new brickwork, for example, the professional allowance is as tiny as 3mm over a 10m stretch of wall.

The works performed should also be solidly fixed, allowing no play in the fitting. Door frames should have no movement at all, likewise shelving, skirting, studwork, window frames, work surfaces, baths and so on. Unless an item (such as a door) is designed to move, then it should be fixed immovably.

If there is any play at all, reject the work until it is sufficiently well fixed. Once again, a builder may attempt to justify the lack of a completely solid fixing, by the difficulty of operating on a defective wall. This is his problem, however, and if he has quoted to do the work, he should have advised you of any reservations beforehand. If something is even fractionally loose when the builder has completed the work, then it will only become looser over time, until it becomes a liability.

Do not be afraid of pulling and pushing against newly done (but finished) work, to ensure that it is properly and strongly fixed. Even walls (once they are dry and properly tied in) can be tested to see if areas within them move. If they do, then it is probable that insufficient strengthening, either in the form of timber or tying-in, has been done.

It is in the area of strong, level and solid that, with a decent spirit level, time and energy, you can most simply check what is being done.

The rest of this chapter deals with the following specific problem areas, in alphabetical order:

- Bathrooms
- Brickwork or Blockwork
- Damp, Rot and Woodworm
- Decoration
- Electrics
- Kitchens
- Plaster and Render
- Plasterboard
- Plasterboard Stud Wall
- Plumbing and Central Heating
- Pointing
- Roofs
- Structural Works and New Building

BATHROOMS

Bathrooms are the source of a number of problems, most relating to inadequate attention to the long-term effects of water. It is critical that the correct materials are used, precautions taken, and sufficient attention given to potential future problems. Look carefully at the following:

Baths

- Baths must be properly supported. The feet should be placed on a firm support – not on inadequate, uneven flooring – and a strong bath surround should be constructed to lock it firmly into place. Ideally, if it runs along a wall, the lower top edge of the bath should sit on a batten fixed to the wall. There should be no possible movement of the bath, either laterally or vertically, once it is in position. If there is, then it must be completely corrected.

- The bath should be precisely level.

- There should be access to the taps and waste, if a solid surround with side panel has been constructed. This must be an easy-to-open door or panel, to allow the plumber access to correct any leaks or problems with the taps or waste.

- It is wise to ensure that isolation valves are fitted to the hot and cold pipework leading to the taps under the bath, so that the water can be turned off locally. This will not usually be done unless specified.

- Any tiling or splashback should be fitted so that it sits on the top edge of the bath itself, rather than leaving a gap, however small, between the tiling or splashback and the side of the bath. With some designs it may be necessary to chase the wall around the rim, to position the bath close enough.

- A good quality silicone must be used between the bath and the tiling or splashback. The finish of the silicone should be neat and tidy. Thick, poorly applied silicone should not be accepted – this will probably indicate that there is too great a gap between the bath and splashback or that the bath has already started to move and crack up the originally applied silicone.

- A steel bath must be connected to the secondary earthing of the electrical system. This can be checked by looking for green and yellow cabling connected to the bath, which should then run back to the fuse board.

Showers

These need very special attention. Poor installation of showers probably accounts for more complaints about bathrooms than any other item. That said, this is an area in which you also have a responsibility in purchasing good quality. Even a competent builder may find it impossible to fit a shower adequately when the base is shoddy plastic and the framework a flimsy steel, surrounding a weak Perspex door and screen.

The specification for the work must stipulate that:

- The shower base must be level, and fixed on a firm foundation, often a thick piece of waterproof board, tightly fixed to the flooring below, unless the flooring is already concrete, which makes a perfect base – though even then shower bases are sometimes, depending on the type, set on a base of render to steady them further. A base comprising pieces of timber should be avoided, as these can move in response to any damp.

- The walls to the shower must be composed of either render or waterproof board. If the house wall has been plastered then ideally the undercoat plaster should be removed down to the brickwork and rendered. If the house wall or a newly built stud wall comprises plasterboard or plaster and lath then, at least, a waterproof board should be very firmly fixed over this.

- The base of the shower must be positioned so that the render or waterproof board drops onto the top of the shower base. The base must not be merely positioned beside the waterproof board or render.

- The manufactured shower door and side (if any) must be very firmly fixed so that the whole structure feels firm.

- After tiling, the vertical corners of the shower walls should be siliconed, rather than grouted, so that any movement of the house walls will be absorbed by the elasticity of the silicone.

  Silicone, rather than grout, should also be applied to the area between the top of the shower base and the tiles.

Sanitary Ware

Frequent complaints concern the damage done to sanitary ware in a property, either during its fitting or during the course of the works. It is the builder's responsibility to take care of these items. You should pay particular attention to ensure that you do not accept, at the end of the contract, sanitary ware that is cracked, scratched or otherwise damaged. If you notice any damage, advise the plumber or builder immediately, particularly if the property is inhabited. The builder may, possibly justifiably, try to blame a member of the household – thus causing a potentially unresolvable dispute.

BRICKWORK OR BLOCKWORK

Common problems with this area of work relate to the cracking apart of brick- or blockwork, or to its separating from an existing wall. A further typical problem is the occurrence of damp, due to an inadequate damp-proof course. None of these problems are likely to become apparent until long after the builder has finished the project as a whole. In order to help prevent them, the following should be checked:

- Any wall which is intended to carry a load should be designed and checked by a structural engineer.

- If the brick- or blockwork is being attached to an existing wall, it should be adequately bonded by toothing into the existing wall, or by some kind of wall-fixing kit. Both alternatives ensure that the new brick- or blockwork is locked into the old structure, so that the two structures effectively become one.

- The foundations should be adequate to support the new structure being built. This is the responsibility of any structural engineer supervising the work. As with all structural alterations, it is mandatory for the builder or engineer to call in the Building Control Officer (BCO), who is under a duty to inspect the foundation excavation, the foundations laid and the damp-proof course prior to any building of the superstructure.

  Expressly check that the BCO has made his inspection visits and given his approval for the works to proceed.

- The brick- or blockwork should look good to the eye, with a consistent depth and spacing between mortar joints, and the mortar a consistent colour. At no point should vertical joints between courses match up.

DAMP, ROT AND WOODWORM

These three problems tend to be linked together and are commonly dealt with by specialist companies.

Damp

There are three main forms of damp: penetrating damp, rising damp and airborne moisture.

Penetrating Damp

This is where water finds its way into a building, not necessarily at ground level, with the potential to cause significant damage. It is more likely to affect properties with solid rather than cavity walls, although the latter can also suffer. Often the cause is related to simple poor property maintenance, and sometimes it is obvious as a patch of otherwise unexplained damp.

Common reasons for penetrating damp are:

- blocked drains and gulleys,
- leaking roof coverings,
- defective soakers or flashing,
- damaged or time expired downpipes,
- cracked, unpainted window sills, and
- degraded mortar between bricks.

Once any of the above factors are present, water will find its way into a building and soak into the fabric of the property. Brickwork, plaster and render can become saturated and any timber will be adversely affected. Considerable damage, with a high accompanying expense, can occur if the damp badly affects such things as wooden wall plates, structural lintels and joist ends supporting floors (see Rot, below).

In the case of penetrating damp, it is vital to establish the cause of the damp before allowing any remedial works to take place. For example, you may find that you have an area of exterior wall where the brickwork needs repointing. Only once you have established the source of the damp and rectified it, should you start on any repair works, having carefully inspected for any other damage that may have occurred. You must nonetheless realize that if a wall, for example, has suffered from penetrating damp then, even after the source problem has been resolved, bricks can take months, and sometimes up to a couple of years, to dry completely. The damp will therefore not disappear from the wall immediately you have mended a leaking drain or repointed brickwork. Accordingly, internally it is wise to have the damp area re-rendered (a sand and cement mix, rather than a gypsum plaster), with a waterproofing agent added to the render. If this is not done, any timber or subsequent decoration may be further damaged during the drying out period.

Rising Damp

Damp that rises from the ground up through masonry is a common problem with old or poorly constructed properties. Invariably rising damp is due to one of two reasons:

- The property has no **damp-proof course** (DPC). This is an impermeable membrane between the wall bricks or blockwork, approximately 150mm above ground level, and below the lowest piece of wood used in the construction. It prevents damp from the ground rising up through a building and by law must be inserted in any new building. Before the 1800s almost no buildings had DPCs, and they were not always put in even up until the 1920s.

- The DPC has been breached, broken down or bridged. This can occur if there has been some form of break in the DPC. This sometimes happens when a building moves or even when poor building works have been done. More commonly the DPC is bridged by a rise in ground levels, so that the DPC can be found below ground – allowing moisture to permeate up through the walls. Surprisingly, ground levels around properties tend to rise inexorably over time. New paving, drives, patios, garden beds and so on develop around individual properties – with little regard for the position of the property DPC.

It is critical that when planning a new drive, patio, garden bed etc. that will adjoin your outside walls, you make absolutely sure that it will not touch or come near the existing DPC. If this is likely, make sure that the existing ground level is reduced first. Equally, it is essential to check that any new building work has a DPC or that if renovatory work is performed on or around the DPC, it remains intact or is replaced with integrity.

   If you find rising damp in your property then, as with penetrating damp, it is something that you must rectify. Not doing this can lead to substantial damage to your property.

   Generally it is wise to call in a professional company dealing with damp.

These companies will firstly try to establish why there is rising damp. An essential part of this investigation is finding out where the DPC is located, in relation to the ground level. If the DPC is below ground level then there are effectively two options:

- To trench around the affected area. This would result in a trench being dug, to end below the DPC, and usually filled with pea shingle. This would allow water to fall below the level of the DPC and then, in principle, to evaporate through the shingle. The British climate does not always make this a viable option.

- To inject a **chemical DPC** such as silicone resin or siliconate into brick, stone or mortar joints at ground level. These materials line the pores of the bricks or mortar with a water-repellent solution. If this is done and there is any timberwork left below ground level, such as wall plates or joists, then these should be isolated from the source of moisture by the creation of sleeper walls, bearing points or joist-end protection.

If it is considered that there has been some breaching of the DPC that is not connected to its being below ground level, then the application of a 'tanking' material may be needed to withstand lateral penetration from moisture below ground.

The injection of a chemical DPC, if performed well, should produce a sound DPC. However, there can be problems with it and, as with all building work, it is reliant upon competent operators and good practice being used.

Once work to create or rectify a DPC has taken place, it is important that there is further attention to the inside of the property. If a wall has been wet for some time then hydroscopic salts form in it. These keep the wall damp and attract further damp, notwithstanding the new DPC. It is therefore necessary to remove all the existing plaster or render and replace this, up to a height of approximately 1.2m, with a salt-retardant render. If the render is not applied in accordance with the manufacturer's specification you will still suffer problems with damp.

A complaint frequently made by specialist damp companies is that the rendering of walls after a DPC has been inserted or corrected is not done properly. Rather than have a specialist company do this work, there is a tendency for householders to get their own (possibly cheaper) builder to do it. However, this is rarely wise and can restrict any guarantee provided by the damp-course company to the DPC alone.

Any injected DPC should last 20 years, and most guarantees will state this time limit.

Airborne Moisture

This is a serious form of damp and has much to do with modern living conditions and the design of structures themselves. Condensation occurs where there is bad ventilation, poor insulation and inadequate control over heating. Double glazing, central heating, lack of continuous ventilation, vinyl paints, floor coverings and so on, all help to create condensation which, if severe, can affect the very fabric of a property. It will be apparent from damp on the inside of windows and walls and, if extreme, on all other surfaces.

The answer to condensation is rarely simple. The watchword is to 'increase ventilation, improve insulation and create an equitable environment' – an all-round attention to the area of the property concerned. However, depending on your property, and the degree of the problem, this could involve a considerable amount of work. It often requires the specific attention of a specialist – and preferably more than one, so that you gain a second opinion. You must be careful that you are not palmed off with the excuse that it is due to a defective DPC. The condensation may have nothing whatsoever to do with the DPC and, if this is the case, requires quite different treatment.

Rot

There are two main forms of rot: wet rot and dry rot. Both are consequences of damp, and you should be aware that as soon as damp is found in your property it is likely that some, or all, of the timber near the damp area may, to some extent, be affected. In particular, take care to have any ground-floor woodwork inspected if it is found that your original DPC is lower than the outside ground level. There is a reasonable chance that timber in contact with damp external walls within your house will have suffered from the rising damp – and it may have degraded very badly. Indications of this are, for example, when your ground floor is leaning or distorted, indicating that a joist-end or wall plate may have rotted, and be unable to support the load.

Wet Rot

This is where timber degrades through being constantly wet. The timber decomposes, loses all integrity and ends up being unable to perform its function – perhaps the bearing of a load, in the case of a lintel, wall plate, rafter or joist. If these rot beyond a certain point, they will need replacing – which, depending on their position, can be an expensive and time-consuming operation. There may also be substantial collateral damage to decorations and plasterwork.

Dry Rot

Dry rot is a fungus that will grow within a property and then spread out from its initial localized area. Rather like a mushroom it thrives on areas that are damp, poorly ventilated and dark, and in the right circumstances certain types can spread extremely rapidly in their search for water. There are spores in the atmosphere all the time, but they only spread when the conditions are right.

This form of rot damages timber by removing all the moisture from it, to the point where the wood crumbles. It can often be identified by seeing timber that is extremely dry, flaky and cracked. Cottonwool-like mycelium growth may be evident. Great care must be exercised when handling or disposing of infected wood as the spores can be easily spread to uninfected areas.

If rot is found in your property then the first priority is to establish the source of the problem and rectify it. On most occasions, you will find that damp is penetrating into your building, perhaps from one of the causes mentioned above such as a leaking drain. Once this has been sorted out, remove all the infected timber and, if there is dry rot, any render or plaster within the immediate area. This removal of affected timber may involve the expense of completely replacing some items although others, depending on their position and the degree of the rot, may only need replacing in part.

If dry rot is found, any affected timber will have to be carefully replaced, ideally with pretreated wood, and all the wood isolated from the wall by using joist-hangers or membranes to protect the timber from further possible infection. Finally, reinstatement works can take place, such as replastering and decoration.

If any dry rot is found then it is often advisable to employ a specialist company to deal with it.

Woodworm

Woodworm can weaken the integrity of timber, if left unchecked. However, the problem when seeing a piece of affected timber is establishing whether or not the woodworm is still alive and capable of doing further damage. This is not an easy matter and is generally best left to a specialist company and an experienced surveyor.

An indication that woodworm is live is when traces of fine powder (**frass**) are evident around the timber concerned. It is also possible, by shining a torch down a woodworm emergence hole, to see whether the hole looks a different and lighter colour, suggesting that it is new and that woodworm has been active recently.

The problem with treating woodworm is that the surface of any affected timber and that surrounding it will require spraying. The process works by covering timber with a solution that will penetrate the timber by 1–2mm. When the adult woodworm start to eat their way out of the timber, in which they were laid as eggs, they will eat into the sprayed wood. This will kill them and prevent them from infesting any further wood. The main visual damage done by woodworm is made by the adult eating its way out of the wood – rather than by eating into it. The spraying is therefore preventative only and will kill the beetle when it makes its way out of the timber.

Any company doing the spraying will therefore need clear access – necessitating the removal of floorboarding, for example, if the woodworm has attacked the joists and flooring. Because of this it is an immensely inconvenient process to have done when you have moved into your home, fitted carpets and completed your decoration. Accordingly, the right time to have any spraying done is before you move into your property. The spray is harmful by contact and you will have to vacate your building usually for at least 8 and possibly 48 hours – and great care must be taken if a member of your family is asthmatic.

Specialist Damp-Proofing, Rot and Woodworm Companies

If you do find that you have problems with damp, rot or woodworm it is generally best to go to a specialist company to perform the work. However, as with all work make sure you do the following as a minimum:

- Obtain at least two quotations and opinions before going ahead with any work. This is particularly important when you are not certain of the source of the problem or the best form of resolution.

- Where possible, it is advisable to get a company which is registered with the **British Wood Preservation and Dampproofing Association**. This association is national, requires an annual subscription and imposes yearly inspections on its members to check on their working practices and safety precautions.

- Make sure that the company you employ provides an insurance-backed guarantee for the work. This is only available from the **Guaranteed Protection Trust**, and only BWPDA members can offer it. Other than annual product liability insurance, all other guarantees are supported by the chemical-producing manufacturers. If you have any doubts about a guarantee offered, double-check that it is valid and has integrity.

- Check carefully, before any work proceeds, the terms of the guarantee, what it covers and for how long. **Tanking** (the construction of an impervious, continuous membrane, such as for cellars) is often not guaranteed.

- Remember that guarantees normally only cover reinstatement of work that is defective – not consequential loss such as the removal and replacement of kitchen units, carpeting etc. So, make certain the work is done well and by a reputable company, notwithstanding any guarantee.

- Do not forget to get any guarantee signed over to you personally, when you are buying a property from a seller who holds a guarantee for work previously done on the property.

DECORATION

Decoration tends to be considered the poor relation of the trades involved in construction. This is unfair, and grossly underestimates the value of a skilled decorator – as opposed to just a painter. Indeed, good decorators are extremely hard to find, and most builders often do not employ more than semiskilled decorators, who have genuine trouble in producing high quality finishes. The work itself is very labour-intensive, and also suffers from a high level of subjectivity as to what is or is not an acceptable finish.

Indeed, one of the main problems you will encounter prior to having decorating done is to define, with absolute clarity, the type of finish you want and are prepared to pay for. It is vital when preparing your specification that you precisely define the quality wanted – whether it is a quick 'tosh' job, a reasonably good finish, or one of the highest possible quality.

Unfortunately, for the most part, checking decoration is difficult until it is effectively completed. Decoration tends to be progressive, with work possibly being done perfectly well but still not looking good, right up until it is completed. You have to be somewhat patient, until the decorator asserts that the work in a given area is finished. It is really only at this time that you can check, authoritatively, that it is to the standard required.

A possible exception to this is exterior decoration. You can check that sufficient making good has been performed in the burning off of flaking paint, and that the surfaces have been adequately rubbed down and filled before painting. You can, and should, also check that sufficient coats have been applied; this can easily be done by asking the decorator not to apply further coats until the last one has been inspected.

There are three main areas in which problems occur with decoration:

Standard of Preparation

The key to all good decoration is the level of preparation prior to beginning. Two problems, however, tend to make this more difficult than it seems. First, you must ensure that the surfaces to be decorated *can* be made good by a decorator. Decorators are not plasterers and cannot perform miracles on walls and ceilings. Be realistic. Make sure, if a surface is poor, that it is plastered, or renewed in the case of defective wood, before any decoration. To do this will, in the long run, be cheaper and more satisfactory than trying to get a decorator to make it good.

Secondly, as the work is progressive, it is hard to know how effective the decorator's making good will be until the work is completed. Certainly, work done by a skilled decorator, with good filling and the hanging of a thick lining paper, can result in very effective concealment of surface defects. Take care to inspect the work at night, however, with the lights on, when surface blemishes tend to show very clearly.

If you expect the work to be of high quality you should check the following:

- All flaking or loose paint should be removed.

- All cracks should be raked out and filled, and all lumps, bumps and coarse areas sanded down.

- All areas of 'blown' plaster – that is, plaster which has become detached from its backing surface – should be removed and filled either by patch plastering or with decorating filler.

- All surfaces should be washed down and cleaned of dust and grime.

Paintwork

It is almost always a mistake to specify in your schedule the number of coats of paint to be used for the interior of a property. Individual paints and colours may require different numbers of coats, before they produce an acceptable finish. Five or six coats of paint, for example, are often required to produce an acceptable finish on bare timber. While subjectivity should be avoided in all parts of small works construction, the quality of paintwork is almost always open to it. The most effective paint specification is one that defines the finish to any interior paintwork as having to be of 'superior, even depth and consistency'.

- Any paintwork, whether on wall or wood surfaces, should be smooth, free of any 'nibs' (grainy particles) and devoid of obvious brush or roller marks.
- Woodwork should not be finished across the grain.
- Paint should not have runs or 'curtains' (waves of coagulated paint).
- Every surface painted should be covered, i.e. there should be no gaps or holes that are bare of paint.
- Delineations of paint colour should be crisp, clear and, wherever possible, in straight lines.

Wallpapering

Wallpapers present a particular problem for decorators, in that the quality varies considerably from one manufacturer to another. Indeed, the variations are so great that the same decorator, hanging several different wallpapers in a property, can end up with several different results. One room may be perfect, another may have some separating of the seams and another will perhaps have suffered from small areas of the surface paper becoming detached. Inspection of another room may reveal that the patterns of a wallpaper do not consistently meet. Sometimes these problems are simply not the fault of the decorator, but the result of poor manufacture – a difficult matter to prove one way or another.

Try to minimize problems by following these guidelines:

- Wallpaper should be bought before the decoration of a given room is started.

- The correct adhesive should be bought for the wallpaper – and the same adhesive used to hang the lining paper.

- The schedule of works or specification should stipulate that all areas to be wallpapered are to be lined first. Good quality wallpapers should only ever be hung on surfaces that have first been lined.

- The wallpaper hung by the decorator should have joints that are butted close together, all cuts to the wallpaper should be crisp and tidy, no residue of glue should be left on the wallpaper (often prevalent along the seams).

Finally, when inspecting completed decoration, check that the area is serviceable and clean of paint. Sockets and switches should be paint-free, as should windows (apart from an overlap of about 3mm at the edges to act as a weather seal), door fittings etc. Also check each and every window and door, to ensure that they all open and close easily. These are all part of the decorator's responsibility in completing a site.

ELECTRICS

Common problems with household electrics are:

- insufficient circuits throughout the property;
- poor or non-existent earthing;
- old consumer units or fuse boards; and
- poor installation of the fittings.

There are also occasions when rewiring has been required and, in fact, little more than renewal of the external fittings has been done – creating the false impression that the entire property has been rewired.

The specification to an electrician, preferably in the shape of a floor plan, should be comprehensive, and should itemize the type and quantity of lighting and sockets that are required, together with their exact locations. It should also clearly set out the type of equipment that may be used, such as washing machines and cookers, so an electrician is able to calculate the loading on each of the circuits that are being installed. Ample additional capacity should be allowed for on each circuit, to take into account the increase, year by year, in the number of electrical items likely to be run.

Once the electrician has done his work, and before you pay any completion money, check each and every socket and switch, to see that they are working satisfactorily. Ideally, at the end of the job a **certificate of completion** issued by the **NICEIC (National Inspection Council for Electrical Installation Contracting)** should be obtained. Failing that, your local electricity supplier can be asked to inspect the work.

During the course of the work, check the following:

- There should be a separate circuit installed for each broad area of usage. In a normal three- to four-bedroom house, there will be separate circuits for the downstairs lighting, upstairs lighting, downstairs sockets, upstairs sockets, kitchen cooker (if it has a 45 amp rating), kitchen/utility room sockets and the garage/workshop if there is one. Any circuit to the garden lighting should also be separate. A good electrician, if installing a new consumer unit/fuse board, should ensure that the fuse board, once wired up, still has capacity for an additional circuit, in case you need greater capacity in the future.

  You can identify the circuits by the fact that on the consumer unit/fuse board, each circuit will be represented by a separate fuse or **MCB (Miniature Circuit Breaker)**.

- All the fuses should be clearly marked, to identify which fuse connects to which circuit.

- The consumer unit ideally should be a new one, with MCBs rather than wire fuses which, while still effective, cut out later than MCBs and are, of course, a fiddle to rewire in order to restore power to the circuit.

- All the new fittings, such as sockets and lighting points, should be checked to ensure that they are firmly fixed, level (in the case of sockets and switches) and positioned correctly. This should be done as soon as possible, as considerable damage is invariably done in moving anything electrical, due to the necessity of hiding the cabling.

- All cabling should be concealed and protected, either under flooring, chased into walls or placed in conduit. If cabling does run up walls to sockets or wall lights, then it should run vertically, not meander across the walls, so that should any pictures be hung, or shelving put up in the future, then the person concerned can reasonably foresee where the cabling is likely to be, to avoid puncturing it. On no account should bare cabling trail along skirting boards, or be accessible to children. It is good practice, although expensive and still not widespread, to place all cabling which runs under walls and floors within conduit.

- The back boxes of the sockets and light switches should be inspected to make sure that they are all made of steel. Old wooden back boxes should never be used. They represent a fire risk, particularly when located in plaster-and-lath walls.

- If steel or brass face plates are used on sockets or switches, then they should be checked to ensure that the cabling is earthed to the switch.

- All old or disused cabling should be removed from site, and not left in place, regardless of its having been disconnected. Leaving old wiring in place only leads to confusion in the future, and makes another electrician's job unnecessarily hard.

- No connection to **VIR** (obsolete, cloth-backed wiring) should ever be made. Where there is any doubt at all, new cabling should be used, and if a rewire of an old property is under way, check some of the sockets and light switches to make certain that new cabling is actually coming into the switch or socket.

- 6mm supplementary bonding should be visible on all pipework to steel basins, baths and kitchen sinks. As for bathrooms (above), this is indicated by a yellow and green cable attached to the pipework, and then running back to the consumer unit.

- The consumer unit/fuse board must be properly earthed in 16mm cable (again yellow and green), and this should be done within 500mm of the gas meter, on the householder's side.

- It is good practice, but not widespread, for an electrician to leave a plan of the electrical system. This is invaluable for the future, and can save considerable time should a problem occur, and the original electrician be unavailable to do any further work.

KITCHENS

Consistent complaints with regard to kitchens revolve around bad design, or poor joinery during their fitting. There is normally little or no excuse for this, and any faulty work, or damage to units during their construction, will be the builder's responsibility, and may necessitate his replacing the damaged part. Normally, faults in this area are all too blatantly obvious , but nonetheless you should pay attention to the following:

- The base units should be firmly fixed together and to the work surface, so that every bank of units is immovable.

- The work surface should be absolutely level – in all directions – and if it is not, then this must be rectified. If this is not done then, among other things, any subsequent tiling will look untidy, and be difficult to do satisfactorily. Some professional joiners or kitchen fitters will fit a batten along the wall behind the work surface, to ensure a constant level, and on which to secure the back of the work surface. This can considerably strengthen the work surface, and prevent any unsightly cracks occurring in the silicone that is run between the top of the work surface and the tiling or splashback.

- The cut between two work surfaces, when they are joined together, should be barely noticeable, and there should be no difference in the levels of the two. This cut is probably the single most skilful part of fitting a kitchen.

- All doors should open and close easily, without touching each other, and should align properly with the doors next to them.

PLASTER AND RENDER

The main problems in this area generally relate either to plaster being used where it should not be – i.e. where there is an area of potential damp, in which case plaster degrades quickly – or to the quality of the plastering – i.e. if when it dries out it is found to be rough. Frequently, both in plastering and rendering, insufficient care is taken to ensure that all levels and corners are true and at a right angle. There are four areas to check:

- Plaster (unless specialist renovating plaster) should not be used externally, nor as an undercoat on the interior surface of a wall that faces the outside. In this case, render (a mixture of sand and cement) must be used. A plaster finish coat (approx 3–5mm thick) can be used internally over the render on exterior-facing walls.

- A **metal edging bead,** or **angle bead,** should be used on all external corners, whether inside or outside the building. This protects the delicate edge of plaster or render, and ensures a straight and level corner.

- Quality plastering or rendering should result in a surface devoid of waves or rolls, and should be tested with a long spirit level or copper pipe, stretched across the surface. All parts of the pipe or level should touch the surface.

- Plastered or rendered surfaces, when finished, should be smooth and devoid of indentations, scratches or bumps. The finished surface of plaster should be suitable for decoration, with little or no prior filling.

PLASTERBOARD

This is used in almost all new construction for ceilings and walls but is often the source of many complaints after the work has been completed. The plasterboarded areas can suffer from excessive cracking along the joints of the individual boards, and the 'popping out' of the nails. Before the plastering takes place, check the following:

- The plasterboard should be nailed to the stud wall timbers with clout nails placed no more than 150mm apart and sunk just below the surface of the board.

- **Scrim** (a fibrous tape or hessian material) or a purpose-made tape should be placed along all the joints between the plasterboards.

PLASTERBOARD STUD WALL

This is the most commonly used material for constructing interior walls. It can suffer from lack of strength due to the builder using too little timber in the construction. You must check five areas:

- The base of the wall must run across any floor joists, or along the top of a floor joist, although the latter may have to be strengthened to take the extra load. The base must not run in between two joists.

- Adequately strong timber must be used, normally either 100 × 50mm or 75 × 50mm, and the uprights fixed with a gap between them of not more than 450mm (for 9.5mm thick plasterboard) or 600mm (for 12.7mm thick plasterboard).

- The sides and top of the wall must be securely fixed to the adjoining walls, ceiling and floor.

- **Noggins** (pieces of timber fixed horizontally between the uprights) should be placed no less than every 600mm up the uprights, and should be fixed wherever the plasterboard does not meet the uprights – i.e. no edge of plasterboard should be impossible to fix onto timber.

- You should, wherever possible, ensure that the stud wall is insulated with at least 100mm thick insulation, or 75mm thick insulation if the wall is constructed of 75mm timber.

PLUMBING AND CENTRAL HEATING

It is difficult for the non-professional to pick up problems during the work of one of the skilled trades such as plumbing, central heating or electrics. Generally, however, a problem within these trades will become apparent quite quickly; most leaks will become obvious as soon as any system is charged, or alternatively something will simply just not work. Likewise, poor drainage of basins, baths and WCs will be clearly obvious, as will any deficiency in the production of hot water. It can be slightly more problematic to establish the adequacy of the heating of the house, if the test has been done in summer, or during warm weather.

The key to dealing with these trades is that you must on no account pay for all the work until a full test of all the systems fitted has been made, and preferably not until several days have passed. In the case of plumbing or central heating the water system should have been pressurized for at least 24 hours. During that time, make every effort to use any of the WCs, basins etc. that have been fitted. The central heating system, if one has just been installed, should be left on, albeit on a mild setting, even if the weather is warm.

There are some things, however, that you can do to check that the work appears to be proceeding properly:

- Pipework should look neat, tidy and well organized, without unnecessary crossing over of pipework or sharp bends. The pipes should also be clipped securely when routed up walls and should be sufficiently protected in conduit, within walls or under floors, to prevent them being damaged during normal use of the property.

- Pipework should never be placed into concrete, unless within a conduit.

- Pipe joints, whether copper or plastic, should be checked for any weeping or dampness, however minor. If this is found, advise the tradesman immediately. No leaking pipe ever gets better.

- Old pipework, whether lead or iron, should not be used or joined onto unless absolutely unavoidable. Both forms of pipework are now out of date and likely to be defective, or may become so at any time. Lead piping is apt to spring leaks, and iron piping to become so clogged up inside as to reduce pressure significantly – and eventually altogether.

- Wherever possible, isolators (small valves that can terminate the water supply to a particular tap or cistern) should be placed on the pipework to WC cisterns, all wash-basins, baths, shower pipework (in an accessible place) and outside taps (the isolator to be accessible internally). The isolators will allow work to be performed on any of these areas without the whole water system having to be drained, which is a slow, inconvenient and expensive procedure.

- The plumber or central heating engineer must pressurize the system he is working on, after he has completed the first-fit pipework, to check for leaks. On some projects the second fit of the sanitary ware etc. will not take place for some weeks, by which time flooring may have been put down, joinery performed above the pipework and so on, making the discovery and rectification of any leak extremely difficult, costly and potentially damaging.

- All valves, stopcocks and isolators must be easily and quickly accessible, as should all wastes and taps, and these should remain accessible once all the other works have been finished – i.e. appropriate access panels must be made to allow a plumber to reach into, and work upon, any area in the future.

- Old or disused piping should be removed from the site. It should not just be disconnected and left in position, as this only leads to confusion in the future, should another plumber or central heating engineer have to locate a problem.

- All hot-water piping, whether central heating or otherwise, should be insulated.

- All piping in the loft space, whether hot or cold, should be insulated, and all water tanks lagged, with their tops covered.

- Wherever possible, metal water tanks should be replaced, as these are now out of date, and can leak seriously at any time, with little or no warning. When tanks are replaced, adequate support must be constructed to spread the load of a filled tank across the loft joists.

- Ensure that no boiler flue is located either immediately below a window or within 500mm of a window. If this is the case, then the window must be permanently sealed to prevent opening.

- If a **gas decorative fire effect** (DFE) is installed, then check that sufficient floor and wall vents have been fitted. These fires are potentially dangerous and have a low efficiency, with most of the energy going up the chimney. They must be fitted properly and checked regularly.

- All new external drainage must be specifically approved by the Building Control Officer, who may require a drains test before giving his approval to the works. He is also responsible (see Chapter 14: Building Regulations and Building Control) for checking the installation of any new boiler, new WCs, hot water systems etc. Make sure you personally contact him to check whether or not he should do an inspection. His supervision of the works is invaluable (and often mandatory).

- A floor plan, however basic, should be drawn up by the plumber or central heating engineer to show the routeing of the pipework, any key valves and the isolators. This should be drawn up during the work, before flooring or concealment of the pipework is carried out, and held by you at the end of the work.

POINTING

Pointing on new work is normally a question of aesthetics. Any competent bricklayer can do it well, but the repointing of brickwork is sometimes inadequately done. The following should be checked:

- A sufficient depth of the old mortar should have been chased out prior to repointing. This should be a minimum depth of 20mm.

- The new style of pointing should match the rest of the property, and be done tidily without marking the faces of the bricks.

- The area of work should be well cleaned, paying particular attention to gutters and drains, which quickly get filled and blocked during the chasing and actual pointing.

ROOFS

Roofs, whether pitched or flat, tend to be the source of many problems. Part of the trouble stems from the fact that people, quite understandably, very rarely go up onto a roof physically to check the problem that has occurred, or the work that is being done or has been completed. As a consequence, particularly when repairs are being done, there is scope for unscrupulous behaviour on the part of roofers or builders. They may overcharge or do work that, if inspected, would be considered unsatisfactory. It has to be said, however, that very few people, even when they do have access to a roof, really know what to look at, and this makes them always vulnerable.

Problems with roofing tend to come from two main sources: costs and workmanship.

Costs

The question of the escalation of costs is always problematic, unless the original schedule of works and specification is extremely precise and allows for the precosting, by the roofer, of an array of potential problems. For example, when reroofing, a roofer may well find that some of the rafters are defective. They may be incorrectly spaced, badly bowed or rotten, particularly at the ends. In this event, their replacement will be necessary before work can continue. The problem is that unless you have an agreed figure for the replacement of a rafter, prior to the work starting, then the roofer is at some liberty to charge what he likes. It is essential, therefore, that any contract made with the roofer or builder clearly sets out prices for any work or material which may be found to be necessary.

It should be stressed that in many cases it is simply not possible for a roofer to anticipate the problems that may lie within a roof, and so their subsequent discovery should not necessarily be blamed on him. Until a roof is stripped of its covering (whether slates, tiles, asphalt, felt etc.), it may not be possible to know for sure what problems, if any, are present. Nonetheless, every roofer should be able to enumerate, prior to the work starting, the potential problem areas, and their likely remedial cost – or, at worst, a day rate that he would charge. If this is done, then you can budget accordingly, or delay starting other works on the property until the variables, if there are any, have been located.

It is absolutely vital that, wherever possible, you go and inspect physically the problem areas that have been revealed, and their extent. It is all too easy for a roofer to claim falsely that there are problems which need rectifying, or to exaggerate the extent of any remedial work. If nothing else, the roofer should leave on site evidence of any defects that he has had to rectify. For example, if some timber is found to be rotten, then the roofer should leave it for you to inspect.

Workmanship

It is extremely difficult to know when works to a roof are being performed properly or do, in fact, need to be done. Indeed, one of the main problems that you will have is attempting to define which works are necessary – particularly if you are not going to reroof a property fully. Normally, you will have been alerted to a problem because of a specific leak, or because the roof itself is looking worn – for example, the mortar around hip tiles is missing in part, or slates or tiles are missing or have slipped. In this case, it is quite likely that the roof may just need some minor maintenance or repairs. Equally, however, the roof may have become time-expired, and on close inspection the slates, for example, may have become porous and cracked.

If there is any uncertainty, then you must employ either a surveyor or a structural engineer to advise you specifically on the condition of your roof. Failing that, get three separate roofers to come and inspect it, and advise you of the works they feel need doing, whether it is basic maintenance, a genuine worthwhile repair or complete reroofing. There should be a consensus between at least two of the roofers, and their advice should then be followed.

A classic mistake, made time and again, is a client's (understandable) reluctance to reroof, but willingness instead to allow unsupervised repairs to be done, many of which no roofer would ever be able to warrant. In fact, repairs are often disproportionately expensive, and they are rarely effective or long-lasting, thus necessitating another visit by a roofer to tackle the same or a slightly different area. Over several years, you may find you could almost have reroofed, for the cost of the repairs. Access is always a problem, and if scaffolding is needed, a minor repair becomes an expensive operation. The roofer may also need to find particular materials to match those already present, and these will be costly in small quantities. All of these factors will contribute to the high cost of repairs.

During the works themselves you are, to some extent, protected by the necessary inspection visits of the Building Control Officer, who must inspect all new roofing, or any complete reroofing. Make certain that he has been advised of the works, and that he makes an inspection visit.

Up to a point, all you can do while the work is proceeding is to gain access to the roof (preferably with the roofer present, as roofs can be lethal), and to have a general look at the work being performed. If it does look as though it is being neatly and carefully undertaken, then it is quite likely that the work is all right. You should still ensure, however, that on completion of the works you do not fully pay the roofer until the roof has had a good test of its water tightness, i.e. a reasonable rain storm or, in the case of a flat roof, a thorough and sustained dowsing of water from a hosepipe. You must also obtain a warranty for the works, wherever possible, as roofs are notorious for allowing the slow ingress of water over a period of time. If the work has not been done properly it does not necessarily mean that there will be a specific noticeable leak – there may just be a gradual dampness that will penetrate walls and timbers.

You should specifically check the following:

Pitched Roofs

- Check whether the work to be performed requires the involvement of the Building Control Officer (see Chapter 14: Building Regulations and Building Control).

- If the roof covering is being changed from a lighter material to a heavier one, e.g. from slates to concrete tiles, the roof structure must be strengthened. If this is not done adequately, then the rafters will bow and/or push the wall plate supporting the rafters off the wall of the property. This is a common problem, and very expensive to rectify.

- **Valleys** (where two slopes meet) are a major cause of leaks, often due to cracks or splits in the lead, zinc, concrete or valley tiles.

- **Hips and ridges** (where two slopes meet on an outside angle) should be bedded in mortar, pointed and, in the case of hips, should have a hip iron at the bottom end.

- Dormer windows and parapet walls (where the wall extends above the roof surface) often leak water internally, due to a lack of **soakers** (lead or zinc upstands placed beneath the flashing), or poor flashing.

- **Verges** (where the roof projects over a gable wall) must overhang by about 50mm, and be raised at the edge to bring the water back onto the roof, and then into the gutter. If this is not done the water can find its way under the roof and into the property.

- Felt must be laid correctly, with vertical and horizontal joints overlapped. The felt should drop halfway into the gutter and not have sags near the fascia board, which will rot the fascia and damage the top of the wall and wall plate. If felt is used, then ventilation for the roof must be installed.

- Lead flashing should look neat and tidy, have no nails within the covering, be tucked well into any mortar joints and be held in by lead wedges.

- The runs of the tiles or slates should be straight and even, with the starting-point of any new work being from the verge inwards.

Flat Roofs

Flat roofs are a constant problem, and have a much shorter life span than a pitched roof. Wherever possible, try to go for a pitched roof. If a flat roof has to be constructed, then, if it is feasible, ensure that the roof has the highest gradient possible, and that the roofer doing the work is very capable, and working to a particularly high-quality specification.

- The **decking** (base of the roof) must be made out of waterproof boarding. When reroofing a flat roof, the decking and joists will frequently be found to be rotten, and require substantial replacement. Beware of this becoming an unanticipated additional cost.

- Avoid any process where a **cold bitumen application** is used to stick layers of felt together. A **heated bitumen** is infinitely better in sealing the layers together, and is likely to be longer-lasting.

- The preference for flat roofs should be an **asphalt covering**. This is more durable than felt.

- **Heat-reflective chippings** must not be placed too thickly on flat roofs. Water is prevented from easily leaving the roof, the roof takes a long time to dry out and gutters fill up.

- Great care must be taken by a contractor to ensure that any joints between the roof and any parapet walls are correctly sealed, with the flashing and/or upstands going up the wall by at least 100–150mm.

Roofing in General

- Check that any scaffolding erected is safe, well tied into the property and not accessible to children or burglars, either during the work itself or, most particularly, after the day's work has been completed.

- All debris from an old roof, once checked, should be cleared from site quickly (the timber element is normally highly combustible), and any rubbish in the eaves, gutters and drains should be removed.

- While the scaffolding is in place, check the condition of the pointing or rendering of the chimney stack and parapet walls, and the state of the guttering, soffits and fascia boards. If these need attention it is best to go to the extra expense while access is available. It will make any subsequent work cheaper and quicker.

- If possible, negotiate for the cost of the scaffolding yourself. Most building or roofing contractors will mark up this item quite substantially. If a scaffolding company is used, then make sure that it is reputable. Your roofing or building contractor should directly liaise with the company about the erection timing and precise location of the scaffolding levels.

- In any project, obtain costs for potential additional works prior to the starting of the project as a whole. It will be rare in the case of reroofing if there are not extras by the end of the job, and these may be very substantial.

STRUCTURAL WORKS AND NEW BUILDING

Works to the actual structure of a property, whether internal or external, should only be undertaken with considerable care. A number of factors may need to be considered and checked before the work goes ahead. Otherwise, an unscrupulous or ignorant builder can cause considerable trouble and, perhaps, damage. Structural works should never be rushed into, and the opinion of a professional such as a structural engineer is always justified, even if it is just to confirm a negative – that the works will in no way affect the actual structure of a property, and that there are no adverse consequences to anyone else or to planning or building regulations.

The structure of buildings is often more complicated than at first sight. For example, the fact that an internal wall is composed of stud work does not necessarily mean that it is not load-bearing, while it is also true to say that not all brick or block walls are bearing a load. The difference between a partition wall and a structural wall is therefore not always easy to tell, and cannot be ascertained simply by knocking at the plaster, to see if the wall is solid or not – it is their positioning within the overall structure of the building that is vital.

Be aware of the potential implications of doing structural works which, by their very nature, can disturb a property, or reveal defective areas unsuspected even by a professional. It may well be that the property was originally poorly constructed, or that an innate flaw is discovered, in which case much more work than originally envisaged may have to be carried out. These works are often very committing and, once started, reversal can be a problem. Be prepared for a climb in quoted costs.

Give due consideration to your lease, if you have one, and any possible planning matters (see Chapter 15: Planning Permission). Leases frequently forbid any structural works unless the lessee has first obtained permission from the freeholder, and this can sometimes be impossible, or entail considerable time and expense. Equally, planning permission can be required even for what appears to be uncontentious work such as knocking through a wall to insert a new window.

While it is the responsibility in law for a builder to comply with building regulations (see Chapter 14: Building Regulations and Building Control), it is the owner's responsibility to ensure that any planning permission, party notices or freeholder's permission has been obtained (see Chapter 16: Law and Disputes). Many builders do have a lot of empirical knowledge of these matters, and can advise you, but it is for you to check that all is in order before allowing the works to start.

Ideally, a structural engineer should be employed whenever structural works are being considered. He will take over responsibility for ensuring that the relevant notices are issued, and that the builder has a detailed schedule of works – with all the necessary drawings and calculations.

Common problems experienced with structural works tend to be that:

- the correct permissions from the freeholder or planning department are not obtained;

- no party notice (see below, p.140) is issued to neighbours;
- Building Control is not notified of the work; or
- the builder does not do the work well, and actually causes structural problems.

In any of the first three, even if the building work is beyond criticism, you can find that you have to stop the works and restore the property to its previous state. This is almost always an expensive and avoidable problem, created simply by not having researched the project properly.

The structural integrity of the building work can be ensured through the employment of a structural engineer, and the most important part of his job will be to ensure that the works are performed safely and correctly. The engineer will personally inspect the work throughout the project, particularly during critical stages for which he will have to give his approval before the builder continues with the work.

The involvement of the **Building Control Officer (BCO)** will also be necessary (see Chapter 14), regardless of whether or not a structural engineer or other professional is involved. The BCO will be obliged to inspect the work at various stages to ensure compliance with the regulations relating to the work. At no time should you try to avoid the involvement of the BCO if it is required. The BCO is certainly your best protection against structural problems during the works, if no engineer is involved. It must be emphasized, however, that the remit of the BCO does not extend to the aesthetic qualities of the work, nor to the builder's charging policy or time-keeping. Furthermore, the actual legal liability of the BCO, while conducting his inspections, is extremely limited.

Check the following, before works actually commence:

- If you are a leaseholder, check your lease, or get your solicitor to do so, to see if the proposed works are forbidden within the lease, or whether they can go ahead subject to stated conditions. You are likely to find that you have to advise the freeholder of the detailed nature of the works and, depending on what they are, you will probably have to employ a structural engineer to advise on the works, and/or pay the freeholder's engineer to supervise the structural aspect of the project. You may also have to pay a reclaimable deposit, in case the works do any damage to the building.

- Whether leaseholder or freeholder, check with your local authority Building Control, to see whether the proposed works come within its remit, and thereby require the monitoring of the BCO.

    In principle, anything that comes within the definition of 'material change' requires the attendance of the BCO (see Chapter 14), but it is generally best to contact Building Control to see if the proposed works actually fall within this definition. For the most part, Building Control are very helpful and they are almost invariably happy to advise whether or not the works may also need planning permission. The BCO dealing with your area will also almost certainly know the property or, as importantly, the type of properties in your road, and will be able to advise whether or not the proposed works are subject to inspection. If there is any doubt, then the BCO will normally attend the property for no charge (although this varies between local authorities), to meet with you to assess the matter. This can generally be done with only a day or two's notice.

- If the advice of the BCO is that the proposed works do come within the remit of Building Control, then a building notice needs to be issued, or full plans deposited with the local authority. The local authority will require 48 hours' notice prior to any works proceeding.

  While for some works a sketch and basic description is adequate for the building notice, for other works such as, for example, the insertion of a load-bearing steel, proper engineering calculations may be required and the BCO will specify this, if asked.

- If the works do require detailed drawings then you will almost always have to go to a structural engineer, architect or surveyor (the former is preferable) to obtain proper plans and calculations. At this time it is worth getting the engineer to draw up a proper schedule of works and specification for the builder. This does not go to the BCO but does help the overall running of the project, particularly if the work is complicated.

- You, or preferably your engineer, may have to issue a **party notice**. This is formal notice to a neighbour that works are going ahead which may affect the neighbour's property. For example, if a steel support is being set into a party wall, then there is the possibility that your builder may disturb the neighbour's wall while performing the work. Likewise if, for example, underpinning is going to take place within 3 metres of the neighbour's property, he should be notified.

  This notification provides you with time in which to instruct a surveyor or engineer to inspect the neighbour's property before the commencement of work, to draw up a **schedule of condition**. This can be checked at the end of the works, to see if there has been any damage to your neighbour's property. If the party notice is not issued, then you could become liable for an action of trespass if your builder has disturbed or encroached on your neighbour's property. You will, in any event, have to repair any damage that is shown in the end-of-works inspection.

During the course of the works you should do the following:

- Find out the name of the BCO who will be inspecting the work, and at what stages he will make his visits. This is useful knowledge as, unless you are employing a professional such as a structural engineer, it is helpful to be present when the BCO makes his first visit. At this time you can get a reasonable idea of the type of person the BCO is, and how he will interact with your builder. Also, as the BCO makes his initial appraisal you can sometimes gain a reasonable idea of the competence of your own builder, in seeing how he deals with the queries raised by the BCO.

- Ensure that the work is being done to your desired standard and is, of course, located in the right position, that the builder is using the specified materials, etc. This will come under the remit of a structural engineer if one is being used, but should still be double-checked.

  It must again be emphasized that the BCO does not have any remit as to the aesthetic quality of the work being performed, nor as to the builder's approach to the work, unless it is contrary to building regulations. He cannot intervene if the new brickwork looks untidy or if the builder is doing the work at irregular times. The BCO is interested only in the integrity of the building work and its compliance with the regulations. Accordingly, it is for you, in conjunction with your engineer, to ensure that the work is being done well aesthetically.

  It is therefore important that you check the work as carefully as possible, and do not make the mistake of abdicating your responsibilities to manage and control the project, just because the BCO is involved.

- Once the structural element of the work has been completed, expressly ensure that the BCO is satisfied, and that he will issue a **completion certificate**. This is normally posted to you, but the BCO can, and will, give an oral approval sufficient for you to allow the works to continue.

13

Movement and Subsidence

FEW things can disturb a property owner more than finding out that his property is suffering from movement. This can be devastating if a sale is being processed, can lead to unexpected expense, a devaluation of the property, an increase in insurance and, at some stage, substantial building works. It can all amount to a most traumatic personal experience and is one that has become very prevalent over the past few years due to the change in the weather conditions, with little sign of a slow-down at the time of writing.

There are, for the layman, two basic forms of movement. The first type, not dealt with in detail here, is when a property has an integral fault such as a large flank wall that may not have been adequately tied in to the rest of the property, possibly during the original construction. As a consequence the wall may start to bow out over time until it will, eventually, collapse. Movement can also occur where new work has destabilized a property, such as when a structural wall has been removed without adequate support being provided. In either of these cases a structural engineer should be called in immediately to advise the property owner. It is unlikely that the owner will be able to make a claim against his own insurance company for the remedial works, although he may have grounds for an action against other parties.

The second form of movement is due to subsidence or heave, when an external pressure is moving the property, and thereby causing damage. **Subsidence** is essentially caused by the downward movement of a property, when the foundations start to slip, or lose firm contact with the soil on which they were built. **Heave**, on the other hand, is the opposite, and represents upward movement normally caused by the swelling of soil under the property. Unfortunately, the pressures, whether upward or downward, do not occur with equal and consistent force throughout a property – consequently there is differential movement that gradually tears a building, or part of a building, apart. While buildings are generally very strong, they have no elasticity, and once there is movement, a building will start cracking along the weakest part of the structure, to a greater or lesser extent.

The only vaguely good news for the property owner is that he will be able to make a claim against his insurance company for repairs to the damage caused as a consequence of this form of movement. This is a long and somewhat complicated procedure, however, and once movement is reported to an insurance company it can take, on average, some two-and-a-half to three years before the remedial repairs are completed. Sadly, until that time, any personal ambitions of the owner for the property are likely to be placed on hold.

Few people are likely to buy a property that is suffering from movement or is the subject of a claim, unless, at best, the price is significantly discounted. Furthermore, there is little point in doing more than basic maintenance to the property until the movement has been sorted out and the remedial strengthening works completed. These works can be extremely messy in themselves, depending on the amount required, and can, in some cases, make the property uninhabitable until completion.

WHY MOVEMENT OCCURS

There are a number of reasons why movement occurs, the most common of which are:

A Change in the Level of the Water Table

This can happen when there are extremes of weather, such as long wet or dry spells that change the water content of the soil and therefore its density. Clay is particularly vulnerable; it shrinks in dry weather and expands during wet, adversely affecting the foundations of a property. If the extremes of weather are great enough then this differential will be quite sufficient to cause movement.

The years 1994–6 have been particularly bad for property due to the long periods without rain, and subsidence claims have risen annually – to the point where loss adjusters are now becoming overwhelmed.

The Action of Trees

Trees can affect a property in three ways. First, they can take an enormous amount of water out of the ground, compounding the problem of dry weather by further draining the soil around or under a property. A fully grown willow tree, for example, takes some 100 gallons (460 litres) of water from the soil daily. The vast majority of subsidence claims, where a property is built on clay soil, are the result of trees or large shrubs.

Secondly, the roots of trees are incredibly strong and in their search for water they will go right under a house, sometimes even where there has been underpinning. In doing so they will exert sufficient pressure on the foundations to cause movement.

Thirdly, roots of trees are notorious for penetrating drain systems. As the roots search for water they can start to push through a small break or crack in piping or piping collars and will then gradually, but inexorably, break open the drain. The drain will then become blocked and leak around the foundations, softening the soil so that it once again becomes incapable of solidly bearing the load of a property.

Drains

If any major leakage occurs due to a damaged drain, whether through the action of trees or otherwise, this can cause subsidence. Unfortunately, drains are also often cracked or broken as a consequence of a movement, regardless of what caused it, and they therefore need a proper inspection before any remedial works are undertaken.

Hillsides

Properties built on slopes do have a tendency to move, depending to some extent on soil conditions, unless their foundations are adequate for the ground on which they are built.

Underground Water Courses

Changes in the level of water passing through these can affect the foundations of a property, particularly if the direction of the underground stream or river has changed. This may be due to a natural geological change, a change in the weather pattern, or even possibly new construction works.

Building Works

Defective building works, such as the removal of a load-bearing part of the building, internally or externally, can destabilize a property.

It should also be stated that the foundations of many older properties are, by the standards of today, quite inadequate. Indeed, the foundations of most Victorian and earlier properties would not pass the stringent attentions of any building inspector or structural engineer in the 1990s. It is not uncommon to find that the foundations of some older properties go down little more than 300–500mm, and accordingly these properties are particularly at risk to climatic changes.

That said, good foundations are no guarantee that movement will not occur, and properties that have reasonable foundations, and indeed even those that have been properly underpinned, may still move.

HOW TO RECOGNIZE MOVEMENT

It is important to be able to recognize the basic signs of movement, although the reasons for this movement, its importance and the ability to decide whether it is historic or not, invariably lie in the hands of a structural engineer. Indeed, the complexity of this area should not be understated. If you have any real doubts at all then you must turn to professional advice as soon as possible. While the damage caused by subsidence and heave is generally slow, and may be progressive over a long period of time, an integral fault may need rapid correction. For example, if some poor building work has been done, adversely affecting the structure of a property, then it may need to be rectified very quickly, before a potential collapse.

In practice, the most that you can do is to recognize the difference between structural cracks and natural shrinkage or settlement.

Natural Shrinkage or Settlement

Surface cracking will often occur after new building and decorating of a property, or a part thereof. The cracks will normally run in straight, uniform lines along natural fault lines, such as between the joint of a ceiling and wall, or along the top of skirtings, where the skirting meets the wall surface. Cracks may also appear where different materials meet, such as plaster and wood. They may be seen along the outlines of the plasterboards in a ceiling, showing up the shape of whole plasterboards, and they will commonly appear in new timber, running along the grain.

Generally, and critically, the cracks will be of even width along their length – and will not extend along their line into other rooms or areas of a property. The cracks will also not greatly alter once they become apparent, and will not open and close over the course of time.

If you investigate by opening up the crack, you will see that it lacks any depth and, most importantly, does not penetrate into the actual solid wall surface – that is, the crack will be superficial, and will not have split the brick- or blockwork. Equally, a crack on a wall will not be mirrored in the same place on the other side.

Shrinkage and settlement cracking occurs as new work dries out, or as a completely new property settles firmly onto its foundations. It will start almost as soon as the work is finished, and is accelerated by central heating which will quickly, and to some extent unnaturally, draw out the moisture still held in many of the building materials used.

It should not be forgotten how much water is used in building, whether it is in the concrete of floors, the mortar between bricks or the very wet process of plastering. Furthermore, bricks are often wet when laid and even internal timber has a high moisture content, all of which takes considerable time to dry out completely. Until this has occurred, some cracking and warping of the new work will take place, and this may be over some considerable time, depending on the type and degree of the work done and the heat applied to the property. Indeed, as a generality, it is not normally worth attending to these cracks until the new work is at least a year old, at which time surface filling is probably sufficient to conceal the cracking for good.

Structural Movement

Structural cracking can occur in a property, new or old, and regardless of whether or not new work has been performed. The cracking can be either hairline or very wide and substantial.

Structural cracks can appear anywhere on a property, and are not necessarily found in obvious areas of structural weakness, although this is frequent. So, although cracks will often be found over doors, at the junction of walls and the edge of bay windows, they can equally run up the middle of walls, whether internal or external.

The cracks are invariably either vertical or diagonal, and not horizontal. They also tend not to be in a uniform straight line, at least until they become very big, but will weave their way up a wall, sometimes in a jagged manner but nonetheless following a constant general direction. They will also continue uninterrupted through a property, regardless of the different rooms. So, for example, a crack in a downstairs room will more than likely continue up through the house, along a fairly constant direction.

The cracks vary in width along their length and, critically, are normally wider at one end than the other. Sometimes a crack, when it is traced through a property, will be substantial at one end, but will become hairline, or even disappear at the other end. The cracks are not always very long, and do not have to stretch the whole way through a property, to indicate that they are serious. Sometimes they may be only a few metres long, and may unaccountably stop.

A structural crack, if investigated, will prove to have gone right through any brick-, stone- or blockwork, and the line of the crack may be visible on the reverse side of the wall.

Structural cracks will tend, wherever possible, to follow a line of weakness, so that on brickwork, for example, in the middle of a wall, a crack will often follow the mortar line between the bricks, before cracking a brick itself, and perhaps then refollowing the mortar, before cracking further bricks as it rises along a wall.

Even non-load-bearing walls, such as stud walls, will be affected, with cracking occurring on the junction where they meet a solid wall. The stud work will be pulled apart from its fixing on the solid wall.

Sometimes, where a wall has been stressed, there will be a number of roughly parallel cracks stretching diagonally along a wall.

If you find that cracks appear to be structural rather than superficial, then you must consider calling in a structural engineer to inspect the property. This should be done very quickly if you have any suspicions whatsoever that it may be the consequence of recent building work, whether in your own property or one nearby. Speed may be of the essence if new building work has been done. It is always just possible that the works were badly done, and may lead to real danger or substantial damage.

If you notice structural cracking either during or after your own builder's work, then act quickly to call in a structural engineer, unless the builder can present absolutely cast-iron reasons for the cracking. If there is any doubt at all in your mind seek professional help to confirm, or otherwise, the assertions of the builder.

If the cracking that has been noticed does not seem to be connected to any new building work, then the chances are that it is due to subsidence or heave, the consequences of which do not need so much haste. Indeed, it is unlikely that there will be any immediate real danger to the property, or those living in it. This form of movement generally causes damage slowly. In the majority of cases, it will not lead to the collapse of the house, or any part of it, for *a long time*. That is not to say that the cracking will not be unsightly, damage the weatherproofing of the property, and accelerate the decay of the fabric of a property and possibly the drainage system.

The only thing that you should specifically look out for is the danger of parts of the house becoming unsafe as they are loosened from their fixing. For example, brickwork may become loose, or perhaps areas of render, which if high up on a wall or on the roof, could fall down and cause injury. Equally, cabling chased into walls or previously hidden behind skirtings could become visible and a hazard for children. Also, beware of old plaster and lath ceilings, which can sometimes fall down spontaneously.

WHAT TO DO

If you suspect movement, and particularly if you think it has been caused by something other than subsidence or heave, then call in a structural engineer immediately. He will advise you, based on the evidence of the cracking and the recent occurrence of other activity, as to the probable cause. The engineer will more than likely be able to tell straight away if the movement could be a result of poor building work or some other one-off cause, as opposed to subsidence or heave, in which case he will be able to advise on the appropriate corrective action.

The action taken at this stage, if the engineer considers that the problem threatens the safety of the building, may be the immediate installation of some temporary supports to arrest any further movement, followed by a more careful assessment of the problem and the cause – the cause may have to be resolved before further remedial works can take place. Obviously, if the movement has been caused by someone other than yourself, then the question of liability will have to be settled before any remedial repairs are undertaken beyond that of making the building safe.

An engineer called in to look at movement-related cracks may well believe them to be related to subsidence or heave. In this case, the matter should be referred to the insurance company responsible for your buildings policy. They will then effectively take over the process of full investigation and repairs. This is a long and somewhat complicated procedure, however, and it is essential that you understand it if you are to ensure the process proceeds satisfactorily.

THE INSURANCE CLAIM

Before advising the insurance company of the possibility of movement to your property, it is wise first to check your insurance policy. This will, almost undoubtedly, cover you for repairs to the property due to movement, although there is likely to be an excess imposed on the cost of the works.

The most common misunderstanding by claimants, when approaching an insurance company, is the belief that the company is responsible for the cost of rectifying the cause of the movement, and always for underpinning the property. This is a misconception which constantly leads to problems between the client, the insurance company and the loss adjusters. You should understand the reality.

If a policy document is read carefully, the terms relating to movement are likely to be that the insurance company 'will pay the cost incurred in reinstatement or repair'. This does not mean that the insurance company will be responsible for paying for the rectification of the *cause* of the movement, nor does it imply that an insurance company will underpin the property as a matter of course.

If the cause of the movement is found, by the structural engineer, to be a tree or broken drain, then the insurance policy will not cover the works necessary to pollard or remove the tree or dig up and renew the drain. This is your responsibility and something for which you will have to pay directly, on top of your insurance excess.

In the case of underpinning, insurance companies interpret the policy very restrictively, while using an equation to work out whether in the long run it is worth their paying for this. Their calculation relies on the fact that underpinning, to any great extent, is extremely expensive to carry out – much more expensive, in fact, than most remedial works to repair the damage caused by the movement. Insurance companies therefore tend to look at the comparative costs of repair, as against underpinning and repair works together. If the repair costs are much lower than the underpinning costs, then they are often prepared to take a risk that the property may not move again, once the remedial repairs are carried out. Even if the property does move, they know that they can afford to pay for the remedial works again, before coming close to the original cost of having to underpin the property and then do the repair works.

For example, if the costs of repair and reinstatement are going to be £5,000 and the costs of underpinning £15,000, then it is worthwhile for an insurance company to do only the repair works, even if, over a course of years, the building continues to move and further repair works of £5,000 are required. If the repair works are likely to cost £15,000, however, and the underpinning £20,000, then the risk for the insurance company of not underpinning is not worth taking, let alone if the cost of underpinning was actually less than that of the repair and reinstatement works.

This strategy of the insurance companies, while it makes economic sense and is in no way deceitful, can be infuriating. You may find that the recurrence of movement is inevitable because the cause of the movement has been inadequately dealt with. Even so, there is little that you can do, apart from either employing a structural engineer to argue the case for underpinning the property with the insurance company, or funding the underpinning or the rectification of the cause of movement yourself.

The next matter that you should appreciate is that the policy document will state something to the effect that the insurance company 'will not pay for the cost of repair or reinstatement of any undamaged part of the building'. It is important to understand, from the start, that even the repairs and reinstatement that *are* paid for by the insurance company will be subject to a restrictive interpretation. So, if there is movement-related damage to an area of a room below a dado rail, for example, then they will pay for this to be corrected and redecorated – but will not pay to have the whole room redecorated, unless there is a compelling reason. Any contract will be monitored on the basis that no 'betterment' occurs. In other words, the insurance company will not pay to improve the property beyond what it was like prior to the claim.

The final matter that should attract your attention is the excess on the policy. This can vary from one insurance company to another, but is generally based on the area in which the property is situated, and whether or not it is one known to be prone to movement. The excess is generally £1,000 but it can be £5,000 or even more. The excess payable used to be required from the claimant as soon as the claim was reported. Increasingly, however, insurance companies do not require the excess to be paid until the structural engineers have completed their inspection report and the company has accepted that there is a valid claim. If you cannot find the excess amount at this time, the claim is unlikely to proceed any further.

DEALING WITH MOVEMENT

The process can be broken down into the following stages:

- Your advice to your insurance company of the possibility of movement.
- Monitoring of the property by structural engineers.
- Report by your engineers to your insurance company, confirming movement.
- Appointment by the insurance company of loss adjusters to deal with the detail of the claim.
- Nomination of structural engineers (normally yours) by the loss adjusters.
- Preparation of schedule of works by engineers for underpinning or, if no underpinning, then the general repair works.
- Agreement of the loss adjusters to the schedule of works.
- Sending out of the schedule of works and tenders to three underpinners with a copy to you.
- Receipt of the tenders, and assessment of them by the engineers and loss adjusters.
- Appointment of underpinners to perform the contract.
- Commencement of the works under the supervision of the engineers.
- On completion of the underpinning, preparation by the engineers of a schedule of works for the superstructure repair works.
- Agreement to the schedule of works by loss adjusters.
- Sending out of schedule of works and tenders to three builders with a copy to you.

- Assessment of tenders by engineers and loss adjusters.
- Commencement of works under the supervision of the engineer.
- Your approval of the completed works, and final authorization for the insurance company to pay the builders.

Realistically, the time between advice to the insurance company and the completion of the works can be up to three years. It is therefore important that you act reasonably quickly to start the process, as any delay will only put off the inevitability of having the work done.

While much of the process, as above, is effectively out of your hands, there are, nonetheless, some matters that you should be aware of and understand:

Monitoring

This is one of the reasons why the claim takes such a long time to settle. Once structural engineers have been appointed, their first task is to establish the cause of the movement, and to find out whether the building is still moving and, if so, to what extent. Among other things, to enable them to do this they need to attach 'tell-tales' across some of the cracks, which will, over a period of time, measure any movement. These tell-tales will measure movement to a thousandth (0.001) of a millimetre, although engineers will not normally be looking for a measurement of less than 0.01mm.

In crude terms, movement of between 1mm and 5mm in a month is serious, and below 1mm minor movement. To give you some idea of the degree required to be noticeable, a movement of the property by 0.5mm will be sufficient to break a plaster surface.

In the first three months the structural engineers will, as part of their initial investigation, also test the drains of your property, and dig a trial hole and place a bore into the ground to test the soil. The samples of soil will be sent to a laboratory for testing, to establish the condition of the soil, relating to its ability to sustain the property's foundations.

The monitoring will always be done for a minimum of 6 months and generally for 12 months. This allows the engineers to gain a clear idea of how the property is moving and to what extent it is affected by the different soil conditions in winter and summer. It is not unusual for cracks to close up during certain periods of the year, or for the engineers to find that the movement has stopped or, indeed, that it was historic and the building has not moved for many years.

Even if it is found that a property has stopped moving, or the cracks have closed up, remedial works are still very necessary. When a crack closes up it tends not to do so perfectly, as grit and dust get into it, and the material reclosing will therefore tend to rotate slightly. Furthermore, once a brick, block or piece of stone has cracked or split, it will never regain its former integrity, regardless of how it closes up, and the building will therefore have lost its previous strength and structural cohesion.

Unfortunately for you, the monitoring of the property cannot be artificially speeded up and there is little that you can do, apart from ensuring that the time taken between advising the insurance company of the movement and the commencement of the monitoring is as quick as possible.

The Schedule of Works

Once movement has been established by the structural engineers, they will report back to your insurance company, who will in due course appoint **loss adjusters** to supervise the detail of the claim. It is the responsibility of the loss adjusters to ensure that the interests of the insurance company are looked after. In reality, the loss adjusters will attempt to keep the cost of the claim to a minimum, thus restricting the works as far as possible within the strict definitions of the policy.

There can therefore be a potential conflict between you, who will want the maximum possible amount of work done, and the loss adjusters, whose aim will be the reverse. In the middle will be the structural engineer who, in theory, will only be interested in getting the works done on a professional and objective basis, although, after he has been nominated by the loss adjuster, the engineer's appointment is formally transferred to you – that is, the engineer, while paid by your insurance company, is working, in theory, directly for you.

You must attend to any schedule of works that is produced by the engineer, however, to ensure that it is properly comprehensive. While the engineer is theoretically an independent expert working on your behalf, the reality is that he may often have to bow to the demands of the loss adjuster, and thereby produce an unduly restrictive schedule of works. After all, it is the loss adjuster who appoints him and will, or will not, put future work his way.

The schedule of works produced by the structural engineer should be made available to you, prior to its being sent out to builders for tender, and at this time you must go carefully through the document (see Appendix 2: Specimen Professional Schedule of Works) to ensure that you agree with the findings of the engineer, and the scope of works that has been formulated. It cannot be too highly stated that you must do this, and check that you agree with every particular of the remedial works, with specific attention to the finishing works. All too often claimants do not look at the schedule until the end of the actual works, when they realize that all that they wanted done, or thought should be done, has not been. They then discover that these works were never in the schedule in the first place. If works are not enumerated within a schedule then they will not be done – the contractor will have quoted only on the items contained in the schedule, and nothing else.

Clearly, it is difficult for anyone with no background in structural engineering to make any meaningful comments on the proposed structural repairs and their adequacy, and up to a point you have to accept that the engineer is a professional and will attend to this properly. If you have doubts about whether or not the proposed structural repairs are sufficient, however, then seek the opinion of another engineer, not connected to the loss adjusters.

Generally, the problems with the remedial works when they do take place

– apart from the perennial question of whether the property should or should not be underpinned – revolve around the mess created and the extent of the finishing works. To some extent both are linked, as the mess and damage caused in performing the remedial works can affect the rest of the house. If a schedule of works is very restrictive then you can find that, at the end of the work, your property has not been returned to its pre-movement state.

The important point to appreciate is that the insurance company must, in doing the remedial works, ensure that your property is returned to the state it was in prior to the damage caused by the movement. For example, if the property was in a poor state before the movement, then it will be returned to you in the same state, except that the necessary restrengthening works will have taken place. If the painted or decorated state was poor, your insurance company may not even pay for any decorating to be undertaken. If the property was well decorated, however, then your insurance company would have to pay to have the same quality of painting and wallpapering done.

It is vital to look carefully at the schedule of works to see what provision the structural engineer has made for the finishing works, and to make sure that there is sufficient latitude in the schedule to take into account the fact that dust, mess and damage will be created as an inevitable consequence of the works. Look carefully at the schedule, and if you feel that it is too restrictive, take this up with the engineer first and then, at worst, with the loss adjusters. If neither of these parties provides you with satisfaction, try the insurance company direct, although this is not normally effective and should be a last resort. The main point is that you must fight your corner productively, to obtain as wide an interpretation of 'repairs and reinstatement' as possible, prior to the works starting – and this must be reflected in writing in the schedule of works.

That is not to say that amendments to a schedule cannot be made during the actual conduct of the works. Indeed, this is frequently done, as the works themselves often reveal previously concealed flaws. In this case a structural engineer will negotiate with the loss adjuster to increase the scope of work originally defined. So, although the schedule of works undoubtedly forms the basis of the works, amendments can be made – although obviously it is harder to get these done during the work than before it starts. If you subsequently find that areas which you thought were going to be dealt with are not, then you should attempt to get them included, regardless of the stage which has been reached.

The Structural Engineer

The conduct of the structural engineer is crucial to the successful conclusion of any insurance claim and, as in any other business, the competence and integrity of these individuals varies greatly. Be careful to assess, as best you can, the engineer appointed to produce the schedule of works, and to supervise the remedial works yourself.

Appallingly imprecise specifications are sometimes produced by structural engineers, on the narrowest possible interpretation of remedial and reinstatement works, with an almost deliberate avoidance of allowing adequate works. Furthermore, flaws found during the actual conduct of the works are sometimes dismissed, and no attempt made to increase the scope of the schedule of works, however essential, through fear of increasing the costs and thereby upsetting the loss adjuster. Some engineers will also restrict their visits to site to an absolute minimum, not supervising the work to any proper extent. When these things occur, you are more than likely going to end up with a poor or unsatisfactory job.

A good structural engineer will produce an immensely detailed, unambiguous schedule of works itemizing every possible function that he wishes the builder to undertake (see Appendix 2). He will also have the confidence in his own professionalism to approach the loss adjuster during the course of the actual works, to make changes to the original schedule of works which take into account any newly identified problem areas, regardless of any additional cost incurred by the insurance company. He will, in effect, while remaining firmly within the policy definition of the works, fight your corner wherever he feels appropriate. Furthermore, and importantly, he will make frequent visits to site to supervise the works and physically check that the work he has specified is done in the way that he wants.

If you find yourself provided with a sloppy schedule of works, or find that the engineer is not properly looking after your interests and monitoring the site professionally, act quickly to try to persuade your insurance company to appoint another structural engineer. Do not buckle just because the engineer is a professional. At the end of the day, do not lose sight of the fact that you are the employer to all parties, whether it is your insurance company or the engineer. Also, whether your excess was £1,000, £5,000 or more, it will also be your own money for which you are not getting proper value (let alone your years of paying premiums).

The Builder

Any remedial and reinstatement works will be performed by the builder who provided the lowest tender for the work – unless there is something so peculiar in the tender that it makes a structural engineer or loss adjuster concerned about his competence. This may seem an indication of trouble but, in fact, the engineer will have vetted the builders and will, furthermore, tend to use the same three or four building companies for all his insurance-related work. This means that the builders will take care not to perform poorly, for fear of being struck off the engineer's list. Equally, the engineer will normally manage the contract carefully, as he will not wish to upset the loss adjusters or the insurance company – who will lose faith in him if there are too many complaints from you.

While you must recognize the importance of your personal monitoring of the work done, the real supervision of the works will be carried out by the engineer, whose job it will be to ensure that the schedule of works is properly completed. Do not neglect to visit the site frequently, however, particularly during the finishing works, to ensure that they are up to standard.

Generally, in view of the very different skills required for the remedial works, two different building companies will be used. The underpinning will be dealt with by a company specializing exclusively in that area, while the more delicate and quite different skills required in works to the superstructure will be dealt with by a different specialist company. Some companies are able to do both functions, but this is not normally the case.

The Remedial Works

The remedial works to be performed on a property that has suffered subsidence or heave tend to fall into three areas, depending on the advice of the structural engineer, and the extent of the works for which your insurance company is prepared to pay.

The first area, where applicable, will be that of correcting the specific problem that has caused the movement, and the direct cost of this will, in any event, be your own responsibility. Following this, or perhaps undertaken at the same time, will be the underpinning of the building, after which the remedial works to the superstructure will take place.

Initial Corrective Works

If the problem located is due, for example, to a defective drain or a tree, then this must be remedied as soon as possible, unless the problem is such that it will require extensive works that could be most efficiently undertaken during the underpinning stage. If a tree is found to have caused the movement then it will most probably be pollarded immediately, to start to reduce its adverse effect on the building. Equally, if a drain is at fault, then if the repair can be conducted reasonably easily, this will be performed as soon as possible and before the underpinning.

Underpinning

As seen above, this may not take place, either because it is unnecessary or because your insurance company takes the economic option of not doing it. If underpinning is carried out, then expect a fair amount of disruption to your property, although this depends greatly upon the extent of underpinning necessary – and its location.

If the underpinning does take place, ensure that all the things that you value are moved well away from the area of work. This should include any statues, plants or shrubs that are particular treasures in the garden or any furniture or furnishings within the house. The interpretation of the 'area of work' should be as broad as possible, as most people not involved in building will not appreciate the amount of mess caused nor the amount of room required. In many cases, the supervising structural engineer will have allowed in the schedule of works for the builders to help to clear the site beforehand, but it is in your interests to do as much of this as possible before any builders arrive.

There are a number of different ways to underpin a property but most require the careful digging of holes around and under the foundations of a property, prior to strengthening the foundations or, in some cases, effectively providing the building with proper foundations – which may never have existed in the first place. The work is arduous and extremely messy, with huge amounts of soil having to be excavated and disposed of, and equivalent amounts of concrete being brought to the property and used to fill up the holes. While most underpinning can be performed outside the property, there are occasions when the work is done inside, such as where an internal structural wall requires underpinning. Understandably, this will completely disrupt the room for the duration of the works, and lead to unavoidable disruption to the hallway as well. This also occurs where the works are being done to terraced houses and underpinners have no separate access to the rear of the property.

Obviously, the important thing is that the works, once they do start, are carried out efficiently and quickly so as to get the disruption over as soon as possible. The last thing you will want, particularly if you are living in the property, is for the works to be conducted slowly or erratically. It is therefore critical for the structural engineer to supervise the works to ensure they proceed properly, and for you to advise him if the builders unaccountably start to reduce their manpower, or fail to attend the site for several days.

Once the underpinning has been completed, the site is normally left for some six to eight weeks before any remedial works to the superstructure take place. The reason for this delay is to allow the building to settle properly on its new foundations, during which time some further cracking may occur, together with a fair amount of moisture penetrating up into the building. The latter is due to the concrete drying out, and this process can cause discolouring of wallpapers and the rusting of some vulnerable metal. It is during this period that the engineer will develop a schedule of works for the superstructure repairs.

Reinstatement Works

There are two reasons for carrying out these works. First, and most importantly, the key aim is to restore the strength and integrity of the superstructure of the building. Secondly, the works are undertaken to restore the building to its pre-movement decorative state.

The restrengthening works revolve around the cracked areas of a building, and are performed in many different ways, depending on the judgement of the structural engineer. Cracked bricks, stone or blocks may be removed and renewed, or they may be retained but injected with immensely powerful epoxy glues that stick the separated materials back together. Stainless steel rods are also used to knit areas together, and concrete lintels are often inserted horizontally along large cracks to tie in weakened walls further. Stud walls that have parted from their moorings to solid walls are also restrengthened with stronger fixings and the use of expanded metal. The computations within this process are many and varied, and outside the scope of the layman. It is really only necessary for you to understand that when this stage has been successfully completed the superstructure of the building should be as strong and cohesive as it was prior to any movement.

One area of the repair and reinstatement process that can cause some controversy, however, is the relevelling of areas of the property that have been moved out of alignment. A typical example will be where a property has dropped on one corner, thus causing a window frame and lintel to lean in one direction. The window may, after comparatively minor servicing allowed for by the loss adjusters within the schedule of works, be made to work and fit well enough, but still be out of alignment. In this case, you will find that although the window has been repaired, it may still not match aesthetically the other parts of the property.

The engineer will only recommend that areas of a building be realigned if the movement causing the non-alignment has happened recently. If the building had moved long before your claim, then this would be considered historic. It is only the problems caused by recent movement that will be dealt with in any works. For example, an eighteenth-century house may have moved considerably over the years since it was built. This movement would not form a part of the claim, as your insurance company will only pay for rectification where there has been new, defined and specific movement.

Once a property has been adequately restrengthened, the final stage of the repair and reinstatement process will take place: the areas damaged by the movement and restrengthening will be redecorated. As we have seen, this will be done within a relatively tight interpretation of the policy, but you must check that the works are completed to the same standard as before the movement. So, if the decoration was previously of a high standard, then the same quality must be maintained in the reinstatement works. If this is not done, then either your insurance company is simply not performing its part of the contract, or the builders are not complying with the schedule of works.

A common problem with superstructure repairs is disagreement between claimants and engineers or builders relating to the finishing of the property, with both parties anticipating different standards. On the whole, the best you can do is to ensure that you are realistic about the standard of your property before the work commences, that the level and detail of the finish that you want is clearly enumerated in the schedule of works and that you carefully check the work done – before signing any completion certificate at the end of the works. At times, you may well have to assert yourself with the structural engineer until a particular area has been done properly or until an essential addition to the schedule of works is made to allow the builder to upgrade the work.

Final Approval

The ultimate assurance that the works are finished to your satisfaction is the requirement for you to sign a **completion certificate** with the loss adjuster.

Until this document has been signed, neither the structural engineers nor the builders will be paid by the insurance company. The payment of the builders' charges is often delegated to the engineer, the client signing a mandate at the start of the work which allows the engineer effectively to take full control over the work done by the builders. Although you will be able to raise objections which the engineer has to heed, he can, nonetheless, authorize payment of the builders. If the engineer is effective then this can save you from some trouble and paperwork. A mandate should not be signed, however, if you have any reason to suspect that the engineer will not be sufficiently tough in ensuring the proper completion of the schedule of works. This would remove your most important leverage, should the work finally not be to your satisfaction.

No payment of the engineer will take place until you expressly sign the completion certificate at the end of the works. This, in itself, ensures that the engineer has a vested interest in your satisfaction with the works.

You should not sign any completion certificate, or definitively agree with the engineer that the works are finished, until every possible agreed snag has been attended to and rectified (see p.106). There is no better guarantee of total completion of all snags, however minor, than ensuring that no payment is received until you are completely satisfied.

The Warranty

You must check, before the works commence, what warranty is provided once the specified works have been completed. As a general rule, there will be an insurance-backed warranty on underpinning which is transferable to subsequent owners of your property, lasting for between 20 and 25 years.

Equally, it is important to be quite clear about the procedure for reopening a claim if your property continues to move and damage the repair works already performed. In this case it is vital that the insurance company does accept it as a reopening of the original claim, as opposed to the forming of a completely new claim – in which case you would once again be forced to contribute your policy's excess figure.

In most cases, when a property has been subject to a claim and remedial works, the value of the property should, in theory, return to its pre-movement value. Indeed, in some cases the property may well be in a better structural state than it was when initially constructed, and as a consequence may turn out to be a better buy than the buildings around it, which may not have had new foundations or thorough repairs.

Always retain the paperwork relating to the works done, particularly the schedule of works and the structural engineer's completion certificate, so that any future buyer, or his surveyor, can see that the movement has been correctly rectified.

SUMMARY

- Be able to recognize genuine signs of movement, as opposed to shrinkage or natural cracking.

- Act quickly to get a structural engineer to inspect the possible movement, particularly if building work has recently taken place on or near the building.

- Appreciate that most insurance claims regarding subsidence or heave take two to three years to resolve, so any claim should be processed as soon as possible.

- Carefully check any schedule of works drawn up and ensure that it is detailed, and specifically covers all the areas of work.

- If a schedule of works is unduly restrictive then fight hard for it to be made more comprehensive. If necessary, employ another structural engineer to assess the schedule of works prepared.

- During the conduct of the work, ensure that the supervising engineer consistently monitors the work of the contractors.

- Do not give final approval for the completion of the works unless you are completely satisfied.

- Advise the insurance company immediately if there is any further movement, so that the original claim can be reopened, thus avoiding the liability to pay a further excess contribution.

PART THREE

Law and Regulations

14

Building Regulations and Building Control

EVERYONE should be aware of building regulations and the function of Building Control. The latter can be of critical help and guidance. Indeed, Building Control represents one of your best safeguards when you are involved in certain defined building works.

If Building Control are involved in a project, then you will know once a completion certificate has been issued that the works have been done in accordance with the regulations. This gives considerable protection and extends to some of the most costly and vital parts of a building – such as its structural integrity.

Both property owners and builders frequently avoid using Building Control. They do this either because they do not know of its existence or, if they do, because they think that Building Control will simply impose costs and delays on a project. This is invariably short-term thinking. Beware of employing a builder who is reluctant to use Building Control when required.

Building Control exists for your protection, not hindrance, and the people working there are generally approachable, fair, efficient and helpful. It is effectively the closest thing to direct consumer protection that exists in construction. In any event, there are areas of building work where it is mandatory to have the involvement of Building Control. To avoid this can rightly open the owner of a property to prosecution.

The remit of Building Control does not extend to all building works, however, and you must understand where their responsibility lies.

BUILDING REGULATIONS

What Are They?

The building regulations stem from the Building Act 1984. They include a series of detailed **approved documents** and refer to a range of **non-statutory documents** such as **British Standards** and **Codes of Practice**. Constantly updated, the regulations cover a wide range of building activity. They specify minimum standards for much of the work performed in building, whether it is for new properties or those being altered or renovated in one way or another. **There are variations in the regulations for Scotland and Northern Ireland, although the gist is similar. Any reference in this chapter applies to England and Wales.**

Broadly, the regulations are designed to secure the health, safety and convenience of people in or about buildings and of others who may be affected by buildings or matters connected with them. Almost every building function of any complexity, importance or size comes within the ambit of the regulations and the controlling definition of 'building work'.

Definition of 'Building Work'

The building regulations only concern 'building work', but the definition is very wide. If you have any doubts at all as to whether they apply to your project contact your local authority Building Control to obtain their advice. You may otherwise find that you, or your builder, are contravening the regulations and thereby becoming liable to fines or an order to remedy or reverse work done.

'Building work' is defined as:

- the erection or extension of a building;
- a material alteration to a building;
- the provision, extension or material alteration of a controlled service or fitting in conjunction with a building;
- work where a material change of use is due to take place;
- insertion of insulating material into a cavity wall of a building; and
- work involving the underpinning of a building.

A **material alteration** is one that could adversely affect an existing building and make it worse, as regards compliance with the regulations, than it was before the works started. For example, if an existing building was altered, and this affected the means of escape or spread of fire, then the regulations would apply. They would operate either to stop the work being carried out, or to ensure that adequate specified works were done to improve on the means of escape and fire spread.

The regulations do not affect a domestic house that has not been altered but is actually contrary to current regulations in many areas. As soon as a material alteration is done, however, the regulations apply, with consequences that may be far-reaching.

So, if you remove a non-load-bearing wall in your three-storey house, the regulations may well apply, if the wall had some function in protecting against fire spread. In this case, a Building Control Officer (BCO) may only pass the work if, for example, you then install adequate fireproofing. This may involve, perhaps, the closing in of the staircase and the fitting of fire-check doors to all the rooms.

Controlled services are baths, hot-water systems, WCs, septic tank drainage systems, boiler and chimney or flue pipes etc.

The regulations are, then, all-embracing when new works are being performed, whether on an existing or new building. Before starting on a building project always find out whether the regulations will affect the proposed works, and if so to what extent. This could considerably affect your budget – and, possibly, the very nature of the proposed works.

Compliance

The onus of complying with the regulations is on the person actually undertaking the building work. This will be your contractor, if you have one, or you – if you are doing the works yourself.

There is no actual obligation to adopt the solutions that are set out in the **approved documents**, which contain detailed practical guidance on how to comply with the regulations. If a problem does occur, however, then the onus is on the person doing the work to show he has complied with them. In reality, it is always wise to follow the official published guidelines, and it will be these that any BCO will follow, unless a very good case is made to the contrary.

There are a number of books setting out and explaining the approved documents, or alternatively you can obtain copies covering the area you are interested in from the Stationery Office. For example, if you are planning to install a new staircase, this will be shown in simple and clear detail allowing you to see how the regulations are applied in reality. Much of the detail is reasonably accessible to someone with DIY experience.

Enforcement

The building regulations are enforced by local authorities. They have dedicated departments (Building Control) whose work it is to supervise building work undertaken in their area. These departments employ **Building Control Officers (BCOs)** who physically visit sites and monitor work being done. The regulations also allow for **approved inspectors** to ensure full compliance with building regulations. In this case, the approved inspectors will carry out the normal function of the local authority.

Building Control Officers are authorized to enter premises at all reasonable hours to conduct an investigation. If access is refused, they can obtain a warrant and then take with them anyone they need (such as a policeman) to inspect the property concerned. If a BCO passes your property and suspects that work is being done that may need his inspection, he can come in to check it.

If a BCO finds that there has been a breach of the regulations and you refuse to rectify the breach, then the local authority can serve upon you, as the owner of the property (*not* your builder), a **Section 36 notice.** If you do not rectify the fault within the time period specified in the notice (normally 28 days), then the local authority can arrange to have the works corrected, and charge the cost to you.

Under another provision (Section 35) the actual person contravening any provision of the regulations also becomes liable to an action in the magistrates' court. This action would be brought by the local authority and could result in a substantial fine, with a continuing penalty for each day the work is not rectified.

Appeal against Local Authority Decision

You do have a right of appeal against any decision of a BCO, although, in practice, this is rarely exercised. There is normally very little opportunity, once building works are in progress, to stop work on a site for any sustained period of time. It is generally quicker to alter the work that has supposedly breached the regulations, than to go through the lengthy process of formal appeal. Normally, therefore, the ruling of a BCO is accepted, however reluctantly.

If you do seriously object to the ruling of a BCO, then your first course of action is to try, informally, to persuade him that his decision is incorrect, perhaps with the help of an architect, surveyor or structural engineer. If this fails, then your next move should be to arrange a meeting with the head of the local authority Building Control department. As a rule the local authority will welcome a consultation period when there is a dispute, and will try hard to avoid having to go to the lengths of serving a Section 36 notice.

If the consultation between you and the local authority results in an impasse, however, then the Section 36 notice will be issued. At this stage you have two choices of action. You can, first, appeal directly to the magistrates' court who will have to be shown, by the local authority, that you have not complied with the regulations. Normally, evidence of the local authority that the relevant approved document has not been followed will be sufficient to place the onus of proving compliance back onto you. This can be an uphill struggle.

Alternatively, on receipt of a Section 36 notice you can notify the local authority in writing that you want to obtain an expert's report on the alleged breach. This will extend the time for compliance with the Section 36 notice to 70 days, during which time you can produce an expert's report. If the local authority are persuaded that this report shows that the alleged breach does not exist, then they can withdraw the Section 36 notice – and *may* pay the costs of your report.

Quality of Work

The regulations impose a duty on the person undertaking any work that 'all building work is to be carried out with proper materials and in a workmanlike manner'. The BCO will be looking at the work done from a very basic viewpoint. His duty is only to see that the works have been undertaken sufficiently well to ensure that the building meets reasonable standards of health and safety. He will not be interested in aesthetic considerations.

For example, the BCO would have to check the works involved in removing a load-bearing wall to make two rooms into one. He would be concerned to ensure that the structural steel support inserted was adequate to carry the load, was correctly positioned on load-bearing piers and was properly fireproofed. He would not be interested, however, if the plastering was poorly finished, the angle beading out of true and the painting of the area appalling.

Equally, the BCO has no remit to look at, or comment on, other works that may be performed within the property which do not come within the specific parameters of the regulations. For example, a BCO may visit to check the integrity of a damp-proof course or a new roof. It will be irrelevant to him that new windows inserted into your property are out of true and clearly the result of bad workmanship – so long as the work of putting the windows in has not affected the structural integrity of the building.

Notification

If works come within building regulations then they have to be inspected during the course of the work to ensure that the regulations have been complied with fully. It is the duty of the person actually carrying out the works to ensure that inspections take place. Any person intending to undertake building work must notify the local authority using one of the three methods described below. Unless this is done then whoever carries out the works will be in breach of the regulations and liable to prosecution. If you are employing a builder, make certain that he has properly advised the local authority (unless an approved inspector is being employed). If you have any doubts as to whether the local authority has been advised, or whether the works come within the remit of the local authority, then expressly check with Building Control.

Unless Building Control is specifically advised that the proposed works are going to occur, they will simply not know about them – and are unlikely to attend the site.

Serving a Building Notice

This is a simple form obtainable free from the local authority. It advises the local authority of the exact location of the property to be worked on and the type and nature of the works. The notice does not have to be accompanied by detailed drawings, calculations or plans, although the BCO can request further details during his inspection of the work. For example, if he is not happy about the size of a structural steel beam that is going to be used, then he can stop any further works going ahead until he has received satisfactory calculations.

There is a sliding scale of fees payable to the local authority on service of the notice. These fees are minimal.

Once the building notice has been served the local authority will require 48 hours' notice before any works start. Normally a telephone call to Building Control is sufficient.

Depositing Full Plans

The normal alternative to a building notice is the deposit of a full set of plans, drawings and calculations of the proposed works. The local authority must either expressly approve or reject these within five weeks – although this can be extended by a further three weeks. If the plans are approved and the work is carried out exactly in accordance with the plans then the local authority cannot take action against you under Section 36.

The works can take place, even without approval, once the plans have been lodged with the local authority. The BCO will assess whether or not the work is adequate when he inspects it on site. Ideally, however, you should not start work until notice of approval has been given. Approval of the plans provides you with an important protection against having to do works that were not anticipated and that could extend the costs of the project.

You must provide 48 hours' notice of commencement of the work, regardless of approval or rejection of the plans.

Employing an Approved Inspector

Approved inspectors are either individuals, who must have approval from a designated body such as the **Institute of Structural Engineers**, or a corporate body such as the **National House Building Council** (**NHBC**). These inspectors have the authority to ensure compliance with the building regulations on a project and to certify it. At present these approved inspectors are rarely used and as yet they have had no real impact on small building works.

If you exercise the option to employ an approved inspector, the BCO still has a right of access to the site, and may require changes.

BUILDING CONTROL AND THE BUILDING CONTROL OFFICER

Local authority Building Control departments tend to go out of their way to help anyone involved in a building project and will go to some lengths to be of particular help to the layman. They should on no account be considered a remote, authoritarian body. Most people, once they do approach Building Control, are impressed by the help and advice that is often enthusiastically dispensed. It really is a wonder that more people, particularly non-professional builders, do not make better use of Building Control.

Building Control departments have BCOs who are generally appointed to look after designated areas of a borough or district. Over time, they tend to get to know these areas extremely well. Indeed, their in-depth knowledge of individual properties and their construction, and any localized problems, are probably unrivalled within their area of responsibility. They also become familiar with the local builders and their methods of working, whether good or bad, and can react accordingly when doing inspections of work.

If you have any queries concerning building work, contact Building Control for advice. This may be given over the telephone straight away, or you may, more helpfully, be referred to the BCO responsible for your area. If the query is a complicated one which requires the officer to make a visit before providing an adequate answer, he will often attend free of charge – although this varies between different local authorities. He will advise you of any misgivings that he may have about the proposed works, the regulations applicable, and how best to go about the work to ensure the work will comply.

This is an extremely useful service and you should exploit it if you intend to do any building work whatsoever. The sooner a BCO is involved, the sooner any potential problem areas can be either eliminated or amended. This will prevent unexpected costs and delays once the work is going ahead.

Normally, the helpfulness of BCOs extends right through the works themselves. The visits can be constructive – particularly if you develop a good relationship with your particular officer. He is normally keen to dispense advice about what he wants to see on his next inspection, and this can result in inspection visits becoming routine and uncontentious.

If for some reason you or your builder do not get on with the appointed BCO then you can approach the head of Building Control to request that another officer is charged with monitoring the work.

Finally, Building Control is structured around the necessity to respond to site visits and an officer is legally bound to make an inspection within 24 hours of notice being given. Often they can respond much quicker, and will attend the same day that you call them.

Inspection of the Works

Physical inspection of the building work being carried out on a site is the single most important function of Building Control and the BCOs.

Inspections go to the core of the regulations. They are the greatest protection that you have, apart from employing a good structural engineer or surveyor, that the works will comply with the regulations, and therefore reach basic standards of integrity and safety. If the inspections are to be of any use they need to be done at critical stages of the work, and these are defined both by legislation and the decision of the BCO monitoring your works.

Inspection visits to site vary depending on the BCO, his assessment of the site and any inherent problems – such as particular complications with the construction or with the person actually performing the work. If the BCO lacks confidence in a particular builder, for example, then he may choose to inspect the work at frequent stages. He may consider this less necessary if the site is being worked on by a competent builder under the direction of a structural engineer.

Normally, the stages that have to be inspected will be agreed between you or your builder and the BCO, before work is started. For example, if a load bearing wall is being removed, the BCO may initially advise that he will want to inspect the work once the structural steel beam is in place, but before any temporary support is removed.

Once this stage has been reached the BCO must be told. He will then come and check that the loading is correct and the beam adequate. He will also ensure that the works have not adversely affected any other part of the building, perhaps with regard to fire spread. If he is happy with the work and the consequences of it, he will give his approval for the temporary supports to be removed. He will then arrange a further inspection visit to see that the fireproofing of the beam has been carried out (work that could not be done before he had checked the bare beam on his previous visit). If he is happy that the beam has been fireproofed satisfactorily then, if this is the only area of work requiring his attention, the BCO may issue a completion certificate for the works.

If, during his inspection, the BCO is not happy about an element of the work, then he will advise you or your builder of this and request that the work be altered to comply with the regulations. There really is little option but to comply. As seen above, there is an appeal process available but it can take a long time to resolve and, of course, time is rarely on your side if works are in progress.

If a BCO comes and finds that the works have gone beyond the stage at which they should have been inspected, then he can request that the finished work be opened up. In the example of the steel beam above, the BCO could order the removal of the fireproofing to check that the beam itself was sound. If this was not done he would not issue a completion certificate, as he would be unable to tell whether the work done was proper and adequate.

Equally, if underpinning has been performed without allowing the BCO the opportunity to check the depth of the foundation holes, then he could order trial holes to be dug. This would allow him physically to check that they had been excavated to the correct depth and dimensions and that the subsoil had load-bearing capacity.

It is in your interest that the BCO is able to conduct his visits at the right stages, and that the work does not just tear ahead. Trial holes and the revealing of completed work are expensive and time-consuming. If the premature action does result in the BCO being unable to issue a completion certificate then you should not accept your builder's work.

Mandatory Notifications of Work

There are a number of areas of building work for which it is mandatory that notification is submitted by you to Building Control, either by way of a building notice or the deposit of full plans. If you have any doubts at all as to whether your work fits into one of the categories then check with your local Building Control who will happily advise you accordingly. It is always wise to do this – even if you are employing your own builder. He may not be up to date on the regulations or may deliberately wish to avoid the attentions of Building Control and their inspecting officers.

Notification is mandatory at the following stages:

- commencement of work (notification to occur at least two days before work starts);
- foundation excavations;
- foundation concrete;
- damp-proof course;
- oversite hardcore;
- drains and private sewers (one working day before these are covered or *haunched*);
- drains and private sewers (within five working days of the haunching or covering of any drain or sewer);
- completion of works;
- occupation.

Examples of types of work which the BCO will want to inspect are as follows – though this list is by no means comprehensive:

- completed foundations;
- damp-proof courses and membranes;
- drainage systems;
- load-bearing brickwork or blockwork;
- thermal insulation for floors, walls and roofs;
- fire protection;
- structural elements;
- weatherproofing;
- flues and vents for appliances;
- ventilation;
- staircases, landings etc.;
- safety glazing;
- facilities for disabled people;
- soundproofing.

Time Limit to Inspection by Building Control Officer

Any building work that has been completed over 12 months prior to the inspection of a BCO falls outside his remit. If a BCO, for example, sees that work has been done without notification to Building Control, but this occurred over a year ago, then the BCO has no remit to inspect the work. This is regardless of the fact that there may be blatant breaches of the regulations.

This is not to say that the BCO may not report the breach of planning permission, if there has been one, to the planning department of the local authority. He may also advise the Land Charges Register, who may place this information on file – to be revealed by a future buyer of your property during his searches.

Completion Certificate

A Completion Certificate will be issued by Building Control once the works have had their final inspection by the BCO. This will only be issued if the officer is entirely happy that the work has been done according to the regulations.

The completion certificate is of particular value to you. It is proof to any future buyer that the works done to your property were carried out properly. Also, if you employ a builder it is proof that the works he has done were properly inspected and approved.

Ideally, any completion certificate should be stored with your property deeds, although Building Control keep records of all work done, and certificates issued.

Common Problems Experienced by Building Control Officers

Building Control Officers tend to have three common complaints:

No Notice of Completion

Often BCOs are not advised by those doing building work that they have actually completed the works, notwithstanding that the officer may have been making scheduled inspections during the course of the works. No BCO will be able to provide a completion certificate until he has made his final inspection. The Building Control file will therefore remain open.

At some stage the BCO will try to make a completion visit and this may be some time after the builder has finished, been paid and left site. Frequently BCOs find on this final visit, however, that a number of matters still remain outstanding. In this event they will certainly not issue a completion certificate – and may even serve on you, as the owner, a Section 36 notice requiring you to complete the works satisfactorily.

It is vital to obtain the completion certificate prior to paying your builder in full. Always expressly check with Building Control that the final inspection has taken place and approval been given.

Under-Use of BCOs

BCOs complain, with some justification, that they are not consulted sufficiently beforehand about works that are due to take place.

Before doing any building work consult fully with the appointed officer and establish what he expects in terms of the detail of the work and the stages of inspection. This can avoid a lot of upset as the greatest loss will always be yours – when you find you simply have no choice but to make any alterations required.

Poor-Quality Work

A frustration experienced by almost all BCOs is their lack of authority to order correction of poor works on site that are outside their remit. If they do see poor brickwork, joinery or any other work that is not directly within the ambit of the regulations they can do nothing about this – even though it is quite clear that you are getting a raw deal. Equally, their remit to inspect works within the regulations is narrowly defined. It is to ensure that the work done is adequate with regard to the regulations – not that the work is done to a fine-quality standard.

Common Problems Experienced by Builders

There are two main complaints aimed by builders at BCOs:

Inconsistency between Officers

Different officers within the same local authority often give their concentrated attention to different areas of the work. For example, some officers will interpret the regulations regarding structural matters harshly, while perhaps being quite lax on matters concerning drainage. Others may concentrate on particular areas, while not being especially interested in an area where a builder is accustomed to very careful inspection.

This element of inconsistency can have awkward consequences when the officer monitoring a site hands over to another officer at any time during the works. The builder can then find himself receiving different instructions, perhaps even contrary to those already received.

There is little a builder can do other than obey the last instructions received or approach the head of Building Control to resolve the matter. BCOs, in practice, have considerable discretionary power.

Delays Due to Inspections

There is no doubt that delays do occur on site while an inspection is awaited. A delay of a day or so can be quite frustrating, and in some works the delays can result in significant costs to the builder, as he may be unable to do any work until the BCO has given his approval. Up to a point this can be mitigated by good planning, organization and anticipation of the required inspections. Nonetheless it is often looked upon as a problem. Certainly, any undue delay caused by a BCO's not arriving at the appointed time is very unwelcome, and you or your builder can do little about it – let alone recover money for lost time.

SUMMARY

- Building regulations have been developed over a long period to protect people from the inherent problems and dangers of buildings and the work done on them. It is in your interest that they are adhered to.

- Specifically check with Building Control before starting any building work, to see whether the works are subject to the regulations.

- Make use of Building Control to provide detailed advice during the works and to ensure that the work will comply with the BCO's expectations, before any actual inspection takes place.

- Understand the remit of the BCO. There are matters upon which he is unable to comment, as his protection only extends to certain defined areas of the work.

- Make certain that any builder employed complies with the regulations, and that the correct inspections are carried out. Any avoidance of the inspections or regulations will reflect badly on the builder and may lead to a conviction in the magistrates' court and an order to remove or alter the work.

- Ensure that the BCO carries out a final inspection and grants his approval to the works done, before you pay any builder in full.

- Always obtain a formal completion certificate from Building Control and retain this with your property deeds.

15

Planning Permission

IT is essential to have at least some idea of when planning permission is necessary. If you inadvertently do something that contravenes the planning laws, the consequences can be severe. You may find you have to reverse building work or alterations that you have done, or you may find the use for which you bought your property is not allowed. For example, you may have bought the property specifically because it would be a good place from which to run your business. If this use broke the planning laws, and you could not subsequently obtain the necessary planning consent for change of use, your purchase might prove to have been a disaster.

Equally, it follows that sometimes you may find yourself next to a neighbour who is doing, or wishes to do, something with his property that upsets you or damages your enjoyment of your property. If this is the case, you need to know what to do. He may be doing something that is breaching the planning laws, or he may have applied for planning permission for something you find offensive. In this case, you need to know who to get hold of, and how to object effectively.

While planning is a very complex area and should not be underestimated, an outline knowledge of how it works is essential for every home-owner.

PLANNING CONTROL

Planning controls are somewhat confusing. The main control is exercised by the regulations enacted within the Town and Country Planning Acts. Within these acts there is special protection for listed buildings, conservation areas, areas of outstanding natural beauty, trees, and national parks. They are not the end of the matter, however; further regulations have to be complied with, such as local authority bye-laws. You may also have restrictive covenants on your property (registered on your title deeds), preventing you from doing certain things. These can be particularly pertinent on newly built estates.

It is vital to realize that the onus is on you, as owner, to have received the correct consents, and to comply with the specific requirements of these authorities – before you make any alterations to your property.

RESPONSIBILITY FOR PLANNING

Planning is the responsibility of both central and local government. Central government defines national policy and sets out guidelines, sometimes very precise, as to the policies which local planning authorities should follow. It is also responsible for the overall supervision of the planning system itself, and decides any appeals resulting from local authority decisions.

For most purposes, however, it is the district councils with whom you will be most preoccupied (see below for exceptions). They have quite considerable latitude in formulating local policies, although they have to take into account governmental instructions and the structure plans produced by, and for, the county as a whole. You will probably find that your district council will have produced its own local plan, specific to your area, and this will give you some idea of the policies that the planning department will operate. Alongside this, there may be some rather informal policies that are relevant, as contained in various leaflets and documents produced by your district council. Unfortunately, there are often ambiguities of policy direction between all the various bodies involved in planning – this can add to the confusion of trying to understand clearly what is, or is not, recommended development in your area.

You have a right of access to all these documents, which, if you can understand the complex language, and have the time, you will benefit from studying. You will then be able to angle your project and application so that it falls clearly within the policy guidelines set out. That said, as a layman, you would be better off spending some time actually speaking to your local planning office, who will be able to indicate to you the local policies in operation. Generally, it is only when you think that your particular project is going to be contentious that you really need to do some in-depth research into policy documents. Often planning departments have booklets or leaflets that are directed at the layman and will be of more initial help to you. Where these are practical and comprehensive they are an invaluable tool.

OPERATION OF THE PLANNING SYSTEM

In England and Wales, planning permission is the responsibility of district councils. The same is true in Scotland, except in the case of the regional councils of Highland, Borders and Dumfries and Galloway, who deal with all applications themselves. In Northern Ireland, the Department of the Environment (Town and Planning Service) deals with all applications.

Except in Northern Ireland, the planning system is run on the basis of a combination of professional and political personnel. Each district council has a planning department (sometimes called the housing or technical department) which deals with applications. The council officers service the paperwork, assess applications and make the necessary consultations with other interested bodies. They will be in charge of any planning application publicity and will, importantly, write a report, with recommendations as to refusal or consent to the application. This report is placed before the elected councillors for your district at the appropriate committee meeting. Some applications are actually decided by senior planning officers themselves – but these are only decisions that have been expressly delegated to them.

Otherwise, the decision whether or not a planning application can go ahead rests with the elected councillors of the district in which the application is being made. Certain of the councillors of your district will have been appointed to the planning committee, and it is when this sits that applications are approved or refused. For the most part, the councillors will follow their planning officer's recommendation – but they are at liberty to disregard this, as they see fit.

If you wish to appeal, because your application has been turned down or because the conditions attached to your approval are too onerous, then this appeal is decided by the relevant Secretary of State (in Northern Ireland the Planning Appeals Commission), using objective, professional planning officers as advisers.

WHAT MATTERS REQUIRE PLANNING PERMISSION?

The planning laws essentially govern the exterior of your property and your surrounding land. They also govern the use of your property. They are widely encompassing, and you should not underestimate their complexity. If you have any doubts about whether planning permission is required, you should specifically check this before performing any alteration to, or changing the use of, your existing property or land. The safe assumption is that permission *will* be required. This is particularly true if you are living in a conservation area, a national park or an area of outstanding natural beauty.

If you are unsure as to whether or not something needs planning permission, always ring your local authority first, and speak to your local area planning officer. It is their job to advise you, and normally they are very helpful. If there is any uncertainty, they will come to your property, look at what you are proposing and advise you accordingly.

Some examples of where permission is required (**this is not definitive**) are:

- extensions;
- construction of new house or rebuilding of old house;
- porches;
- replacement windows (if different in style or material from existing);
- fire escapes;
- cladding or rendering of exteriors;
- dormer windows;
- new chimneys;
- subdivision of a property into flats, etc.;
- converting garages;
- change of use, e.g. from home to business or vice versa;
- outbuildings;
- construction of new access to a highway;
- diversion of public right of way.

Examples of where planning permission is *not* required:

- general repairs and maintenance;
- small alterations;
- works to interior of property;
- removal of buildings under 50m³;
- new windows or doors of same style;
- new roof with same slates or tiles;
- use of part of property for business, depending on nature or size of business;
- reconstruction of fences and walls.

The examples above are not meant to be comprehensive. You must also be careful of how some matters, which appear not to need planning permission, are defined by the planning laws and enforced by your local planning officers. For example, you may decide to repaint your house, considering it only general maintenance. It is possible, however, to breach planning permission if you change the colour. You may be in an area where radical changes of colour are not allowed without express permission. This is often the case in national parks or in conservation areas. Equally, you may decide to remove an architectural aspect of your house that you dislike. This may also require permission. Business use of your property can also be subject to interpretation. It is one thing to use a room for an office, but it can be quite another to start repairing cars in your back yard as a commercial operation.

PERMITTED DEVELOPMENT

The strict operation of the planning laws is mitigated greatly by **permitted development**. This term covers a range of activities and projects that would normally require planning permission but are allowed to go ahead without it. The thinking behind this is that if every minor alteration to a property had to receive permission, the planning system would be unable to cope. Accordingly, within quite strict parameters, certain things can go ahead without the express consent of the planning authorities. But even here you must be careful. First, your development must come strictly within the specific rules which allow you to make alterations without permission. Secondly, councils can withdraw permitted development – most commonly in conservation areas. So it is always worth double-checking that what you intend to do falls safely within the definition of 'permitted development'.

Below you will find two examples of how permitted development operates. There are numerous other forms of development to which it applies.

Porches

These require no planning consent in England and Wales, unless they are in a conservation area or are a part of a listed building, so long as the following rules are applied:

- The floor area must not exceed 3m².
- The height must be no more than 3m.
- The structure must be over 2m from the boundary of a public road.

Extensions

These require no planning consent, so long as the following rules are applied:

- The height must be no greater than the highest part of your house.
- If the new structure is less than 2m from the boundary of your house, then it must not be higher than 4m.
- It must not be located beyond the front edge of your house, when facing a public road.

In terms of size, every extension must satisfy the following criteria:

- It must not be more than 70m³, or 15% of the volume of your original property, whichever is the greater – up to a maximum of 115m³.

  (If your property is a terraced house, or in a national park, conservation area or area of outstanding beauty, then the total volume allowable is reduced to 50m³ or 10% of the volume, whichever is the greater, up to a maximum of 115m³.)
- It must not cover more than half your garden or land.
- The extension must not increase the volume by which your house has been extended, since 1 July 1948, beyond the total allowable volume.

This does not mean that you will not get planning consent if you happen, for example, to be in a conservation area – but to build, say, a porch would require your making a full planning application. This would then be looked at in the same way as any other application – and consent granted or refused on its merits.

The benefit of doing a project that is within permitted development is obvious. You avoid having to go through the planning process, with all the delay and cost that it involves. With this in mind, it can be worth scaling down the size of your proposed extension, for example, to bring it within the permitted development.

Obviously, if you do start on a project that you believe is a permitted development, then you must make sure that you stay within the rules. In the case of something like an extension, you will have to get your local authority Building Control involved. If, when doing an inspection, they suspect that you have exceeded the rules, then you may find they report you to the planning authorities. In this event, you could end up with problems.

APPLYING FOR PLANNING PERMISSION

There are essentially two types of planning applications, as detailed below.

Outline Planning Application

You would make this type of application to find out whether, in principle, you could obtain planning permission for a project on a particular area of land. For example, you may make this application to see if you could build an extension on the side of your house. You would have to give dimensions, and rough details of the building that you wish to construct, together with its exact location (a copy of the relevant Ordnance Survey map is required to a scale of 1:2,500). It is wise to enclose also an illustrative drawing showing the new alteration as it would look when finished. You would not have to produce full drawings, however, or indeed specify every detail of the proposed structure. It is therefore cheaper to make this type of application, given that less detailed work on the proposed structure has to be done.

Outline planning applications are often made when you are considering selling your property. To obtain outline planning consent can result in the property having greater value, as it demonstrates to any purchaser that the land has positive development potential.

If you do receive consent, having made an outline planning application, this is valid for three years. Should you want to go ahead with the project, you will have to make a **reserved matters** application within this period. Unless this is consented to, you have no permission actually to start your development.

The reserved matters application must contain full drawings and all details of your proposed project. It must, of course, relate to the proposal for which you were originally granted outline consent. If you obtained outline planning consent for an extension, you cannot propose, in your reserved matters application, the construction of a four-bedroomed house. You would have to make a fresh application. This is not to say that you cannot make several different reserved matters applications, showing different variations of design for your extension. This can be a helpful bonus if your proposals are controversial.

Obtaining consent for both outline planning and reserved matters amounts to full planning permission.

There is a scale of fees applicable when you make both an outline planning application and a reserved matters application. The two fees together will be greater than applying for full planning permission.

The route to obtaining outline planning permission is the same as for applying for full planning permission (see below), less the production of detailed drawings and plans, etc.

Full Planning Application

This differs from the outline application in that fully detailed plans will have to be submitted at the outset. If you achieve consent for full planning permission then, unlike outline planning permission, you can start the works for which the permission is granted straight away – subject to any imposed conditions, or the effect of any other relevant bodies such as Building Control. As with outline planning permission, there is a scale of fees payable on any application. Your local planning office will provide you with details of these.

There are effectively seven stages to applying for either full or outline planning permission:

- Preparation
- Application
- Acknowledgement
- Publicity
- Checking Progress and Lobbying
- Planning Officer's Report
- Planning Committee Meeting and Decision

Preparation

It is vital that, if you do apply for planning permission on a given project or activity, you do not do it half-heartedly. The process is comparatively expensive, depending on what you are applying for, and can be time-consuming and stressful. Furthermore, if your application is refused, it can be hard to get approval in the future. Your refusal, the planning officer's report and other details will be held on record and can work against you, and any subsequent owner of the property, in the future. There is therefore no point in being tentative about your application. All aspects of the presentation must be done as carefully as possible. You must be proactive in any application – it really is not good enough just to sit back and allow an application to wander its way to a conclusion.

If the matter is complex, or of critical importance to you, then you may be wise to place the application in the hands of a professional (see below). Most matters can be dealt with by a layman, however, albeit relying on professional help for such things as the creation of plans and drawings.

As a matter of course, you should do the following:

Define Precisely What you Wish to Do

This may seem obvious, but it is surprising how imprecise some people are. Define clearly the type of alteration you intend to do, the sizes, positioning and rough design, as appropriate. Check to see whether it would fall within the definition of permitted development or if, with design adjustments, it could be made to do so. A telephone call to the planning department at this stage may be all that is necessary to confirm that the project does not actually need planning permission. It may be outside any of the planning regulations. If there is any doubt, then make sure that you see your planning officer in person (see below). Do not rely on your builder to do the checking. It is your property, and it is against you that the planning authorities will act.

Research the Planning History of your Property

Go to the planning department of your district council and ask to see the planning history of your property. This is likely to be kept in the form of a card index, with a card briefly itemizing any applications made on your property, and the outcome of the applications or any appeal. Once you have found that applications have been made, then ask to see the file on each application. This will contain all the relevant documentation. From this you can see what precise applications were made on your property, together with the planning officer's report. This can be very useful. You may find, for example, that an application similar to the one you are considering was made in the past. If this was turned down, you will be able to see the reasons given, and even any objections from third parties – such as your neighbours.

If an application pertinent to your own has been turned down, try to assess whether this was for reasons of policy. If so, then it is well worth making a note to research further, to see if that particular policy has now been relaxed. If the application was turned down for technical reasons – perhaps the proposed alteration was out of keeping with the character of your area – then note this down, so that your project does not fail for the same reason.

Having done this research you may well decide that it is not worth pursuing the matter further, or that you are going to need professional help to overcome obvious obstacles.

Pre-Application Meeting with your Planning Officer

It is essential that, before you make any application, you have a face-to-face meeting with the planning officer for your area. The best place for this is on site, as opposed to at the council planning office. When you meet the officer, have a sketch of what you propose to do. You should take some trouble to ensure that this reasonably represents your intentions. It does not have to be a detailed architectural drawing showing every detail, but it should be clear and do justice to what you have in mind. A thumbnail sketch on a grubby piece of paper will be of little help.

Try to strike up some form of good relationship with the planning officer. He is important to your application, and his advice and help can be invaluable. At the meeting, find out whether your project fits, or could be made to fit, within permitted development. If this is not the case, then sound out the officer as to whether he thinks your project is likely to receive consent and if not, why not. If your particular officer is helpful, he may well give you considerable guidance on what aspects of the project will make it more acceptable. Take careful notes of his comments, so that you or your designer can make amendments to your final plans that might make them more workable.

After the meeting, write to your planning officer confirming what has been said. If the officer has said that the project is within permitted development, get a letter from him confirming this.

Remember that the officer's comments cannot be considered as definitive, one way or another. The final decision as to whether or not you actually receive consent for your application depends not on him, but on the planning committee of councillors, or a senior planning officer where delegated decisions are concerned. That said, the officer is doing this work full time, and he will have a very good grasp of what will, or will not, be acceptable. You should bear in mind, however, that officers can sometimes be overly cautious in their advice.

Neighbours

It is important to try to limit objections as far as possible. It is therefore well worth visiting all your immediate neighbours, and speaking to them about your proposals. Show them an easily comprehensible sketch of what you are considering doing, and listen to their views. If possible, try to counter any of their objections, even if this means agreeing to make some alterations to your proposal. If you can get them to put in writing that they have no objections, then so much the better.

There may also be a **residents' association** in your area, and it is worth meeting some of the leading lights. Their opposition can be very damaging, particularly if it is an active community association. Equally, their approval in writing is helpful.

Local Councillors

At the end of the day, planning consents have a political, subjective and human angle, in so far as local councillors will be the people to approve your application. It therefore makes sense to get at least your local councillor on your side. Arrange to meet with him, and show him what you are intending to do. Tell him that you have seen your neighbours and any local residents' organization. He will certainly want reassurance that the proposals you are making are not controversial. The last thing he will want is to be seen supporting something local people are up in arms about – particularly if an election is approaching. If the meeting goes well, record a summary of it in a letter to him. This should act as a prompt, and help to commit him to you. The more councillors you can gently lobby before the application, the better – although beware of making yourself too much of a nuisance at this stage.

Application

The appropriate forms for applying for planning permission can be obtained free from your local planning department. These will be accompanied by guidance notes, applicable to each section of the application. If possible, try to get two sets of the forms, as this allows you a spare in case you find you have made initial errors, or that the form has become unduly messy.

When you fill out the form, do so accurately, tidily and concisely, and do not avoid any of the questions asked. Some of the questions, such as those concerning drainage or waste disposal, may need the advice of your intended builder, if you do not have other professional help.

You must include with your application full plans and drawings of the proposed alteration. These must be properly drawn with accurate dimensions

– and they should look good. If your application is for full planning permission, depending on your project, you may need to produce site layout plans, block plans and building plans, including elevations and floor layouts etc. You may also choose to enclose a coloured illustrative drawing of your proposed finished project. Unless you have experience in technical drawing you would be wise to leave this aspect of the application to a professional. Good drawings are an essential part of the argument that you are putting forward in your application, and it is from these that planning officers will mainly work. Competent, well presented drawings are worth a thousand words.

You must ensure that you enclose the relevant fee for the application. If you are uncertain of the fee chargeable, then check with your planning office.

You can write a statement supporting your application. This is not necessary but, if written well, it can be a further tool to persuade the authorities that your application should go ahead. Take great care in writing this statement. It should not just reiterate what is shown in the drawings and plans. Set out any facts that will support your application as a whole, such as the way your design matches neighbouring buildings, the support you have for it from neighbours, how it complies with the council's own local plan or guidelines, and how you have attempted to make the best of the physical constraints around your development, such as by preserving trees or not having windows which overlook other properties. A well drafted statement can be a persuasive document, and can materially help your case, although it should not be unnecessarily lengthy. Keep your comments brief and to the point.

For tidiness' sake, enclose your application with a covering letter itemizing the contents – application form, fee, plans, statement etc.

Acknowledgement

You should receive an acknowledgement of your application within about a week – depending on the efficiency of your planning department. If you have not heard from them by that time, ring up and make sure they have received your application, and that it is working its way through the system. When you do receive the acknowledgement, this will advise you of the date it was received, the time it will take for a decision to be made – within eight weeks of receipt – the name of the planning officer dealing with the matter, and a reference number for your particular matter. This should be quoted in any correspondence.

Publicity

Depending on your type of application, the council will publicize it. This can be done in a variety of ways, including advertising in local newspapers, a site notice and letters to immediate neighbours, inviting anyone who has objections to state these, in writing, to the planning office. Your plans will be made available at a local office for public inspection.

Checking Progress and Lobbying

Approximately one month after you have received an acknowledgement (but not much later than this), contact your planning officer and see how your application is progressing. Much before this time, your application is unlikely to have been properly assessed, or the results of any consultation with interested bodies received, by the planning officer.

This communication with your planning officer is an important move to make, and you must try to obtain as much information as possible from him, as to the status of your application. Depending on council policy, officers can be very helpful, and can indicate the nature of any objections they may have concerning your application. Try to see what suggestions the officer has to overcome the objections – it may be that you have to resite windows, or perhaps change the intended cladding of a property. There may have been valid objections from neighbours (although you will not be given their names), and it is useful to know their nature.

It may well be that the objection to your application is fundamental – perhaps it directly contravenes a council policy decision. In this case, there is little you can do. It is probably worth withdrawing your application – which is better for the property file than a recorded decision that went to committee and was refused. You can then reapply having rethought your project. There is no further fee if your new application is made within 12 months.

If objections are raised by the planning officer, you can attempt to overcome these by revising the relevant area of the project. For example, in the case of windows overlooking a neighbour, you could advise the planning officer that you wish to revise the drawings of this aspect. You must make absolutely certain that the planning officer understands what you are doing, and does not allow your application to go to the final committee meeting until the new drawings or information have been received and assessed. If the alterations are considerable your officer may decide to republicize the application so that the changes can be viewed by the public.

Good communication with your planning officer is therefore essential, together with your willingness to make a quick decision to overcome objections. This can make all the difference to the success of your application.

Planning Officer's Report

If the application is to be decided by a planning officer (rather than the planning committee), as in delegated decisions, then you will be advised formally of the decision made, and the reasons. The report made by your officer will have been given to a senior planning officer, who checks it and then makes a final decision.

Normally, your application will be decided by the planning committee. In this case, the report will be available for you to see some three days prior to the committee meeting – so long as you go to the planning office and obtain a copy. The report will make a recommendation to grant or refuse you permission, and will give reasons for the decision.

You must try to see the report before the committee meeting. Remember that the report can only *recommend* a particular decision. Although the committee will generally follow what he advises, it is at liberty to disregard the planning officer's recommendation.

If the recommendation is for refusal, then you must look closely at the reasons given. If you are fortunate, there may be errors of fact in the report which help to discredit what the officer is saying. If his decision is based on a matter of opinion, then this may allow you an opening to argue against his opinion, or to persuade your local councillor to speak out at the committee meeting. Either way your best initial recourse is to try lobbying as many local councillors as possible, to ensure they actively support your application when it comes before the committee. Try hard to get them to come to your property, to get a clear idea of the proposed alterations. Most of them are not trained in planning, and will be able to assess a project much better by seeing the site. If you can get some councillors to side with you, then there is the chance that they can persuade the committee to grant your application. Make sure to attend the meeting yourself, and to warn the councillors that have promised to speak up that you will be there.

If you are unable to persuade some councillors to fight your corner at the committee meeting, then you are really only left with three choices:

- You can withdraw your application. This prevents your property record being marked with a refusal, and allows you (within 12 months) to reapply for permission with a new scheme – and one that should avoid the failings of the last one. You can withdraw at any stage before receiving written notification of refusal from the planning department. So, even after the committee meeting which decides your application, you can still technically withdraw it – but you must move quickly.

- You can allow the committee to assess and refuse your application, and then take the matter to appeal (see below).

- You can request that the application be deferred, while you see if you can find a way of satisfying the planning officer's objections.

Planning Committee Meeting and Decision

Unless your application is particularly controversial, or is raised as an issue for debate by one of the committee members, it will be decided on quickly, with no discussion. In essence, the application will be rubber-stamped on the recommendation of your planning officer. Some councils will allow you to speak in favour of your application – but this is rare.

The committee will refuse or consent to the application, or they can defer (see above) or delegate a decision. Delegating a decision would occur when the committee decided to refuse or consent to the application in principle, subject to a final matter being sorted out. This defined matter would be attended to by a senior planning officer, who could then make a final decision on your application and issue the permission.

Any consent to your application will have conditions attached, and you must look at these carefully. The conditions will vary, depending on the type of project that you are proposing, although there will always be a condition specifying the time period the permission will last – five years. Other conditions may relate to a number of matters to do with the property. For example, you may have to get approval in writing from the planning department for the cladding or roof materials that you use on your new building project.

If you do not accept the conditions, you can either ignore them – this is unwise – appeal to the Secretary of State (see below) or make an application to the council to have them removed. The latter option is the safest and most cost-effective action to take.

APPEALS

You have a right of appeal:

- if your application for planning permission or for reserved rights has been refused;
- if you consider any of the conditions set on the planning permission consent unreasonable;
- if certain matters are only approved subject to conditions; or
- if your planning application was not heard within eight weeks from the date of receipt.

The decision whether or not to appeal against any of the above should not be taken without serious consideration. The process is complicated and time-consuming, and there is a very real prospect that you will lose the appeal. You would be wise to take professional advice and use a planning consultant to handle the appeal.

All appeals are made to the Secretary of State although, in fact, he appoints professional inspectors, reporters or commissioners (depending on whether it is in England, Wales, Scotland or Northern Ireland) to deal with them. Most appeals are conducted by written representation only, but there are also informal hearings and inquiries. The latter are generally only for matters of considerable public importance. Your appeal is likely to be heard in writing only, thus necessitating very well argued documentation. This is normally beyond the capacity of the layman and is outside the scope of this book.

ENFORCEMENT

If you change the use of your property, or develop it in any way, without having first obtained the necessary permission, you may find that your local authority takes enforcement proceedings against you. These will have serious repercussions and could, in the worst case, result in your having to remove altogether a building that you have constructed. Whenever you are in doubt about whether an activity or alteration needs permission, check before you do anything. (See above, What Matters Require Planning Permission?)

If you have broken the planning laws you are likely to be contacted by a planning officer, probably following a complaint from a neighbour. The officer will want to see the nature of the breach and discuss it with you. At this stage, he should be able to give you a clear idea as to whether or not you have broken the law. If you have, he will advise you of the specific breach and how to remedy it. This will subsequently be placed in writing to you. You may be advised by the officer to apply for retrospective planning permission to cover the breach, if he thinks it is likely that permission would be granted.

If you do not remedy the breach – which may involve a serious amount of remedial work – or apply for retrospective planning permission, the council will serve an enforcement notice on you. This will define the breach of the planning laws and order you to remedy it within a set period. If you do not comply with the enforcement notice, then the council will start legal proceedings against you. If successful, they will be able to rectify any breach themselves – with you having to pay all the related costs. You can appeal against an enforcement notice; times set for complying with the notice will then fall into abeyance until the matter has been heard.

If you are served with an enforcement notice and the breach is serious, you would be wise to take professional advice. It may well be that the council cannot act, as the planning laws were broken so long ago that the council have no right of enforcement. If, however, they have a right to act, then the stakes for you can be high. Removing an extension that you have just built, or having to change the location of your business, could be disastrous.

EFFECTIVE OBJECTION TO AN APPLICATION FOR PLANNING PERMISSION

If you object to a building matter proposed by another individual for which planning permission is required, then you must make sure that you act quickly and effectively, and use all the weapons at your disposal. That said, this can be very committing in terms of personal relationships. Your objections will not be looked on kindly by the person applying for permission.

You may hear personally from the person intending to apply for planning permission, before he actually makes his application. Alternatively, you may see that the application has already been made, and is publicized either in the local papers or in notices stuck on lampposts around the relevant site or property. If the latter is the case, then you have less time in which to make your objections. The application will already be working its way through the system and may be close to a conclusion.

Whichever is the case, your first priority is to find out what exactly the applicant is applying for, and how long you have before the matter is decided. Find out immediately where you can inspect a copy of the plans, lodged as part of the application, and the date the application is due to go before the committee. If you ring the planning department of your local authority, they will be able to advise you. Normally, for a set period after the application has been made, they will be available in a council office near the property concerned. You can go and inspect the plans, and satisfy yourself as to what exactly the application is for. You usually have three weeks in which to make an objection in writing although, in practice, objections can be registered right up until the committee meeting.

Reading plans is not always easy for the layman, and you must make sure you fully understand what is set out. If the plans are complicated, it can be helpful to take someone skilled in reading plans with you. This may be a builder, a friend or a professional employed only for this purpose. It is all too easy to misread the plans, and become offended about something that will actually not concern you. For example, you may interpret the plans as showing windows overlooking your property when, in reality, they face in a different direction. Alternatively, you may have no real understanding of the dimensions of the proposed project, and how it will really affect you.

If the application is something about which you feel compelled to object, you have two main choices of action:

Direct Negotiation with the Applicant

This is probably the best way to object, if your aim is to maintain a good relationship with the applicant. The latter will want to keep any objections to his proposals to a minimum, and it is quite likely that he will make minor alterations to satisfy you. He may genuinely have not realized the offence that he will cause, until you point it out to him. Many aspects of a plan can be changed relatively easily, by a good designer, to achieve the same end result for the applicant, but without causing anyone else problems.

If the applicant does agree to alter his plans to suit any objections that you have made, ensure that these are shown on revised plans before the matter proceeds to the planning committee. This can be done by contacting the planning officer in charge of the application. Preferably, you should physically check the redrawn and resubmitted plans at the council offices.

Objecting Directly to the Planning Department

If the applicant will not negotiate with you about abandoning his application, or making changes to his plans, you must fight the application for all it is worth. There are two main ways of doing this, and both should be put into operation.

Lobbying

Do not forget that planning is subjective and, importantly, decided by elected officials, your councillors. These officials have to stand for re-election every four years, and depend on your support to stay in office. They will respond if they find that, by not doing so, their political position is made insecure. Find out who your local councillor is and lobby him to oppose the application. Do not stop there. The more councillors you can speak to, the better. If you can, get the councillors actually to visit your property, so that you can show them what detrimental effect the proposals within the application will have.

Get hold of your immediate neighbours and persuade them to object to the application. For this to be effective they must object in writing, or sign a petition. Approach your local residents' association and, if appropriate, your local chamber of commerce, and obtain their active support. If at all possible, try to get the support of your local paper as well – this can be a real bonus. The more people and associations you can get on your side, the greater the pressure you can bring to bear on the councillors who will make the final decision. Always try to obtain support for your objections in writing. Oral support has little power.

Make sure that if councillors do promise you their support, they know that you will attend the committee meeting – and bring with you as many other objectors as possible. This will help to ensure that the councillors perform.

Your reasons for the objections may not be particularly sound factually, but you should not underestimate the sheer persuasive power of many people strongly objecting.

Presenting a Sound Case Against the Application

You should do the same as someone about to apply for planning permission. Firstly, research the history of the property concerned. Go to the planning office and ask to see the card index for the property, which will itemize its planning history. Look at any previous applications made, and then check the planning files, which will give the reports and reasons for past decisions. It may be that the proposal in question has been turned down before. While at the planning offices, pick up any brochures or leaflets that state or describe the planning policy for your area.

Go to your library and look up the **local plan**, which will advise you of the council's own policy guidelines for use when considering applications. Request **county structure plans** at the same time. Try to find out any principles or guidelines that the application may be transgressing. Make a careful note of these, where they are written and precisely what they say. These documents, together with national policy documents, are not easy for a layman to read, so be prepared for some quite complex jargon. If you can, try to get this research done by a professional or a friend competent in this area. Your objective must be to create a strong argument, to show that the application should not be consented to as it goes against existing guidelines and principles.

Apart from looking into the principles of the application, also look at the actual plans themselves. Ask yourself how they will adversely affect you.

- Will you be overlooked?
- Is your natural light going to be reduced?
- Are you going to be facing an unsightly brick wall?
- Do the proposals change the character of the street?

- Will there be increased parking problems?
- If the application is for change of use, are you going to be disturbed by noise, increased numbers of people coming and going, lorries arriving and so on?

The examples are numerous. Be able to list coherently the adverse effects on your life and property if the application were granted.

Finally, write a letter of objection to the relevant planning office. Make sure that you quote the reference number of the application and that the letter is addressed to the planning officer dealing with the matter. Make your letter cogent and precise, and separate your arguments into numbered paragraphs, so that points are made clearly. When lobbying neighbours and councillors, it can be handy to have copies of this letter for them to sign individually – not everyone has the ability, time or will to write a letter. If you can give them something that they just have to sign, you can pretty much guarantee it will be sent. Sample letters are given in Appendix 5.

Make sure that you also contact the relevant planning officer by telephone. Ask him to come to your own property, so that you can show him the effects of the proposed development on site. At this time, try to find out the officer's own feelings about the application. If you are lucky, he may be able to present you with arguments that you could use in any objection.

If you are forceful and energetic, you can be very effective in objecting against an application. The key factor, however, will always be obtaining the support of councillors. They are the people who make any final decision and, wherever possible, they should be targeted.

In the event that the application is refused, but the applicant takes the matter to appeal, you would certainly be wise to employ professional advice. Appeals are dealt with on a much more objective basis than initial applications to your district council. It is at this time that a good planning consultant with experience of appeals will come into his own, not least because one limb of your strategy – the subjectivity of your councillors – will have become ineffective.

THE PROFESSIONALS

While both applying for planning permission, and effective objecting to it, can be done by a layman, you may well choose to use a professional. This is wise if the matter concerns something of critical importance, is contentious or requires detailed drawings and plans. The latter tend to be the greatest obstacle to the layman in processing his own application, all the way through the system. If plans and drawings are required, they must be to a proper, professional and technical standard – and they need to comply with any building regulations. This is beyond most lay people, and usually a professional of some sort will be employed to produce the necessary plans.

Apart from producing drawings and plans, professionals are of considerable importance to you, in terms of their design ability and knowledge. A well thought-out design is obviously going to be of benefit in maximizing the potential of your particular project. Just as important, though, is the fact that the design produced should be something that the local authority will like, and will accept as being in keeping with local principles and guidelines. A professional who is used to dealing with your local planning office will know what they find acceptable. Over time he is also likely to have built up a relationship with the planning department, and possibly even with some of the committee councillors. This will enable him to angle a project correctly, and to sound out planning officers effectively on a particular matter. If the professional has a good reputation for design and implementation, then this in itself can carry weight with the authorities.

You can use a professional in a couple of ways when making an application for planning permission. You may choose to have the professional design your project, produce all the plans and drawings, fill out and present the application, and communicate with the planning officer, thus taking the matter to its conclusion. Alternatively, you may decide to use a professional only to produce drawings and plans from your designs. The rest of the application you may do yourself, although generally you would get your professional to fill out the form.

If you decide to use a professional, then choose carefully. Make sure the person you employ has the right experience to deal with your application. Before employing him, be sure to see some of his work, in terms of both plans and completed building projects. You should also make certain that his charges are clearly laid out in writing, and that they itemize exactly what work he will do for you, the stages of payment required, and any disbursements expected. If at all possible, get him to give you a written quotation for the work. Also, check that he has professional indemnity insurance that will protect you against any negligent work that he performs. Finally, always be sure to specify what you actually want – before your professional starts work. You may not be able to decide on every possible facet, but try to narrow down your requirements – the more design time you waste, the more expensive your professional's bill will be at the end of the day.

The professionals involved in planning are:

Architects

These are highly qualified individuals, registered with the **Architects' Registration Council**. They should have indemnity insurance to practise, and you must expressly check that they have. They are normally the most expensive professionals to employ, although this can depend upon their experience and the area in which the project is located – and their fees are normally negotiable.

Surveyors

Anyone can call himself a surveyor – so beware. Check that the person you wish to employ has qualifications pertinent to the work you need doing. There are a number of professional organizations, the most highly recognized being the **Royal Institution of Chartered Surveyors (RICS)**.

Draughtsmen, Planning Consultants and Architectural Technicians

There is a miscellany of different people who offer a design and planning service. They can be very competent and, if you choose carefully, there is no reason not to use them. They can be less costly than architects or qualified surveyors.

Builders

Some builders will also offer a design and planning service. Make sure that they have insurance to cover this type of work, and isolate carefully their design and planning fees.

SUMMARY

- Check whether any alteration to the building itself, or any change of use, requires permission before you start your project. Check this personally, even if you are employing a builder.

- Understand the difference between 'permitted development' and those matters that require planning permission.

- If in any doubt about whether you need planning permission, contact your planning officer and get his response in writing.

- When applying for planning permission, be proactive. Talk to your neighbours and your local councillor, and research the history of your property. Have a pre-application meeting with your planning officer and listen to his comments.

- Present the application with good-quality drawings and plans, accompanied by a persuasive statement.

- Make sure you keep in touch with your planning officer during the assessment process, and be prepared to make amendments to your application.

- Lobby your local councillors if a refusal appears likely.

- If you are going to object to an application, try first to have a friendly meeting to dissuade the other party. If this fails, use every means possible to persuade the local councillors to refuse the application.

- If you use a professional at any stage, check his competence: that he has insurance, his costs are clearly itemized, a proper quote is given, and he has experience specifically relevant to your type of application or objection.

16

Law and Disputes

I T is essential to have a basic understanding of the civil law.
  You are probably a party to contracts every day, whether it is buying
  some shopping, or the more critical contracts involved when properties are
bought and sold, or when professionals are employed to perform a service. It
is important, therefore, to understand the basic nature of the civil law, the
protection afforded by statute and the way that the legal process works.

It is also important to have some idea of how to monitor and manage a
dispute, a court case and any employment of a lawyer. All too often, disputes
end up in litigation, embroiled in a process that is difficult to understand, and
over which you can find you have dangerously little control.

While the complexity and subtlety of the law should never be
underestimated, much of the basic framework is reasonably accessible.

OUTLINE LAW (ENGLAND AND WALES)

Most problems stem either from breach of contract, or the negligent actions
or advice of some professional.

Contract Terms

As seen in Chapter 9: The Contract, a contract must comprise three
components in order to be valid: an offer, an acceptance, and consideration.
These components must be absolutely clear, so that an agreement is certain and
the intention of the agreement evident to all the parties involved. The contract
can be made orally, or in writing, with no theoretical difference in
enforceability. Oral contracts should be avoided, however, as they are difficult
to prove either way in the event of a dispute.

A contract may be unenforceable if, prior to the making of it, one party has
seriously misrepresented any matter concerning the contract to another party.
If you, as the injured party, had relied on that misrepresentation – and would
not have gone ahead with the contract if you had known it was a
misrepresentation – then the contract might be deemed unenforceable.
Alternatively, you may have the right to claim compensation for your loss, due
to being misled.

Most contracts consist of a number of terms, which can be divided into
conditions and **warranties**. Distinguishing between what is a condition and
what is a warranty is not always easy, however, although the distinction is

absolutely critical. It is vital when you are agreeing to a contract that you and the other party are agreed about what category the terms fall into. This is not always as easy as it sounds, and lawyers do sometimes talk about **innominate terms**. These can be either conditions or warranties, depending on the exact circumstances. That said, do your best to define and name the terms appropriately.

Conditions

Terms that are absolutely crucial, or central, to the overall intention of the contracting parties are called conditions. Helpfully, lawyers sometimes say that conditions go to the 'root of the contract'. The performance of these conditions is pivotal to the contract.

If a condition is broken this can give the injured party a right to terminate the entire contract, as well as a claim for compensation (damages).

Warranties

These are terms that are incidental to the contract, although obviously still of some importance. If these are broken, however, this does not affect the core of the intention of the parties.

If a warranty is broken the injured party can claim compensation (subject to proving the loss), but will be unable actually to terminate the contract.

An example of the distinction between conditions and warranties can be seen from a contract for the delivery of a length of steel, such as a rolled-steel joist (RSJ). The agreement for the steel may be that it should conform to certain specific dimensions and, when delivered, be left under cover in the back garden of your house. If the dimensions on delivery are wrong, then this would be a breach of a condition. If the steel was of the correct dimensions, however, but left in the front porch, uncovered, rather than in the rear garden as specified, then this is likely to be a breach of a warranty, rather than a condition. That said, depending on all the circumstances, this may be a breach of condition, if the position of the delivered steel was absolutely critical to the contract. For example, your house may be terraced, and the only way that the steel could be of any use to you would be if the steel provider's crane carried it over your roof to its desired position.

Such shades of meaning are grist to a lawyer's mill. As a layman you must use your common sense and make every effort to make quite clear, at the time of any agreement, what you consider to be the conditions of your contract. As with any contract, this should be in writing, and important terms expressly called 'conditions'. Be warned, however, that if you call a term a condition and it is broken, and you then go to court to terminate the contract, the court may find that the term is, in fact, not a condition but a warranty – as it concerns a trivial aspect of the contract. The court may then say that common sense should prevail, and refuse to allow the contract to be terminated. The opposite can also occur, where a warranty is found to be a condition. So beware, as you may be in for a surprise. You must always look carefully at the contract as a whole, to ensure that what you call a condition is, in fact, exactly that.

Be especially careful when making stipulations about time (for example, time of delivery, time for reaching a certain stage, etc.). If you want to be able to rely on time stipulations, then always state that **time is of the essence.** This magic phrase should be used each time a date or time is mentioned, which you regard as crucial. If this is not done, then you may find your right to insist on compliance with the time stipulation is curtailed.

Implied Terms

Terms are often 'implied' by courts when assessing a contract which is in dispute. This implying of terms occurs for two main reasons. Firstly, contracts are rarely drawn up in sufficient detail to cover every possible eventuality. While the basic purpose of the contract is clear, there are often gaps in the detail. In this case a court, if there was a dispute, would be able to imply terms that would give the contract a business efficacy – to make it workable, given an objective view of the intentions of the parties.

Secondly, terms are implied to protect the interests of the parties involved in the contract. This occurs to a large extent when private individuals (consumers) are involved. In this case, if there is a statute implying terms into a contract, then this will generally override any contrary terms to which you (as an individual) may have agreed, or been forced unknowingly to agree.

For example, a term implied to any building contract is that a builder must comply with building regulations. This would hold good even if a plan and signed contract conflicted with the regulations. Your builder, in this case, could be liable to you for breach of contract for carrying out works contrary to the building regulations – notwithstanding that his work complied with your plans.

It is critical to appreciate this area, as implied terms, particularly those implied by statute, are frequently a consumer's chief protection against unfair contracts. (See Consumer Protection below.) Apart from consumer protection, however, courts will always try hard to let a contract stand in the form in which it was negotiated.

Breach of Contract

A breach of contract occurs when one party to a contract does not comply with the terms, whether express or implied. When this happens the injured party can seek redress for the breach by taking legal proceedings against the party breaching the contract.

As an injured party, you can go to court to claim compensation (**damages**) if you have suffered a quantifiable loss. Alternatively, you can ask a court to enforce compliance by the other party to the terms of your contract. This is called asking for an order for **specific performance.** A judge always has a wide discretion as to whether he makes an order for specific performance, instead of, or in addition to, ordinary monetary compensation. An order for specific performance is not always an option – not least because, as the injured party, you must not be in breach of the contract yourself. You must also be ready, willing and able to perform your own obligations within the contract, on time and unconditionally.

If the breach of contract is serious, and fundamental to the performance of the contract – that is, it significantly undermines the essential agreement between the parties – then, as the injured party, you can end the contract completely and sue for any loss sustained. You must always be careful in terminating a contract, however, because of another party's breach. If a court finds that the breach did not justify termination, then you could find yourself being sued for wrongful termination of the contract. This could prove to be a very costly error.

Wherever possible, before taking any irrevocable steps, you must try to get an objective third party to look at your particular contractual problem. As an injured party, you are probably too emotionally charged to be able properly to assess the scale and importance of any breach. At this time a lawyer can be most valuable, in advising on the nature of the breach that has occurred.

Negligence

Negligence can be an extremely difficult matter to prove, and is not one that is often tackled by a private litigant without professional help. Part of the problem lies in identifying the standard of conduct that the courts will recognize as negligent – the knotty question of whether bad conduct is merely unfortunate, rather than negligence capable of redress. What may seem bad or shoddy to you, as a layman, is by no means always deemed by the courts to be negligent. Almost invariably, establishing whether or not there has been negligence takes the skills of a good lawyer (particularly if it is to help you prove that another lawyer may have been negligent).

It can also be difficult to prove negligence because often you, as the injured party, simply do not have, or cannot obtain, sufficient evidence to prove the facts conclusively. This can be the case particularly with professionals, whose knowledge, records and control over events is often much better than the layman's. They are often able to place a spin or gloss over events sufficient to cloud any negligent act, and prevent a successful court action.

Negligence has been described as a 'breach of a legal duty to take care resulting in foreseeable damage'. While this may seem reasonably straightforward to the layman, actually proving the elements of this definition to the standard required by a court is extremely difficult. One of the main problems is proving that the element of care expected was not properly exercised. In terms of professionals, such as solicitors, surveyors, engineers and so on, the error made would have to be one that a reasonably competent professional, exercising the ordinary standards of his profession, would not have made. So, not every error of judgement is actionable – only those that go beyond a general standard nominally set by the relevant profession as a whole. If someone professes to be a specialist in a particular field then the standard expected is higher than that of a general practitioner. The standard is relatively vague, however – and not easy to define precisely.

Negligence, if it is suspected, is something that will invariably take professional help to prove, and requires a high degree of caution, prior to any accusation or legal action. It is also something that a professional will fight hard against, firmly backed up by his professional indemnity insurers. They are likely to take the matter a long way through the court process, which can be stressful and very expensive, particularly if you are funding it yourself. Suing for negligence is not something for the faint-hearted and, before setting out on this course, you must check that you have a valid case and the funds with which to proceed – or can get legal aid.

Consumer Protection

There are a number of crucial statutes that have been enacted specifically to protect you, when acting as an individual. These acts automatically imply terms to contracts, and give you rights that you would otherwise not possess. These terms cannot be avoided by another person or company, even if they draw up a contract that tries to exclude them. The protection of these acts tends to extend only to individuals in a non-business capacity, and not to businesses or corporate bodies.

There are a number of key acts that specifically aim to protect the consumer, such as: the Trade Descriptions Act 1968, the Consumer Credit Act 1974, the Consumer Protection Act 1987, The Sale of Goods Act 1994. Appendix 4 summarizes the basic protection afforded by these acts.

A good example of consumer protection in action is when you buy a tin of paint. The Sale of Goods Act will imply into the contract for sale that the paint is fit for purpose, and of merchantable quality. If the paint does not come up to these conditions then, regardless of what the seller claims, the courts will find that there has been a breach of contract. This legislation provides significant protection to you as an individual consumer.

Overall, as an individual, you have considerable protection inherent in the operation of the law, to prevent you from suffering under an oppressive contract. This presupposes, however, that you know about the protection afforded and, at worst, are willing to go through a court action to assert your rights. The protection afforded must certainly not be considered as an excuse for entering contracts carelessly, on the basis that any problems can be resolved later. This can be a recipe for disaster, as legal action tends to be very slow and expensive – and there is always the danger that a court may not find in your favour.

The best approach that you can take, when entering any contract, is to have in mind the legal principle *caveat emptor* – 'let the buyer beware'. At the end of the day you are free to enter into contracts at will, and it really is up to you to ensure that you do this wisely. Protection offered by the courts and consumer legislation should only ever be considered as a bonus.

It is essential that any contract to which you are a party is entered into carefully, cautiously and with a view to removing all vague areas, prior to any purchase or work being carried out. This will always concentrate the mind of the other party and will, on its own account, prevent many problems from occurring in the first place. It also makes any legal action much easier to conduct, when it is quite clear what specific terms and conditions existed in a contract.

Appreciate that the standard of performance that a court will read into a contract with a professional, builder or other person, is, in practical terms, low. If you want a high level of service, top-quality work or a superior level of skill, then this must be expressly stated in your contract. If it is not, and if the contract is for building works, for example, then a court is likely to base its judgement on the principle that a builder should do work in a good and workmanlike manner, using good and proper materials and, if he is responsible for the design, provide a building fit for its intended purpose. This may not be acceptable to you, when really you required attention and skill to a much higher standard.

DISPUTES

It should be your express aim to avoid a dispute going to court, while giving the impression to the other party that this is a course of action that you are not afraid to take – what lawyers call 'consolidating your negotiating position'.

It is rarely of value for anyone to take a matter all the way to a final hearing as the risk, expense and stress are considerable. It is therefore worth committing time and effort to settling a matter as soon as possible, even if a small loss is sustained or your ego left unsatisfied.

Preparation

Most disputes should never reach the stage of a court action, and can be forestalled by good preparation and attention, both when drawing up a contract and during its actual operation.

The starting-point when entering into a contract must be the absolute expectation that problems and disputes are likely to arise. Most people, by contrast, tend to enter into a contract blithely, giving little consideration to any problems that may occur. They therefore do not monitor the detailed progress of a project until long after a dispute has become serious – by which time their options are often reduced. As a consequence, they are often not prepared for any dispute, and rarely have any evidence of their own to prove their arguments one way or another. Accordingly, even when an individual has a good moral case against another party, he can often not afford the risk of taking the matter to court.

In fact, many cases would never get as far as a legal action, if the preparation for and control over a contract were adequate from the start. Most disputes occur through misunderstandings, which cannot be immediately and conclusively disproved.

The following are absolutely essential:

- Any contract entered into should be clear, unambiguous and in writing. All foreseeable problem areas should be dealt with and written in as terms of the contract. Do not avoid contentious areas at this stage. Ask yourself what problems there could be – and deal with them head on within the contract. Decide what are the conditions, and what are the warranties, within the contract.

- Wherever possible, include a clause in the contract that specifically deals with the resolution of disputes. This should allow a course of action that is cheap, quick and certain, without having to resort to a court or legal proceedings. Nominate a form of resolution appropriate to the matter in hand (see below, pp.197–9).

- Open a specific file for all the paperwork on the contract and neatly collate this paperwork in date order. Enter anything and everything relating to the matter at hand, and retain it until some time after completion of the work. Wherever possible, send letters confirming instructions or the material content of conversations – and keep copies.

- Make **attendance notes** of telephone conversations and face-to-face meetings throughout the duration of the project, specifying actions or conversations that take place but have not been confirmed in writing. These attendance notes should be timed and dated, and give an accurate précis of what each party said or agreed. As contemporaneous notes, they have evidential value in a court, and will often be sufficient, with other paperwork, to persuade the other party that the evidence on your side is so overwhelming that it would be suicidal for them to allow the dispute to proceed.

- By the end of the contract make sure you have a full and detailed history of the contract in date order.

The importance of maintaining a full record of the contract is always critical – never more so than when professionals, such as architects, surveyors, engineers, solicitors etc. are involved. The latter will, as a matter of course, record every action and conversation. When disputes occur they invariably have a considerable advantage over private individuals, who rarely have the same detailed record. They are therefore able to win many disputes, purely because all the hard, detailed evidence is held by them. If you are opposing them with vague dates and inaccurate statements, this will rarely be sufficient to persuade anyone conclusively, let alone a court – and you will inevitably have to back down.

Few things will deflate an opposing party more than being shown contemporaneous attendance notes, or letters itemizing agreements or actions, which contradict what they are maintaining. They will know that any attempt to deny them will be an uphill struggle and, as a consequence, will be forced to accept that their position is unsustainable.

It may well be boring, and seem like a waste of time, to be nit-picking about retaining paperwork and making notes. If this results in disputes being prevented from going to court, however, then the effort is well worth while. Sometimes it stops a dispute even arising, because you will find that you are monitoring the detail of the ongoing contract, and can thereby nip problems in the bud.

Dispute Resolution

When a dispute occurs, always assess the matter dispassionately and attempt to resolve it before any legal action takes place.

Quite often disputes occur through simple misunderstandings or miscommunications, rather than any deliberate breach of contract. Much of the time, problems arise from differences of perception, rather than facts. It is important, therefore, for emotional responses to be put to one side and the problems behind the dispute clearly isolated. It may well be that the dispute has no real grounds. It is at this stage, therefore, that direct lines of communication between you and the other party to the contract are so valuable – and must be preserved for as long as possible.

It is vital that any dispute goes through managed stages of escalation, rather than flying straight from a disagreement, to a court action. The latter course should always be considered a last resort, not least because it is an expensive and lengthy route to follow, and will rarely provide the quick satisfaction that is required. Furthermore, a court action always has a significant element of uncertainty, and it is quite possible to lose a good case through poor presentation.

Prior to any formal legal action you should do the following:

- Carefully analyse the dispute in an attempt to break it down and isolate the core problems. Often, the real reason for a dispute can become lost in ancillary arguments that overshadow the true problem. It is essential that there is clarity over what the dispute concerns.

  Be prepared to recognize the strengths of your opponent's case, as well as its weaknesses. If your opponent has good points, assess whether you have valid answers to them.

- Arrange a face-to-face 'without prejudice' meeting, preferably on neutral ground, to discuss the dispute in an effort to settle the matter amicably.

  If a meeting is arranged, prepare a written agenda so that each distinct aspect of the problem is dealt with. Draw up any agenda fairly, to take into account the points that are being contended by the opposing party. Ideally, a mediator acceptable to both parties should attend the meeting, to ensure that the agenda is kept to, and the points discussed rationally. The meeting may well resolve the dispute altogether, or at least narrow down the disputed matters to a few core points, while settling ancillary matters.

  Make sure that any meeting, conversations or correspondence are **without prejudice** (as opposed to **off the record**), so that they cannot be referred to in any court case. This will allow you and your opponent to be candid, and negotiate openly.

If you do achieve agreement, even if it is partial, then make sure that a written, dated note of the agreement is produced as soon as possible, and is signed by all parties. This will stand as your record and is itself a contract. If your opponent will not sign the document, then at least sign and date your copy.

- If a resolution cannot be agreed on, it is often worth checking to see if you can resolve the dispute through mediation. There are effectively two forms of mediation:

  - Many professionals, such as large firms of solicitors, surveyors, architects and so on, will have a senior member of staff whose specific responsibility it is to deal with complaints against the firm. This can be an easy way to settle a dispute, and can be particularly helpful if both sides wish to preserve a future working relationship. Failing that, there are professional bodies who are responsible for the discipline of their members, such as the **Office for the Supervision of Solicitors (OSS)** in the Law Society, and a miscellany of trade organizations, who can sometimes place pressure on their members.

  - Third-party mediation is increasingly being recognized by the courts as having an important role in dispute resolution. Indeed, there are indications that it may become compulsory at least to consider this before going to trial. Even if you are being represented by a solicitor in a dispute, it is well worth asking for his advice about **Alternative Dispute Resolution (ADR)**. It may provide you with a quick and cheap way of avoiding a long and costly court action. Your opponent may oppose this, in which case there is little you can do. It is an option well worth exploring, however, and you should place considerable pressure upon your solicitor at least to try this route.

- Your contract may well have a clause specifying that in the event of a dispute you have to use an arbitrator. If this is the case, then, unless you can come to an agreement after a 'without prejudice' meeting or mediation, this is the course that you must follow. Ensure that the arbitrator is a member of the **Chartered Institute of Arbitrators**, and that you are happy with his qualifications. You should be given the opportunity to say whether or not you agree to his appointment – and you must insist on this. Once he is appointed it is usually too late. Before agreeing to an appointment, ask for his CV and details of his relevant experience. If you do not agree to his appointment, then there is normally a fall-back position, where an arbitrator can be appointed by the head of a governing body, such as the President of the Royal Institution of Chartered Surveyors (RICS) or the Law Society.

The arbitrator chosen, once he has heard the evidence, will be able to make a legally binding and enforceable decision regarding the dispute, with very limited possibilities of appeal. This can be of benefit in bringing the dispute to a head quickly and finally.

In arbitration of this kind, the evidence concerning the dispute is often sent to the arbitrator in writing only, and on this he makes his decision. However, arbitrators can dictate how a case is presented to them. An arbitration can be an oral hearing, similar to a court trial, but this significantly increases the costs. The parties to the hearing have to pay for the hearing venue and, of course, the arbitrator's time. In a court trial you at least get the court and judge for the minimal cost of the court issue fee.

Arbitrators do have the further benefit to the parties of not always having to observe the strict rules about evidence that are followed in a court trial. This can be of help in the presentation of the case. Arbitrators also have the power to make their own investigations, unless the parties expressly agree that they may not.

- If a dispute remains unresolved, or if arbitration is not possible, advise your opponent in writing, clearly and concisely, what the problem is, what must be done to rectify it, and how soon it is to be done. Make sure the time-scale that you specify is feasible. It may be that you wish certain works to be redone at no extra cost, or that you want compensation to make up your loss. Finally, advise the other party that legal action will be taken against him within a set period, normally seven days (as long as this is realistic and fair in all the circumstances), without further notice, unless rectification is forthcoming. This makes this document a formal letter before action. This is an important step which should always be made in writing.

  This document must be objective, unemotional, unambiguous and open. It is not a negotiating document, so do not put anything in it that you would not be prepared to say to a judge or arbitrator. It may need to be supported by the relevant part of the agreement that has been transgressed, and could be accompanied by an expert's report.

  It can often be worth involving solicitors to draw up your letter before action. Sometimes the mere fact that you have consulted one, and that he has written a letter for you, will force an opposing party to recognize your determination. This letter on its own can be sufficient to settle a dispute.

  The courts like to see that a defending party to an action was advised of impending legal action, and the reasons for it, prior to its being commenced. It is also an accepted final warning-shot that most people will recognize as being the last time that negotiations can take place before legal action.

  If you do not write a clear letter before action then you may find yourself penalized in costs, even if you do win your case. More frustratingly, a court may well allow extensions of deadlines in the early stages of a case, because it thinks that you have not given sufficient time for your opponent to marshal his case.

Assessment of the Case

It is vital that before legal proceedings are started, or after a letter before action has been received, a further thorough assessment is undertaken of the merits of your case – whether you are the person suing (the **plaintiff**) or being sued (the **defendant**). While it is cost-effective, and tactically sound, to threaten to sue, and to use solicitor's letters to exert pressure or to intimidate, the moment an action actually starts, the potential expenses and risks escalate.

The best people to assess the legal merits of a case are, of course, solicitors or barristers. In most matters, however, you will normally have a good idea of the reality of your position, unless the matter is very complex. Also, only you will know what you can afford, the risk you are willing to take, and the strategy you want to pursue.

Whether suing or being sued, consider:

The Strength of the Case

Marshal all the paperwork and evidence available, and look carefully to see whether the facts alone would suggest a winning case. The difficult factor here is the dispassionate investigation that must be carried out. A court will not be swayed by purely emotional, hypothetical, speculative or theoretical arguments. You must be able to prove what you are maintaining, and actually document any losses that you have sustained.

It can sometimes be helpful to give a copy of the relevant paperwork to a friend to look at, to see what someone objective would say. Alternatively, the **Citizens' Advice Bureau** can be helpful, or you can employ a solicitor purely to assess the matter on its merits. It may also be possible at this stage to obtain **legal aid** with which to employ a solicitor. This is a matter which a solicitor, or the Citizens' Advice Bureau, will be able to advise on.

Generally, unless you really have an overwhelmingly strong case, it is probably not worth fighting the matter with a view to taking it all the way to a final hearing. This does not mean that the case could not win, but that the risk and escalation of costs could be too high to be worth while.

Emotional Involvement

Ask yourself how emotionally involved you are in the dispute. Is the fighting of the dispute more about pride and ego than the cold facts of the matter? If so, then realize that although going ahead may result in having your day in court, it will probably be a losing one – and infinitely more painful than a climb-down before the action proceeds further. Most lawyers will rub their hands with glee if you tell them your case is a matter of principle.

The Value of the Dispute

Coldly assess the actual benefit that will result from winning the case. If the monetary value is likely to be small or incidental, then the wisdom of proceeding needs to be looked at in the light of the costs, the time taken, the stress and the ever-present possibility that you may not win.

Ability of the Opposing Party to Pay a Judgement Debt

Assess the opposing party's financial means. There is little point in suing a person or business that, at the end of the day, will not be able to pay a judgement debt. Indeed, you could find yourself not only being unable to recover the sum sued for, but having to pay for all your own legal costs, thus actually increasing your original loss.

There are many private investigators around who will do financial checks of individuals or businesses. For a modest fee, it can be worth employing them to make an investigation before you issue legal proceedings.

Legal Costs

The legal costs on a case you conduct yourself are quite low, although you should not underestimate the hidden cost of the time you will actually spend on it – which is largely irrecoverable. If lawyers are involved on either side, however, then the costs soar, and can quickly become disproportionate to the value of a dispute. Even if you do win your case, and are awarded all your costs, you will, in fact, never fully recover all your own legal costs, which reduces the value of any gain.

It is vitally important to recognize that when a court awards you your costs, they will not be the same as what your solicitor can, quite properly, charge you. There are set amounts that the courts allow for work performed in an action by your lawyer, but these are generally much less than you will be charged in practice. You will personally have to make up the difference – and this can be considerable.

The risk of having to bear your opponent's legal costs is a very real prospect and must always merit serious attention.

Be wary when your opponent is receiving legal aid to pursue the case. This can be an indicator that he does not have the money to pay for any judgement debt that may be awarded – although this cannot be relied upon conclusively. What it does indicate, however, is that he does not initially have to worry unduly about the legal costs of the case – and can afford to pursue the action without this being a constant concern. That said, if you are receiving legal aid and win a case, and are awarded money, then the Law Society will expect some, if not all, of that money from you to defray the costs of the legal aid provided.

Strategic Suing and Defence of an Action

There are occasions when you may need time, for example, to gather sufficient money together to settle a dispute. In this case, defending a court action is one way of putting off having to settle a matter too soon. It is possible to fight a delaying action that effectively puts off any final hearing for a long time. Bear in mind, however, that this may be expensive in legal costs, and possibly in terms of the interest on money claimed by your opponent.

It can also be well worth fighting a case as a spoiling action. So, even if you do not have a good and winning case, you may decide to fight, just to give the impression that you are willing to take the action all the way to a trial. This may increase your leverage to obtain better negotiating terms from your opponent. He may decide just to settle the matter, albeit for less, to terminate a potentially long, stressful and time-consuming case.

Be warned, however, that strategic litigation carries a high risk. You cannot always abandon a case at will. Even when you can discontinue an action without having to ask the court's permission, your opponent will be entitled to recover his legal costs; or perhaps he may have brought a cross-claim against you which he decides to continue.

THE CIVIL COURTS (ENGLAND AND WALES)

There are two types of court that deal with relevant civil matters: the County Court and the High Court.

The County Court

This court historically deals with smaller claims, such as for breaches of contract, possession of property, arrears of rent and damages caused by negligence or wilful damage. This court will be the one with which you are most likely to deal, as an individual. Most reasonable-sized towns have their own county court, so they are very accessible.

The county court is very user-friendly, and has been increasingly developed to allow a private litigant to conduct and present his own case, without a lawyer. There are excellent pamphlets, freely available, clearly setting out the process of an action. The court staff tend to be helpful and informative, although they are not allowed to provide any advice concerning the detail of a particular case.

Claims made in the county court for a value of less than £5,000 (as at September 1997) automatically proceed to arbitration, unless the parties disagree. This form of process is ideal for the private litigant. The procedure is simple, accessible and kept as straightforward as possible, with little formality. The arbitration is adjudicated on by a district judge, used to dealing with private litigants.

Claims made over £5,000 follow a more conventional process, although emphasis is still placed on allowing a private litigant to conduct a case. The information and directions on conducting a case are clear and in plain English, rather than legalese, and there is no real reason why, in cases of reasonable simplicity, you cannot dispense with a lawyer.

The High Court

The High Court generally deals with more serious matters than the county court. It can be very quick and effective when used properly, but it is also rather more formidable for litigants without lawyers. The court procedures tend not to be very accessible to individuals. The costs of actions also tend to be greater, with the scale of claimable legal costs more than would be allowed in the county court. Geographically, there are far fewer venues for the High Courts than there are for the county courts.

Solicitors

There is nothing whatsoever to prevent you from conducting your own case in the High Court or a county court. You have full rights of hearing in all courts, and you can be prevented from presenting your own case only in exceptional circumstances. That said, there are some special rules that govern the presentation of cases by companies, even small ones. In this event, you may have to employ a lawyer to attend for you.

In reality, most people will employ lawyers for matters that are complex or where the sum of money at stake is considerable. It is also wise to employ a lawyer when a case is being conducted in the High Court, where the inherent complications are difficult for a layman to grasp effectively.

Many county court actions do not require a solicitor, and you should be able to conduct an action quite satisfactorily, including the presentation of the case at trial. Indeed, employing a solicitor may be far too expensive for minor matters, where the legal costs may outweigh the value of the claim itself.

Solicitors often have as bad a press as builders, surveyors, financial advisers and estate agents. Common complaints concern their high, indefinable costs and the slow conduct of cases in which they are involved. While there is some justification in these complaints, they tend to derive from an incorrect perception of solicitors and their work. Part of the problem is that people still tend to consider a lawyer as a person primarily engaged in his work because of a driving sense of justice. The common perception is that they are rather like the bank manager of old, who would be available to dispense good, altruistic advice for a reasonable fee.

In fact, with exceptions, solicitors are businessmen, who operate a business where the overheads and staff costs are high, and the pressure of maintaining cash flows and obtaining clients is as tough as in any other field. There is often tremendous pressure on staff to meet their targets for invoicing clients. Increasingly, firms of solicitors are becoming more commercial and entrepreneurial in their approach.

This is, of course, fair enough, and no one can expect solicitors to be non-profit-making. After all, they operate in a competitive market and have every right to make as much money as they can in the area of work that they have chosen. You should understand that, at the end of the day, the relationship between you and your solicitor is a commercially driven one – albeit with some limiting factors imposed by the Law Society (the solicitors' governing body).

You will face two main problems when employing a solicitor. The first is that of obtaining an assessment of the cost of an action, prior to commencing proceedings. Unfortunately, this is virtually impossible for any lawyer to foresee, due to the erratic and unpredictable course of litigation. Cases can settle very quickly and suddenly, or they may proceed, though rarely, all the way to a full hearing. Even then, it can be hard to predict exactly how long a hearing may last, given the fact that the case may still settle halfway through a trial. Accordingly, you can find yourself engaged in a court case, but with no idea of your own legal costs.

The second problem is that without precise knowledge of the process of a case you can quickly lose control, and effectively have to trust your solicitor to conduct your case. It is therefore hard to monitor progress, and to know whether or not your solicitor is taking the right approach and pushing the matter forward efficiently. The only answer is for you to have a reasonable knowledge of the process.

Finally, it must be said that your solicitor is not the only controlling factor in the progress of your case. Significant delays (and costs) can be caused by your opponent or his solicitor – either intentionally or through incompetence. The court process can also create delays, either because of cumbersome procedure, or sometimes because a judge allows your opponent what may seem an inordinate amount of time to process his part of the case.

A Specialist in the Area

Ensure that the solicitor chosen specializes in litigation; if the area of the case is very particular, then he should also have specific knowledge. If the matter concerns a building problem then a solicitor specializing in this area should be employed. Equally, if you are suing another solicitor for negligence, employ a solicitor who specializes in conducting actions against other solicitors. The Law Society can provide details of solicitors specializing in different matters.

Competence

Solicitors, like all other professionals, differ in their levels of competence. Properly research the firm of solicitors that you are going to use, and find out how good the firm actually is and, importantly, how effective is the partner or assistant solicitor who will be dealing with the matter.

Choosing a good solicitor is as difficult as trying to establish how good any professional is. A personal recommendation is probably the best way of choosing one. Even this can be less than reliable, however, unless the person recommending the solicitor has actually had dealings with that particular individual, and on the type of matter in which you are involved.

Find out whether your proposed solicitor has experience as an advocate – and if so, how much, and whether he has a good reputation. This may save you the additional cost of employing a barrister to present your case at trial. All solicitors now have rights of audience in county courts, but only some have the same rights in the High Court. Make sure that you discuss with your solicitor the pros and cons of his acting as your advocate at trial. If he is evasive about this matter, then seriously consider going to another solicitor. It should be stressed that the fact that a solicitor is not a good advocate, or chooses not to present cases personally, does not indicate that he is a poor solicitor. It can mean, however, that at some stage you may have to rely quite heavily on a barrister. This is not necessarily a more expensive option – it depends on the circumstances.

Charges

Obtain from your solicitor a full breakdown of the charges that will be made for any work performed. Solicitors charge for their time and that of their employees at hourly or part-hourly rates. Each member of staff will have a standard rate within the firm, so there will be a scale of decreasing charges between a partner, assistant solicitor, legal executive, trainee solicitor, unqualified clerk and so on. All letters, attendance notes and other actions will be costed on a time basis, depending on who did the work.

You must know exactly what all these charges are, what level of solicitor will be dealing with the day-to-day matter, and the terms of payment for the work. You must be particularly fierce about what are called **disbursements** – non-timed costs, covering a vast range of miscellaneous items – which can significantly increase your bills. Examples of these are postage, document deliveries and photocopying (ask how much you will be charged per sheet and the likely volume, given your case). Other disbursements will relate to any travelling your solicitor may have to do, for example to get witness statements, and to court fees, witness expenses, experts' fees and barrister's fees. Do not be embarrassed to ask about these costs in detail, and again, if you feel your solicitor is reluctant to tell you, then find another one who will. Disbursements are not just incidental to your main bill – they can amount to a great deal of money.

It is now a rule of professional conduct that solicitors clearly explain the basis on which they charge. This does not mean they have to quote an all-in price at the outset, but you must be told what charges will be included and how the pricing structure works. Failure to inform you may result in disciplinary action – at worst, 'striking off', leaving the solicitor unable to practise.

Generally, solicitors will want money on account – that is, in advance – before they will commence work. If you are legally aided, this is irrelevant to you. It is wise, however, even if you are legally aided, to insist on interim billing throughout the course of your proceedings, so that you can keep track of your lawyer's bill. You can insist on being billed monthly, or perhaps bi-monthly, or once an agreed figure has been reached – for example, £500 or £1,000. Any of these methods is a real help, because your solicitor constantly has to talk to you about the costs. Be absolutely clear what is or is not VAT-inclusive. Also, if you ever want to change solicitors, it is easy to do so when you have paid up to date. Otherwise, your solicitor can retain your files until he has been paid – a most effective way of preventing you moving.

Even after a clear negotiation as to costs, it can still be quite hard to see how a solicitor costs his actual time, and you must be wary of being invoiced with high charges for ill-defined matters such as 'perusing the file' or 'collating documents'. Equally, ask your lawyer directly if, and when, he will apply the notorious **uplift**. This may be added to your bill in the light of complexities that your solicitor may have had to work on. Obtain an assurance that this will not occur without fair warning to you.

Never be afraid to challenge any part of an invoice you feel is unjustified – and always check any bill rigorously. Always record in writing (preferably in a confirmatory letter to your solicitor) all agreements about costs, and complain straight away, in writing, if you have any objections.

Finally, try to make sure that you do not unwittingly increase costs by not telling your solicitor everything he needs to know, however obvious or trivial you may think it. This does not mean that you should spend hours going over every point. It does, however, mean that thought and preparation when briefing your solicitor can keep costs down. Before you actually instruct a solicitor, sit down and write a full, objective account of the situation. Do this chronologically, and cross-reference it to documents detailing the problem and its background.

Try not to telephone your solicitor without first making a note of everything you want to tell or ask him. Clients who make frequent telephone calls with snippets of information or uncollated questions will find their bills running out of control. Remember, every call and conversation will be timed, and is costing you money – even if most of the conversation is about the weather. Alongside this, try to give your solicitor notice of the best time of day, and location, where he can contact you, and any times during which you may be unavailable. He should reciprocate, so that your lines of communication are clear, open and cost-efficient.

Managing your Lawyer

Manage and monitor your lawyer. It is simply not good enough to behave as if the lawyer is a superior type of human being, who instinctively knows right, and can be left free to conduct your case. Uppermost in your mind should be the fact that the solicitor dealing with the case has nothing to lose and, rather like a broker, makes his money regardless of the outcome. Indeed, the longer the case continues, the more it is to the benefit of the solicitor – in providing him with work and fees.

Litigation solicitors can be particularly aggressive in conducting actions. This is a valuable quality in many ways, and you certainly do not want to employ a docile lawyer. This quality needs to be tempered, however, with a readiness to find a way of resolving the dispute before a court hearing.

Ensure that your solicitor is constantly trying to find a way of resolving the matter as quickly as possible, rather than just single-mindedly pursuing the court action. In some ways it is easier for your lawyer to go through the process of the legal action than to exercise ways of negotiating and settling your case.

Litigation solicitors often have formidable case-loads and are under considerable pressure, both from clients who are stressed and emotional, and the driving business pressure to do work that is billable. Accordingly, many cases can suffer from insufficient analysis. It is therefore critical that you ensure your solicitor gives due consideration to your particular case – and that a clear, agreed strategy is followed, with frequent in-depth reappraisals.

You must understand, from the start, the process by which your case will proceed. Get your solicitor to write out briefly, and explain, the anticipated court process, the approximate time-periods involved, the costs applicable, the options available and the optimum periods for negotiation and reappraisal. This should knit in with the interim billing process, and your solicitor should be able to indicate to you the cost-intensive periods (in terms of both your time and his).

An outline understanding of the process, and what it involves, will enable you to follow what is happening right from the start and monitor the case together with the performance of your solicitor.

Barristers ('Counsel')

Apart from presenting cases in court, barristers also prepare technical court documents (**pleadings**) and affidavits, and assess the merits of individual cases. The sooner the latter is done the better, although a barrister can only assess the case on the cold facts presented to him, and these facts, to be adequate, may take some time for your solicitor to obtain and collate.

Barristers are well placed to assess disputes objectively, having had little, if anything, to do with you personally. Their day-to-day experience of the realities of trials also enables them to assess the viability of a case. That said, they sometimes have a disconcerting habit of being very bullish about a case when you first see them but losing confidence in it as the trial approaches.

It is vital that you know how good or bad your case is as soon as possible and, in an important matter, try to get your solicitor to brief a barrister early on. You must see a copy of your solicitor's written brief to check that the barrister has been given an accurate summary of your case.

If a case does go to trial, and a barrister is employed to present it, then ensure that he is familiar with the case and knows the full details of the matter. If possible, have a conference with him not more than a week but not less than 48 hours before the start date of the trial. At that meeting, satisfy yourself that he is capable of dealing with the action. Occasionally, a barrister will not have been adequately briefed by your solicitor, or had enough time to give the matter the attention it deserves. There is also the unnerving prospect that the barrister who has been dealing with your case and is scheduled to present it may be unable to do so because of a clash of commitments. If this happens, satisfy yourself that the new barrister has a proper working knowledge of the case, and all its details and subtleties.

In any meeting with a barrister make sure that you understand what he is saying. Ask questions, and seek any clarification you need. At the end of the day, it is you who are paying for his experience and judgement; you are the employer. Do not be intimidated. Your viewpoint is valid and should be considered. Furthermore, you may raise a matter that your lawyers might have missed or forgotten. Certainly, this is no time to be a shrinking violet.

The importance of a well presented case cannot be stressed too highly, both in terms of the oral delivery of argument and the paperwork, which should always be orderly, clear and in paginated bundles. A judge can only react to what he sees and hears, and if the presentation is poor or omits pertinent information, then your case may fail. Money and time is well spent to ensure excellent presentation. There really is no place for penny-pinching if the matter is to be heard at a trial, and you must ensure that you hire the best possible barrister for the case, even if this is very expensive – the risks of failure at this stage are too great to do otherwise.

THE COURT PROCESS (ENGLAND AND WALES)

While the intricacies of conducting a case and taking it all the way to a hearing can be very complex, the basic framework is reasonably simple to follow. The principle behind civil cases is that all the material facts and arguments must be in a state acceptable to a court, prior to any final hearing. Each side in a case also has the right to see what evidence the other possesses, and to know before the trial what evidence is going to be presented. The final hearing or trial will then result in a presentation of both sides' cases, which will be assessed by a judge once he has seen and heard all the evidence.

Matters tend to take a long time to get to a final hearing. The courts insist on allowing a fair time for each party to prepare their case properly, and to disclose to the other party the evidence that they intend to use. There are fixed stages for the process of an action, which have to be completed before a court will be willing to hear the actual trial. These stages can involve sometimes lengthy and acrimonious interim court hearings (**interlocutory hearings**) to deal with the administrative process of the case. They are normally presided over by a district judge, whose responsibility it is to see that the case proceeds to trial within a given time-frame, and that the case is in a condition fit to be heard at trial. The trial judge needs to be assured that the case will proceed without technical or administrative impediments getting in the way.

TYPICAL COUNTY COURT ACTION (ABOVE THE ARBITRATION LIMIT)

Prior to Court Action

The following is an account of an idealized or 'normal' case. In reality few cases are normal, and timings and procedure can vary significantly.

Pre-action Correspondence

A detailed letter should be sent to your opponent, clearly itemizing the reasons for the dispute. This must give the other party the opportunity to make rectification. The letter may set a deadline after which court action will be taken without further notice. Alternatively, a further letter (letter before action) will be sent, stating that legal proceedings will be started after seven days, should the dispute remain unresolved.

Court Action

Summons

A summons is the formal claim of the injured party and will be issued to set out clearly the facts of the dispute, and detail the loss that the plaintiff (the injured party) has sustained. At this stage nothing is stated about how the loss will be proved, or by whom.

Defence

A defence, with a possible counterclaim, must be filed at court by the party sued (the defendant), from where it will be sent to the plaintiff, usually within 14 days of service of the summons.

Counterclaim

A **counterclaim** is where the defendant claims for a loss sustained by him due to some action of the plaintiff relating to the matter at hand. If the defendant has filed a counterclaim with the defence, then the plaintiff must also file and serve a defence to it, normally within 14 days.

Once a defence has been issued the court will send a schedule to each side, setting out the time-limits for the steps below. Dates will be given by which the specified functions should be carried out. If they are not, then either party can apply to the court, either to extend the scheduled time or to force the other party to comply. Sometimes non-compliance brings automatic failure to a case. If you are the plaintiff, always be clear as to the date by which you must apply for the trial date (**setting down for trial**). Failure to do this can bring a premature and disastrous end to your case.

List of Documents

Each party must prepare a list of the documents relevant to his case, whether helpful or harmful. These documents must be made available to the other party for inspection, who can then also request copies (although he will have to pay for the photocopying). You can only withhold **privileged** documents – usually your lawyer's advice and correspondence.

Witness Statements

Any witness statements, including experts' reports, must be exchanged between the parties. There are effectively two types of witnesses. The first are those whose involvement in the matters under dispute has to be presented to prove the case one way or another. The second type is the expert witness. These are allowed to comment on the evidence in the case, both documents and witness statements, and to say why they support your case. Only experts can give **opinion** evidence. Normally there is a limit to the number allowed to be called by each side. Make sure that you can justify to a district judge why you need an expert witness.

Photographs and Sketch Plans

Prior to the trial, these should be provided to the other party and an agreement as to their accuracy obtained.

Listing Information Form

This standard court form should be filled in by both parties and sent to the court. It specifies the estimated duration of the trial, the likely number of witnesses and any dates or special factors that could be material to the scheduling of the trial by the court.

Defendant's Documentation

At a specified date before the trial, the defendant must advise the plaintiff of the documents that he intends to use during the trial.

Court Documentation

At a specified date before the trial the plaintiff must prepare a bundle of all the documents relating to the case, including the defendant's documents, witness statements and particulars. These are then sent to the court. It is a vital part of the plaintiff's responsibility to ensure that these documents are neatly indexed and paginated into a bundle. You must, of course, keep a copy of the bundle yourself and provide the defendant with one if he so requests – although he has to pay your copying charges.

The Trial

The vast majority of cases never get to trial and are settled one way or another before the trial itself – sometimes very soon after a summons has been issued. However, brinkmanship often occurs where one party may wait right up until the day of the trial before suddenly settling the case. Indeed, it is quite common for negotiations to settle a case to be conducted not just at the door of the court, but also during the proceedings themselves, particularly during lunch breaks or at the end of the trial day.

If the case does go to trial then it will be heard and decided by a judge who, before the trial starts, will sometimes have read the court papers on the matter. He may therefore have a reasonably good idea of the outline of the dispute. However, this cannot be taken for granted, and a plaintiff (or his lawyer) should always open the case by summarizing the dispute and presenting evidence to support their arguments. They must do this orally, explaining the matter fully and directing the judge to any key documents, or parts of documents, that support their case. The plaintiff may also call witnesses to help him, who may be either expert or lay witnesses. The former are particularly important as they can present evidence of opinion as well as facts, whilst the latter can only recount facts.

Any witness called by the plaintiff to give evidence will first be asked questions by the plaintiff. Once this has occurred the defendant (or his lawyer) will be able to question the witness, in an effort to give the judge a look at the circumstances of the case from his perspective. This may place the plaintiff's evidence in a wholly different context. If necessary, the plaintiff, and then the defendant, can again question the witness to clarify any of the evidence.

Once the plaintiff has finished presenting his arguments and evidence in support of his case, the defendant will then be able to present his side of the dispute. As with the plaintiff, he will argue his case both orally and by using relevant documents. He can also call witnesses, whom he will examine first, before the plaintiff is allowed to question them.

When the defendant has finished presenting his evidence, the judge will be in a position to give a judgement on the matter. This is normally done immediately after the defendant has finished, but the judge may delay giving judgement, perhaps for some days, if he finds he needs time in which to consider the matter. In this event, the plaintiff and defendant will be given a time at which to return to the court to hear the judgement. Sometimes, where a prompt judgement is vital, the judge will make his decision and then reserve his reasons until a later date.

When giving judgement, the judge will usually first give a summary of the case and the evidence he has heard. He will then give reasons for his judgement, before finally making the judgement order that he considers correct. Once he has done this, he will give the parties an opportunity to address him on who should pay the costs of the case.

Costs

The basic rule is that 'costs follow the event' – that is, whoever wins the case has his costs paid by the loser. However, there can be good reasons for departing from this, such as where there has been a payment into court (see below) or where a judge decides one party has acted unreasonably in his conduct of some or all of the case. In particular, a judge can make **wasted costs** orders against parties to an action. This is important to realize. Ensure when you are conducting a case that you present only relevant evidence. If you do not then, even if you win the case, you may be penalized on costs.

Payment into court can be of vital importance in a case where payment of a sum is claimed. Once a summons is issued a defendant can 'pay into court' a sum that he says represents the proper amount due from him to the plaintiff. He must include any interest owed when making this payment, which stays in a court account until either the plaintiff accepts it in settlement of the dispute, or a judge gives his judgement on the issues.

If the sum paid into court is equal to, or more than, what the judge awards (including interest) then the defendant will have to pay the plaintiff's costs up to the date of the payment into court. However, the plaintiff will have to pay the costs of the case (including the defendant's costs) from the date of the payment into court.

Payment into court is a very important tactical device. If a plaintiff is given notification of the payment of a sum of money into court, he normally has 21 days to decide whether to accept the 'payment in' or not. Not accepting a sensible payment into court can result in dire consequences for costs, should the case proceed to trial and the plaintiff be awarded only the amount paid in, or less. This tactic enables a defendant who pays a well-considered sum into court to place very real pressure upon a plaintiff to settle the case. The judge at the trial is not allowed to know about any payment into court – until he decides upon the matter of costs.

Judges

Judges in the County Court are used to people representing themselves (**litigants in person**) and on the whole take pains to ensure that a litigant is able to present his own case, notwithstanding his lack of legal experience. They will not allow bullying in court by a more experienced litigant or lawyer, and are usually genuinely concerned to establish the truth behind a dispute. Certainly, there is no reason why, if you are fairly articulate and organized, you cannot represent yourself, even if a lawyer is acting for your opponent.

During the trial it is critical to remember that the judge can only decide the matter on the basis of the evidence that has been directly presented to him, either in oral or documentary form. It is therefore imperative that you attend the trial and make sure that the evidence supporting your arguments is actually used. If you have a lawyer, and you think that he has forgotten, or is neglecting, to present certain evidence then you must bring this to his attention. During the trial, you can pass your lawyer notes and whisper to him if necessary. Make certain that you know why evidence that you believe to be material to your case is not used, if your lawyer will not present it to the judge. This is no time to be shy, and if you wait until after the judgement to query what your lawyer has done, it could then be too late. That said, there is a balance to be maintained, and you should take care not to disrupt your lawyer too much, particularly while he is in the middle of submitting an argument.

Apart from the critical role of making a judgement at the end of the case, the judge has two main functions. He is responsible for ensuring that the trial is an orderly affair, conducted fairly and following a proper procedure. Secondly, the judge is responsible for ensuring that rules of evidence are followed. In principle, evidence is admissible if it is relevant to the case, although for real value it needs to be independently supported. So, while hearsay can be admissible and relevant, it can suffer from a lack of corroboration.

It is important that you take careful note of the judge's reasoning for the judgement given, while he is speaking, as you may subsequently decide that you disagree with his reasoning and wish to appeal. In this event, an accurate note can be invaluable, since you (or your lawyer) can immediately study it in detail for any flaws.

Giving Evidence and Cross-Examination

It is not always necessary to discredit the other side's witnesses to secure victory. Disputes rarely arise because somebody is lying – more often it is because perceptions of a problem differ. Cross-examination can draw out more background on a case and place a different context on the issues, rather than breaking a witness down Perry Mason fashion. Most judges will stop lawyers, or indeed litigants in person, from haranguing a witness, and particularly from wearing them down with repetitive questioning.

If you are giving evidence there are two golden rules:

- Always listen to the question and answer what you are asked. Don't answer the question you *want* to hear, only what you *do* hear. Keep your answers short – yes or no if possible, and *never* volunteer additional information. If you don't understand something or need a moment to think, say so; if you don't remember, say so. Don't say what you assume the questioner wants to hear. If you feel your brief answers lead to your evidence being dealt with out of context, this can be cleared up in **re-examination** – by your lawyer asking you to clear up confusion, or, if you are a litigant in person, by doing so yourself. There is no reason why, if you are a litigant in person, you should not ask the judge if you can make a note to remind yourself of the points you want to deal with in re-examination.

- Never argue or lose your temper. This is always disastrous, whether it is with your opponent, his lawyer or the judge.

When giving evidence or cross-examining it is likely that the judge will be taking notes by hand himself. Watch his pen and slow your evidence or examination down to tie in with the speed with which he can record what is being said.

Finally, you cannot speak to anyone else about your evidence while you are giving it. If there is an adjournment for lunch or overnight then you will not be able to speak to your lawyer at all except in very exceptional circumstances. It is vital therefore to have gone through everything thoroughly with your lawyer before the trial, and certainly before you give evidence. This is why plaintiff and defendant always give evidence first in their respective cases – so that, once they have finished giving their evidence, they can talk to their lawyer when other witnesses are called.

Appeals

Appeals are normally available only if a judge goes wrong on a matter of law. A judge cannot be appealed against because he drew adverse conclusions on facts, such as preferring one witness to another – unless to do so was completely irrational, or what lawyers would call 'perverse'.

Most appeals must be made within 28 days of the judgement. This makes clear note-taking during a case important, as obtaining court transcripts can take up valuable time, and it may be vital to know exactly what the judge said in order to assess whether or not to appeal. A judge can be asked to amend his own judgement.

Enforcement of Judgement Order

Unfortunately, obtaining judgement against an opponent is not always the end of the matter. If your opponent does not obey the judgement order, then you will have to take measures to enforce it. This is not something that a court will do unless you initiate the appropriate action first, so do not rely upon the court to do anything at all after a judgement order has been made. They will not try to extract money from a person – unless and until you make the appropriate enforcement application.

If the judgement is for money to be paid to you by your opponent, then you have four main options to choose from, if he refuses to pay you:

Warrant of Execution

This gives a court-appointed bailiff the right to go to your opponent's home and demand payment of the money owed. If this is not forthcoming the bailiff can then seize your opponent's possessions to the value of the debt, and sell them at an auction. Any money gained will be paid to you, until the debt is fully paid off.

Attachment of Earnings Order

This is an order that tells your opponent's employer to deduct a nominated sum from his salary and send it to the court, who will then pass it on to you. The amount to be deducted will be decided by the court once they have considered how much your opponent can afford to pay. He will be able to retain sufficient money from his salary to enable him to cover his basic expenses.

Charging Order

This is an order that prevents your opponent from selling or transferring his property (i.e. land) until he has paid the judgement debt to you. You can also apply to the court for an order to force him to sell his property in order to pay the debt, although complications arise where, as is common, property is jointly owned – for example, between husband and wife.

Remember also that although anyone can now 'inspect' the records held at the Land Registry, not all land is registered, and you have to be able to identify property correctly to be able to search for its proper owner. You cannot just ask the Land Registry to do a search on all land owned by Mr X.

Garnishee Order

This is an order that prevents your opponent from removing any money from his bank or building society accounts. The money will be paid directly to you. A garnishee order can also be sent to someone who owes your opponent money. In this case, they would have to pay the money directly to you, not your opponent, until the debt was fully paid.

All of the above methods of enforcement must first be formally applied for, by yourself, to the court. A fee attaches to each method and, depending on the circumstances of your opponent, the court may refuse to make one of the orders as they are all fraught with individual complexities. The courts have no power to remove from anyone every possession they own, and if your opponent is poor and has few possessions you may well end up with a derisory court order for your opponent to pay you a tiny sum, each month, over a long period. If this is the case, then your judgement against him will, in reality, be worth very little – and may have been a costly exercise.

A further way that you can place pressure upon someone who has not paid you, after a judgement debt has been awarded against him, is to start the first steps towards publicly declaring him insolvent. If someone has not paid a judgement debt then you are entitled to conclude that he is unable to pay the debt and is insolvent. You can therefore obtain and serve on the debtor a special type of request for payment, called a **statutory demand**, which will threaten bankruptcy for the debtor or, in the case of a company, liquidation. You may need a lawyer to help you process the paperwork correctly.

Statutory demands do not themselves begin the relevant insolvency proceedings. They are only the precursor, but their service on a debtor does tend to concentrate the mind and can produce payment where other means of enforcement are unlikely to succeed. That said, the courts do not like insolvency proceedings to be used for debt collection and it would be unwise to go beyond the statutory demand stage without taking legal advice.

If you are uncertain which enforcement order to apply for, you can first apply to the court for an **oral examination**. This means that your opponent will be told to attend the court with relevant documents on his asssets, earnings and outgoings. You can then attend and examine this paperwork, and ask your opponent, in the presence of a court officer, what money or other assets he possesses. With this knowledge you can choose the most effective enforcement order to apply for. However, although the court formally 'conducts' the investigation they will not undertake any preliminary work, and to some extent you have to accept what the debtor says unless it is obviously unlikely, contradictory or downright incredible. Wherever possible it is worth making your own investigations, prior to the examination, to find out all you can about the debtor's means. It can sometimes be well worth employing a professional enquiry agent or private detective to do this work.

Enforcing a judgement can be a slow and depressing task, particularly if your opponent does not co-operate. In this case, he can delay matters for a long time, particularly as the courts are normally very reluctant to imprison a debtor for contempt of court when he has not complied with court orders. Also, at the end of the day, if your opponent has no money or possessions, then no amount of applying for enforcement orders will ever get the debt paid. It really is vital to check, before starting any court action, that your opponent is worth suing – if not, then it is better to swallow your pride and not bother to take action!

The above is a somewhat simplistic picture of a county court process, but it does provide the basic framework. Remember that at any point in the procedure a settlement may be reached, or you and your opponent may ask the court for time in which to negotiate. The process can often be somewhat erratic, as either you or your opponent may need further clarification of each other's case, or may be slow about meeting the requirements of each of the above stages, which would require further court involvement. Further particulars may be required of a claim or defence, and these may also take some time to obtain.

There may be occasions when you need more time to complete one of the above stages, perhaps because you have been ill, or are simply having trouble obtaining the necessary evidence. If this is the case, always apply to the court for further time as soon as possible. Otherwise, if you do not comply with the timings set out in the schedule, or as ordered by a district judge, you can find that, as plaintiff, your case is **struck out** or, as defendant, that judgement has been entered against you. Either way this can be disastrous.

A useful tip for litigants presenting their own case is that deadlines are set by the dates that they are deemed (by court rules) to arrive at their destination – not the date of posting. Whenever possible, go to or telephone the court to check that your documents have been safely received. If you think that your opponent should have filed documents at court, but you have not received them, then find out why not.

The critical parts of the process, apart from the trial itself, are essentially the first five points above (before the preparation of the pro forma court form), during which time you and your opponent will be assembling the evidence for your respective cases. As this becomes available you will be able to assess the strength of the other's case, and decide on the risk of continuing the action. There is nothing to stop 'without prejudice' negotiations taking place during the course of the court action.

SUMMARY

- A basic knowledge of civil law, particularly consumer rights, is essential.

- Try hard to resolve a dispute long before lawyers and courts become involved.

- If you enter into a contract, be prepared for it to end in a dispute.

- Keep a full record, during the term of a contract, of all actions and conversations and put into writing anything of importance.

- Manage escalation of a dispute stage by stage, allowing maximum opportunity for the matter to be resolved.

- Use mediating services wherever possible.

- Consider going to lawyers or court only as a last resort – but do not allow the other party to recognize your reluctance.

- Assess a case with great care before suing or being sued and work out a clear strategy with which to deal with the dispute.

- Do not be afraid to litigate without a lawyer if the dispute is reasonably simple or the value low.

- Manage and monitor your lawyer, his actions and performance, and ensure you have an outline of the process the case will follow.

- Constantly appraise the case as it proceeds to trial, and recognize when a climb-down may be necessary.

Appendix 1

Buying and Selling Property in Scotland

THE process for buying and selling property in Scotland is different from that of England, Wales and Northern Ireland. The general consensus is that it is a more efficient process, and it is quite likely that elements of the Scottish process will, at some stage in the future, be adopted into English conveyancing.

The chief benefit that Scottish law brings to conveyancing is that once the offer has been finally accepted the contract is binding. This allows greater certainty to the purchase process. In English law, an offer is not binding and can be withdrawn right up until contracts are exchanged. This makes the problems of **gazumping** (where a new buyer makes a higher offer than the one already accepted) and **gazundering** (where the person whose offer has been accepted subsequently changes it to a lower offer) common in England. In Scotland this cannot easily be done. Once the offer has been made and accepted, that is the end of the matter. There is a binding contract in place for the sale of the property. If the property is not conveyed, then there is a breach of contract.

This degree of certainty has benefits for both the buyer and the seller. The seller knows that once an offer has been made by the buyer, and he has accepted it, the sale will go through. He can therefore confidently make a firm offer on any other property he finds. This would not be the case in England where chains of property conveyances can form, with everyone in the chain awaiting the catalyst of exchange of contracts. Until this occurs, all the buyers and sellers are left dangling in a stressful limbo.

For the buyer, the Scottish system is of benefit because he knows that, once he has made his offer and it has been accepted, the purchase will go ahead – no other offer from another buyer can be accepted by the seller, regardless of how much it is.

THE SYSTEM

Unlike the English property system of freehold and leasehold, in Scotland there is a system of **feudal tenure**. In this form of property holding the original estate owner or developer of the land (the **superior**) can impose conditions on a property regarding its future use. These conditions will affect new owners of the property, and can prevent them from doing what they wish with their land. For example, there may be a condition preventing any alterations to the property or restricting its use. These conditions are permanent, although they can be waived if the original owner or developer of the property so allows (usually for a fee). If the superior is unreasonable, then you can apply to the **Lands Tribunal of Scotland,** who will rule on the relevant condition. The title deeds of a property should always be carefully checked for conditions before you buy.

Property is normally put up for sale on the basis of either **offers over** (also known as the **upset price**) or a **fixed price.** 'Offers over' indicates the minimum price for which the seller will sell his property. He will not usually negotiate below this price. A 'fixed price' indicates that the seller will accept the first offer made at the price stated. This latter is normally put forward when a quick sale is required, and you should recognize that you may have to act fast.

If the seller finds that he has more than one person interested in buying his property, he may choose to set a **closing date** by which time all offers must be forwarded to his solicitor. None of the prospective buyers will know the price offered by the others. The seller is, however, at liberty to choose which offer he is prepared to accept – regardless of whether or not it is the highest price.

All conveyancing is performed by solicitors; Scotland has no licensed conveyancers as yet. The solicitors have a greater role in property than their English counterparts and also act as estate agents in selling and negotiating the sale of most properties. It is critical that you go through a solicitor, and that you are careful not to make any written offers or acceptances – except through them. Oral offers and acceptances to buy are not legally binding, but remember that offers in writing are, once they have been accepted.

BUYING PROPERTY: THE LEGAL PROCESS

There are seven stages to buying a property in Scotland:

Preparation

Because the process of buying is often quick, you must first find a solicitor to act for you on any purchase. He will be able to advise you in detail about the procedure for buying, and his input will be critical once you find a property you like. As with all professionals, make sure that you obtain a quote from him for his work and any outlays (**disbursements**). If you have little experience of Scottish conveyancing, make sure you get him to write you a note as to the procedure and your part in it.

Before seriously going to look for a property, obtain a mortgage offer in principle, for the amount you need to cover you for any intended purchase. Then locate a surveyor who will be able to undertake a survey of any property you find. He must be acceptable to your lender. Your solicitor will be able to help you find a surveyor, and should be able to advise you on your mortgage.

Initial Interest

Once you have found a property that you like, advise your solicitor, so that he can inform the seller's solicitor of your interest. At this stage there is nothing to stop you negotiating orally with the seller about the property and any fixtures and fittings. You can also try discussing the price, although this will normally result in your being asked to place this in writing. Do this through your solicitor; do not agree anything *at all* in writing directly with the seller.

Finance and Survey

Advise your lender (if you need a mortgage) that you have found a property you wish to buy, and arrange, normally through your solicitor, for a survey to be done on the property. All lenders will require this as a matter of course. If you do not need a mortgage, then it is not compulsory to have a survey, although it is always wise to have this done prior to any binding agreement.

Before you make any formal offer to buy the property, make sure that your lender will provide you with the amount you will require should your offer be accepted.

Offer to Buy

Once you have received the results of the survey, and confirmation that your lender will provide you with the necessary mortgage, you are in a position to make an offer. This must be done through your solicitor. He will write a formal letter setting out your offer, subject to various conditions.

The conditions expressing the terms on which you are willing to buy the property will be set out in a schedule attached to the offer letter. These conditions will concern matters such as the **entry date** – the date on which you pay over the price and obtain access to the property, and the date by which the seller must leave. The conditions will also concern miscellaneous matters such as any purchase of fixtures and fittings, legalities as to title and any outstanding local authority proposals that may be material to your purchase.

Missives

The seller's solicitor (subject to the seller's acceptance of your offer) will then write back to your solicitor with a qualified acceptance of your offer, subject to conditions. The solicitors will then negotiate, through a series of letters (**missives**), the conditions of sale. The seller may also put forward specific conditions, perhaps the entry date that would suit him, which need your attention. You must therefore be available to answer your solicitor's queries as the negotiations proceed.

Negotiation through the missives may take only a few days, or greatly longer if the matter is complex. You must leave all the writing of the missives to your solicitor, as these documents have legal importance in their own right. Once full agreement over the missives has been reached between you and the seller, there will be a binding agreement in force for the sale of the property.

The date of entry is crucial to this agreement, and will be specified, often some six to eight weeks in advance. The agreement will comprise the written offer and the other formal letters, which together are known as the missives.

Concluding Legalities, Mortgage

Once the missives have been finalized, your solicitor will examine the title deeds of the property and make any further necessary investigations concerning the title of the property. These will include investigations into local authority matters such as roads and sewers and any planning proposals or notices affecting the property. He will also prepare a **Disposition**, confirming the change of ownership of the property to the purchaser's name.

You should finalize your mortgage application, if any, and ensure that you have the finances ready and available for the entry date. Your solicitor will help with this and make sure that the loan required will cover the amount you need, and be ready for the entry date. You will have to sign a **standard security**, which is the deed securing the loan on your property.

Settlement

On the entry date your solicitor will have the cheque for the purchase price of the property delivered to the seller's solicitor in return for the title deeds and Disposition – the document that formally sets out the change in ownership on the title deeds. You will obtain the keys to the property and now have full rights of access.

Finally, your solicitor will forward the Disposition to the Inland Revenue for stamping if the price is over £60,000 and will register the Disposition, showing the change of ownership, together with the standard security in favour of the lender with the **Land Register** or **Register of Sasines**.

SELLING YOUR PROPERTY: THE LEGAL PROCESS

There are six stages to selling your property.

Preparation

When you decide to sell your property, you should contact your solicitor and advise him of this. Often it will be your solicitor who actually sells the property, but there is nothing to stop you from trying to find a buyer yourself, or placing the sale in the hands of estate agents. Either way, your solicitor still needs to be involved straight away. He will need to check the title deeds of your property, any loan still outstanding from your lender and the status of any charges on your property. He will also make local authority searches in readiness for any buyer. If your solicitor is both selling the house for you and performing the conveyancing, you should negotiate a package of costs before he starts any work. Be warned that you must not agree anything in writing with a potential buyer, except through your solicitor. If you do, you could find yourself with a binding agreement that could be very disadvantageous to you. Always take legal advice first.

Offers

Your solicitor will advise you of any interest in the property. If a formal offer is made, and you accept this, then you will instruct your solicitor accordingly – having first discussed any conditions that you wish to impose. It may be that you need time in which to find another property. In this case one of your conditions might be that the entry date should not be for a long time – perhaps two months. You may wish to agree other conditions, such as your removal of some particular fixture from the property. You may also find that the buyer is asking you to warrant certain aspects of the property such as the central heating. Make sure you understand and accept all the buyer's conditions – through your solicitor – before finally agreeing to his offer.

Missives

Your solicitor, having sent a qualified acceptance of the offer, will negotiate with the buyer on all the various conditions put forward by yourself and the buyer. Once the conditions of sale have been agreed on to the satisfaction of both, there will be a binding agreement. You cannot then change your mind and decide not to sell, or accept a higher offer.

Legalities

Your solicitor will send the buyer's solicitor your title deeds, and searches will be performed to advise the buyer's solicitor of any impediments to the title of the property. At the same time your solicitor will be arranging with your lender (if you have one) for the redemption of the mortgage, and he will prepare a **discharge document** that the lender will sign before settlement. Your solicitor will also agree the terms of the Disposition (deed) drawn up to recognize formally the change of ownership of the property.

Settlement

On the day of settlement you will sign the disposition showing change of ownership and provide your solicitor with the house keys. Once the purchase price has been received by your solicitor you have no further right of access to the property.

Redemption of Mortgage

Once settlement has occurred your solicitor will pay off the loan to your lender, deduct his own fees and outlay, and then give you a cheque for the balance of the purchase price.

Appendix 2

Specimen Professional Schedule of Works

THE specimen schedule of works below has been extracted from a lengthy schedule, relating to remedial repairs to be performed on a house that has suffered from movement. The schedule was prepared by reputable consulting structural engineers. You should observe the following points:

- Note the detail that professionals such as structural engineers, architects and surveyors will go to in specifying the works they want done. The exact location where the work is to be carried out is stated, to avoid any doubt. The form the work is to take is clearly specified and, where appropriate, related to the relevant clause in the specification.

- Each and every aspect of the work is separately itemized. This allows for easy checking of the work and provides a full breakdown of all the costs into manageable quantities. This helps to ensure that changes in quantity, and variations to the work, are costed in a fair way.

- The four columns running down the right-hand side of the page are for the contractor to fill in, as appropriate, against each and every item. When he returns the schedule of works, his costings for the work can easily be analysed by the structural engineer and assessed against the other bidders. In practice, not all contractors will fill out all four columns. Frequently, they will just place a total cost figure against each item. This is the absolute minimum you should allow.

- Note that the costings enumerated in the columns will be net costings. Unless the contractor is not VAT-registered, VAT will be added to the end total. Check this specifically before deciding which contractor to accept. It could make a significant difference in the overall cost of the works.

- If you commission a professional to develop a schedule of works for you, make sure that it is at least as specific and detailed as the one below. If not, and there are no detailed drawings and plans, your professional may not be doing his work properly. To be effective, a schedule of works must be comprehensive and very detailed.

- The specification (see Appendix 3) answers both general and specific queries a builder could have concerning how to perform the work. It ties him to practices that the structural engineer expressly wishes to see performed during the work.

If you develop your own schedule of works, specify what you want done in as much detail as possible. You may be unable to state exactly how the work should be done technically, but you must define clearly the works or alterations you require. Separate every item into its smallest denominator. This will concentrate your mind, and will also allow you to cut out areas easily, if the costings returned by the contractors exceed your budget.

Attach any photographs or drawings to the schedule that may help further explain the work you want done.

Appelbie and Co.
Consulting Structural Engineers
51 High Street
Allshott
Essex T1B 1FU

1 May 1997

Schedule of Works for 4 The Willows, Long Lane, Allshott, Essex T1B 1UF.

To be read in conjunction with the attached Specification of Materials and Workmanship

	Time	Labour Cost	Material Cost	Total

1 *Preliminary*

1.1 Provide and use dustsheets as necessary to protect the furniture, fittings and contents.

1.2 Remove all furniture, furnishings and contents out of areas affected by the works, and allow for replacing same on completion of the works.

1.3 Ensure the security of the property throughout the works.

1.4 All rooms and areas to be left neat, clean and tidy, and free from dust etc. on completion of works to a 'builders' clean standard'.

	Time	Labour Cost	Material Cost	Total

2 *External Front*

2.1 Prepare and repair crack at junction of door frame to party wall full height (left-hand side). Plug and screw frame to wall at 500mm centres, rake out existing broken mortar, refill and cover with a silicone mastic to form a seal.

2.2 Repeat works in Item 2.1 but for full height crack on right-hand side of door frame.

2.3 Rake out crack at junction of top door to porch ceiling, repack and make good with silicone mastic.

2.4 Prepare and repair crack in stone lintel over entrance porch in front wall on left-hand side in accordance with specification clauses 3.1.1 and 3.1.2.

2.5 Repeat works in Item 2.4, but for continuation of crack in Item 2.4 up through brickwork over, in accordance with specification clauses 3.1.1, 3.1.4 and 3.2

2.6 Allow for repair and making good of all windows on front elevation, to ensure all sashes open and close fully, and where necessary add material to sashes where movement has left gaps between sashes and framework. Make good all timberwork to frames and joint between frame and stone/brickwork.

2.7 After completing all works in Items 2.1 to 2.6 allow for redecoration of front elevation. Allow for all stone and brick surfaces to receive 2 No. coats of masonry paint, all timberwork to receive 1 No. undercoat and 1 No. gloss top coat, all in accordance with the specification. Colour to be brilliant white.

	Time	Labour Cost	Material Cost	Total

3 *Landing, Main Stairs and Entrance Hall (Top Down)*

3.1 Main ceiling to upper landing is badly cracked from junction to front room wall back to downstand over top of stairs, also existing plaster is loose. Allow for taking down this area, plasterboard and skim coat as replacement, approximate area 1.6 × 3.5m.

3.2 Prepare and repair cracks over door to front room, allow for cutting back plaster, securely fixing expanded metal lath and replaster to match existing and to form a smooth, flush finish.

3.3 Prepare and repair crack in party wall of No. 6 at top of stairs, allow for insertion of 6mm diameter stainless steel ties 1.0m long across crack at 450mm centres for full height of wall above stairs, and in accordance with specification clauses 3.1.1, 3.2, 3.3 and 3.3.2.

3.4 Ensure existing door at bottom of stairs opens and closes correctly and ease as necessary.

3.5 After completion of all works in Items 3.1 to 3.4 allow for redecoration of area. Allow for lining paper to both walls and ceilings and 2 No. coats of Vinyl Silk emulsion paint to walls and ceilings, 1 No. undercoat and 1 No. gloss top coat to all woodwork, all as per specification. Colours to client's choice and approval.

(Schedule of Works continues)

Appendix 3

Specimen Professional Specification

THE sample below has been extracted from a specification produced by consulting structural engineers for insurance works to a property that has suffered from movement. It illustrates the use of a specification, which would form part of any contract with a builder. You will see that it effectively binds the builder to perform the works in a specified way. Most uncertainties concerning the way the builder tackles various jobs are eradicated.

The specification is also in clear English, and quite accessible to the layman. If you are preparing your own schedule of works for a project, it is well worth approaching structural engineers, architects or surveyors, to see if they will give you a specification to attach to your schedule. This will not normally cost very much, but is well worth while. It goes a step further towards tightening up the contract you have with your builder.

Appelbie and Co.
Consulting Structural Engineers
51 High Street
Allshott
Essex T1B 1FU
1 June 1997

Specification for 4 The Willows, Long Lane, Allshott, Essex T1B 1UF.

1 *General*

1.1   Prices to include for moving and/or protecting furniture, furnishings, fittings, fixtures and contents as necessary for access, and replacing on completion.

1.2   Heavy-duty plastic sheets should be taped down to all existing carpeted areas within the proposed work area with a double-sided tape, to ensure that no dirt or dust can be trodden or swept onto the carpets. Where sheets are lapped they should be doubly taped. Should the sheets need to be lifted prior to completion the builder should obtain agreement from the client, and before retaping, satisfy the client that the carpet is clean and undamaged. If the client should require the sheets lifted prior to final completion of the works, any dirt or damage occurring would be at the client's risk.

1.3   Each item on the schedule to be priced separately, as the insurance may pay for only part of some of the items.

1.4   Works to be phased to enable the use of the premises to continue, in agreement with Mr V. Cross.

1.5   Any variation from the works as laid down in the schedule of superstructure works or extra works which the builder or structural engineer deem to be necessary is to be agreed in writing with the structural engineer prior to the works being carried out, and any works done without prior agreement will not be considered for payment, or an allowance made on the completion date.

1.6   When extra works have been agreed with the structural engineer he will issue a structural engineer's instruction to all parties, on which the works and the time required will then be added to extend the agreed completion date.

1.7   Waste materials to be disposed of in accordance with byelaws and regulations.

2 Materials

2.1   Bricks to be clay facing bricks to BS 3921, to match existing on external surfaces.

2.2   Cement in mortar and pointing to be sulphate-resisting Portland cement to BS 4027.

2.3   Sand for mortar to comply with BS 1200.

2.4   Sand for rendering to comply with BS 1199.

2.5   Mortar and render to be of 1 : 1 : 5–6 cement : lime : sand.

2.6   Mortar for pinning-up shall be of 1 : 3 cement to sharp sand mix, with sufficient water to provide coherence but such that no water shows on the surface when the mortar is squeezed in the hand.

2.7   Epoxy mortar shall be Epoxy Plus Low Slump Mortar supplied by SBD. It shall be used in conjunction with Epoxy Plus Bonding Aid as a primer. (SBD literature attached.)

2.8   Plaster undercoat to be Carlite bonding coat, finishing coat to be Carlite finish, both supplied by British Gypsum Ltd.

2.9   Paint for the external stonework faces shall be a solvent-based undercoat and gloss paint, matching the existing. Colour to client's choice.

2.10   Paint for internal joinery shall be Dulux or similar approved paint manufactured by ICI Ltd, and the gloss finishing coat is to be the client's choice, and the recommended undercoat is to be used. The emulsion paint for ceilings is to be to the client's choice of colour; priming paint is to be lead-free and compatible with the undercoat.

2.11   Wallpaper and ceiling paper shall be to the client's choice, and of similar quality to the existing. Allowance per roll as noted in items in schedule of superstructure works. It shall be trimmed to give straight, parallel edges.

Rolls of each type shall be carefully matched for colour. Adhesive appropriate to each paper type shall be used.

2.12 External wall: After thorough preparation of the surface to receive the paint, it shall be painted with 2 No. coats of Dulux Weathershield paint or similar approved at the interval recommended by the paint manufacturer.

2.13 Tie rods to be 6mm diameter stainless steel.

3 *Workmanship*

3.1 Brick/Stonework Repair

3.1.1 Where repair by resin bonding is required in the schedule, this shall be by resin injection, and carried out either by a specialist approved by the structural engineer, or by the contractor using the method given by SBD Construction Products Ltd in their Specification 4 (copy attached, together with details of their injection kit) or Sealocrete Plus Bond 25 (copy attached, together with details of their injection kit).

3.1.2 Where resin injection is into stonework, after the injection the exposed faces of stone on each side of the crack are to be cut to form a 12mm deep neat straight groove. The surfaces of the groove are then to be primed with Epoxy Plus Bonding Aid and while this is still tacky the groove is to be solidly filled with an Epoxy Plus Low Slump Mortar. Surface to be made smooth and flush with existing stonework.

3.1.3 Where brick stitching is required to be done (*Note*: on interior, first cut back existing plaster for a minimum of 250mm each side of crack), cracked bricks are to be removed, and replaced with matching bricks. All joints are to be fully filled with mortar. Bricks are to be laid frogs up. Mortar joints on the external face are to be either struck or pointed to match existing.

(Etc.)

Appendix 4

Consumer Protection

THERE is a considerable amount of legislation protecting you, as a consumer, when you make or enter into a contract.

The principle behind the legislation is to provide consumers with a large degree of protection which they would not otherwise possess. Without this protection, the weak, or those with little knowledge of the law, would constantly be under threat from unscrupulous traders. Accordingly, terms are implied into contracts, placing restrictions on the organization or person with whom you make the contract, whether or not they are specifically written into that individual agreement (see above, p.192). If these implied terms are breached, you have a right of action against the party who has broken them. Terms in a contract which conflict with the implied terms will be found by a court to be unenforceable.

The consumer legislation, and the common law supporting it, is now comprehensive and quite complex. Consumer rights and law in Scotland broadly correspond with the law in England, Wales and Northern Ireland, although the Scottish consumer should specifically check any variations with respect to what is written below. Either way, if you think that your rights have been breached, always check the situation with your lawyer. Alternatively, go to your local **Citizens' Advice Bureau** or consumer advice centre, or contact your local **Trading Standards** (sometimes, **Consumer Protection**) **Department**. In Northern Ireland the Trading Standards Department comes under the **Department of Economic Development**. You can also contact the **Office of Fair Trading** – a government department concerned with protecting consumers and encouraging competition. They have a wide variety of free pamphlets, on a range of consumer-related matters, that clearly and simply set out your rights. The information is set out in non-legalese English and is very accessible to the layman.

The definition of 'consumer' changes between various acts, but you are safe to assume you are within the definition if:

- you are making or entering into a contract as a private individual;
- you are not making or entering into the contract as part of a business transaction to make money;
- the other party is in business, or a trader of some kind; or
- the goods are of the sort normally supplied for private use.

Consumer protection is relevant to you in several crucial areas, with regard to your property. Below is a brief outline of some of the protection afforded:

- Unfair Imposition of Terms in a Contract
- Loans and Credit
- The Supply of Goods and Services

UNFAIR IMPOSITION OF TERMS IN A CONTRACT

Broadly, the **Unfair Contract Terms Act 1977** restricts a trader's ability to limit his liability, and states that a trader cannot:

- exclude or restrict his liability for death or personal injury, or
- exclude or restrict his liability for breach of contract.

A trader can, however, restrict his liability for loss or damage due to negligence (not taking reasonable care and skill), so long as any exclusion clause is 'fair and reasonable'. Reasonableness would be looked at by a court in the light of all the circumstances known by you and the trader (or those that should have been known), your relative bargaining strengths and any special inducements, such as discounts, offered to persuade you to enter into the contract.

A trader has to negotiate any terms in a contract individually with you. If he does not do this, and you agree to a whole raft of terms that are presented to you, then the terms may be deemed unfair and therefore unenforceable by the trader. This will be the case if the unnegotiated terms are not in good faith, or create a significant imbalance in the contract between you and the trader, which is disadvantageous to you as a consumer.

It is possible to agree expressly with a trader that implied terms do not apply on a certain transaction. For example, a pot of paint may be of appalling quality, but you may nonetheless want it. If you agree to buy it, notwithstanding its quality, then this agreement will be binding. However, any agreement that purports to allow the trader to exclude the terms set out in the Unfair Contract Terms Act with regard to liability for personal injury, breach of contract etc. will be unenforceable.

Alongside the 1977 Act, the **Unfair Terms in Consumer Contracts Regulations 1994** empower the Office of Fair Trading to take action against unfair terms in a contract; under these provisions the unfair terms become void but the rest of the contract stands.

LOANS AND CREDIT

The **Consumer Credit Act 1974** regulates all credit agreements, whether cash loans, loans on goods and services supplied, or credit, hire purchase or conditional sale agreements. The loans must be for more than £100 and less than £15,000 (except where they are extortionate; see below). A consumer is defined as anyone who enters a credit agreement as an individual – and this includes partnerships, sole traders and unincorporated associations.

The four main forms of protection afforded by the Consumer Credit Act are as follows:

Equal Liability of Credit Supplier and Trader

If you use credit to buy something for over £100, up to and including £15,000, then the credit company is equally liable with the trader for any defects or problems with the goods bought. You have a choice of remedy against either the trader or the supplier of credit. It can therefore make sense to use a credit card, for example, as a further form of protection whenever you are buying goods and services. You must make sure, however, that when you enter into a credit agreement, the total amount of credit borrowed is no more than £15,000. If it is £15,001, then the Act will not apply (except in the case of an extortionate loan – see below).

Licensing of Companies Offering Credit

Anyone, whether a company or an individual, who supplies credit for amounts of £15,000 or less, as his business or as part of his business, must be licensed. It is a criminal offence if they are not, and they should be reported at once to Trading Standards officers or the police.

Clarification of Agreement

Any agreement to supply credit must be clear to the person borrowing the credit. In particular, it must make clear the total charge for credit, the **annual percentage rate** (**APR**) being charged and the exact number of payments to be made. The agreement must be personally signed by the person receiving the credit and he must be provided with a copy of the agreement with a further copy sent to him in the post.

Cancellable Agreements

The Act makes an exception to normal contract law. In certain circumstances, even when signed, a credit agreement is cancellable, albeit within a set period. This is an important protection. The reasoning behind it is to give protection to individuals who may have signed a credit agreement after pressurized selling, before they could really give the matter their full consideration.

You can cancel the agreement made and signed by you if the following apply:

- The agreement was not signed at the premises of the dealer, creditor or trader involved in the credit or the goods to be sold. If you were at home with the salesman when you signed the agreement it would be cancellable.

- There were any oral representations made at the dealer's, creditor's or trader's office, concerning the credit agreement. The agreement would not be cancellable, for example, if you walked into the creditor's offices, signed the agreement, and then talked about it. If any sales pitch was done before you signed the agreement, however, it would be cancellable.

A credit agreement will not be cancellable if you do all the negotiations through the post, and then send the agreement to the creditor.

If you do have second thoughts about going ahead with a cancellable agreement, then you must act within the set **cooling-off period**. This is any time after you have signed the agreement and up to five days after you have received the second copy of the credit agreement. You can cancel by telephone or in writing to either the trader himself or the creditor. It is generally best to follow up any cancellation by a letter, recording the date you cancelled, if this was done orally.

If you do cancel the agreement within the cooling-off period, then you must be refunded any money that you have paid as part of the agreement. You are under a duty to take reasonable care of the goods for 21 days after cancellation.

Extortionate Loans

The Consumer Credit Act 1974 gives the courts power to act when they find a consumer has entered into a credit agreement (even over £15,000) that is extortionate. In this case, the courts can alter the agreement – even to the extent of forcing the creditor to pay back excessive amounts of interest that he has received from you.

The credit agreement will be looked at as a whole, in case the excessive interest payments have been in some way disguised – as, for example, inflated costs for some other matter in the contract. For the courts to be prepared to act, however, the credit agreement must specify payments that the law defines as 'grossly extortionate', or such that they 'grossly contravene the principles of fair trading'.

THE SUPPLY OF GOODS AND SERVICES

Your rights of any action for breach of contract, with regard to goods and services, will always be firstly against the trader with whom you have contracted – the person from whom you bought the goods or services. As above, however, if you have bought the goods on credit, and they are over £100 and £15,000 or under then you can also claim breach of contract against the credit company. Depending on the nature of the breach, you may be able to reject the goods or service and ask for your money back, and/or have a right to claim compensation for any loss, or ask a court for an order for specific performance (see above, p.192).

Goods

Under the **Trade Descriptions Act**, it is a criminal offence for a trader to say, or write, anything which is untrue about what is being offered for sale. If you have been misled, then you should always advise the **Trading Standards (Consumer Protection) Department**, who may well prosecute the trader.

By civil law, any goods sold to you for cash, or hired, or the subject of a hire purchase, credit sale or conditional sale agreement must, by law:

- be of 'satisfactory quality', and fit for their normal use. 'Satisfactory quality' is what a reasonable person would consider satisfactory, given the description of the goods, all relevant circumstances and the price paid. So the standard of 'satisfactory' must be looked at in the light of the purchase. If you buy a second-hand, battered cement mixer for £50, you cannot reasonably expect it to give the same type of performance as one bought new for £300. If the new one broke down within two weeks you could rely on implied terms. If the old one broke down, you probably could not – subject to any other terms of the contract.

    A trader will not be liable for selling you goods if he has clearly advised you of specific faults, and you still buy the goods concerned – and then complain about the faults previously advised. Neither will he be liable if you have used the goods for something that they are not designed to do. If you buy some plaster and use it outside, then you will have no rights against him if it degrades quickly (as it will).

- match the description under which they are sold. If the goods you buy are a different size, colour or shape than you specified, or in some way do not match the description under which they were sold, then this will be a breach of an implied term. Equally, there will be an implied breach if the bulk of any goods does not match samples shown to you. If you have carefully inspected the goods, however, and still bought them, recognizing that the description is inaccurate or that there are flaws, then there will be no breach.

- be reasonably fit for the purpose for which you have told the trader. There will be no breach, however, if you did not rely on the trader's skill when choosing the goods, or if it would be unreasonable to do so. If you asked a trader whether a sheet of board would be suitable for outside use, and he said he did not know, then he would not be responsible if the board subsequently proved to be for interior use only. If, however, you relied on the seller's assurance that the item you bought would perform a specified function, and you subsequently found it did not, then this would be a breach of the implied term.

Delivery of Goods

If you expressly agree a delivery date for goods, then you have a right to cancel the order, and have your money returned, if the time for delivery is not met. If no date is defined when you buy goods, they should be delivered in a reasonable time. If they are not, then you must contact the trader and agree a reasonable time for delivery. If they still do not arrive, then you can cancel the order.

You are under no obligation to accept unsolicited goods. Indeed, if they have not been collected within six months they become yours, free. If you have advised a trader, in writing, to collect his unsolicited goods, he must do so within thirty days – or they become your possession.

Acceptance

You must take care that you do not negate the protection afforded by implied terms. You can do this by 'accepting' the goods. This occurs in the following cases:

- If you tell the seller that you have accepted the goods, notwithstanding any faults that you have found.

- If after a reasonable opportunity to inspect the goods, you do something that is not consistent with the previous owner's still owning the goods. If you sell the goods, or give them away, then you will have no further rights against the seller.

- If you keep the goods for a reasonable amount of time without telling the seller that you want to reject them. You cannot keep and use something that is flawed for a few months, and then decide to rely on an implied term to reject the goods. You must advise a seller as soon as a defect is discovered.

Services

Any contract for a service will have a term implied to it that the work is carried out with reasonable care and skill, and is performed within a reasonable time for a reasonable charge. In building contracts, for example, the work will be expected to be carried out in a good and workmanlike manner with materials and workmanship of proper quality.

The key to assessing when an implied term will apply is the factor of 'reasonableness'. A court will look at all the circumstances of the contract, and the intentions of the parties, to assess what is or is not reasonable. The standard that a court would use is, however, quite low. If the service that you have received is adequate, rather than exceptional, a court may not find any implied breach of contract.

Appendix 5

Specimen Letters of Objection to Application for Planning Permission

NEW SUPERMARKET

The individual in this example is objecting to an application to build a new supermarket close to a small village. Note that the correct reference number has been quoted, and that the objector has produced an argument which is unemotional, objective and shows that he has researched the local planning policy guidelines.

> 4 The Willows
> Long Lane
> Allshott
> Essex T1B 1FU

R. L. G. Leeson DipTP, FRTPI, DMS, MI Mgt
Director of Planning and Economic Development
Allshott District Council

1 May 1997

Dear Sir,

RE: Application no. ALL/97/1199

I have inspected the above planning application concerning the new supermarket for Tall Beans & Co., and make the following observations:

1 The proposal would involve the loss of high-quality agricultural land, and affect a green wedge with a public right of way, important to the amenities of adjoining and local residents. The council's policy is that in such circumstances there should be an overriding need to justify development.

2 The envisaged scale of retail space is some 12 to 15 times that presently serving the day-to-day needs of Little Allshott, and therefore quite inappropriate in

scale. It would require substantial local housing development, which is not envisaged in the local plan, in order to support the proposal. Failing this, trade would be drawn from the existing main road shopping centres. Furthermore, the survival of the existing small supermarket would be endangered. The council's policy is to safeguard the future of this village and the local centre stores.

3 There happens to be scope within the existing village retail frontage for some extension of the day-to-day facilities, but the fact that this has not been taken up indicates a lack of local demand. There is adequate public and private transport available to reach easily all the existing major local and main shopping centres.

4 The traffic capacity of the adjoining main road and nearby road junctions is extremely limited, and the proposed development would involve the authorities in a substantial cost were it to be upgraded.

Yours sincerely,
V. Cross

NEIGHBOUR'S EXTENSION

Note that the objector's argument is presented both from his own point of view, regarding the direct consequences he will suffer on his own property, and that of the neighbourhood. Once again, he has looked at the local plan and found that the application goes against the local policy guidelines.

4 The Willows
Long Lane
Allshott
Essex T1B 1FU

R. L. G. Leeson DipTP, FRTPI, DMS, MI Mgt
Director of Planning and Economic Development
Allshott District Council

11 July 1997

Dear Sir,

RE: Application no. PIP/97/0497

I have inspected the above planning application for an extension at 2 The Willows, Long Lane, Allshott and I should like to register the following objections:

1 The extension is shown projecting from the main elevation in Long Lane by some 5m in front of the building line of adjoining residential properties. This extension will therefore be in close proximity to the public footpath. Indicated as some 6m wide, the extension will look both conspicuous and incongruous in the street.

2 The extension will detract harshly from the architectural distinction of 2 The Willows which presently contributes to the character of the road. The local character will also be adversely affected by the loss of lawn from this attractive house, the removal of the two oak trees standing in the garden and the construction of a high brick wall around the property.

3 The large windows on the south side of the extension will look directly into the garden of my house (4 The Willows), and the scale of the extension, and its proximity to my house, will place our front garden in shade for most of the day.

4 Long Lane is part of the Allshott conservation area, and it is the policy of the local authority, as set out in the local plan, to retain the character of the unique buildings in the area and to resist major alterations to the residential houses.

Yours sincerely,
V. Cross

Appendix 6

Professional and Trade Organizations

FINANCIAL

Association of British Insurers
51 Gresham Street
London EC2V 7HQ
Tel. (0171) 600 3333

The British Bankers' Association
105–108 Old Broad Street
London EC3V 9EL
Tel. (0171) 216 8800

British Insurance and Investment
Brokers Association (BIIBA)
BIIBA House
14 Bevis Marks
London EC3A 7NT
Tel. (0171) 623 9043

Building Societies Association/Council
of Mortgage Lenders
3 Savile Row
London W1X 1AF
Tel. (0171) 437 0655

Corporation of Insurance and
Financial Advisors
174 High Street
Guildford
Surrey GU1 3HW
Tel. (01483) 539 121

Independent Financial Advisors
Association
12–13 Henrietta Street
London WC2E 8LH
Tel. (0171) 240 7878

IFA Promotion
17–19 Emery Road
Brislington
Bristol BS4 5PF
Tel. (0117) 971 1177

FINANCIAL REGULATORY AUTHORITIES

Personal Investment Authority (PIA)
7th Floor
1 Canada Square
Canary Wharf
London E14 5AZ
Tel. (0171) 538 8860

Securities and Investment Board (SIB)
Gavrelle House
2–14 Bunhill Row
London EC1Y 8RA
Tel. (0171) 638 1240

FINANCIAL OMBUDSMEN

Banking Ombudsman
70 Gray's Inn Road
London WC1X 8NB
Tel. (0171) 404 9944

Building Societies Ombudsman
Millbank Tower
Millbank
London SW1P 4XS
Tel. (0171) 931 0044

Financial Ombudsman
63 St Mary Axe
London EC3A 8NB
Tel. (0171) 621 1061

Insurance Ombudsman
City Gate One
135 Park Street
London SE1 9EA
Tel. (0171) 928 7600

Investment Ombudsman
6 Frederick's Place
London EC2R 8BT
Tel. (0171) 796 3065

LEGAL/DISPUTES

Chartered Institute of Arbitrators
(CIAB)
International Arbitration Centre
24 Angel Gate
City Road
London EC1V 2RS
Tel. (0171) 837 4483

Citizens' Advice Bureau
(Located in most towns)

The Consumers' Association
2 Marylebone Road
London NW1 4DF
Tel. (0171) 486 5544

Council for Licensed Conveyancers
16 Glebe Road
Chelmsford
Essex CM1 1QG
Tel. (01245) 349 599

Department of the Environment
Public Enquiry Point:
Room P2/162
2 Marsham Street
London SW1P 3EB
Tel. (0171) 276 0900
Publications Dispatch Centre:
Blackhorse Road
London SE99 6TT

Director General of Fair Trading
Field House

15–25 Bream's Buildings
London EC4A 1PR

The Law Society
113 Chancery Lane
London WC2A 1PL
Tel. (0171) 242 1222

Law Society Northern Ireland
Law Society House
98 Victoria Street
Belfast BT1 3JZ

Law Society of Scotland
26 Drumsheugh Gardens
Edinburgh EH3 7YR
Tel. (0131) 226 7411

Land Tribunal of Scotland
1 Grosvenor Crescent
Edinburgh EH12 5ER
Tel. (0131) 225 7996

Leasehold Advisory Service
8 Maddox Street
London W1R 9PN
Tel. (0171) 493 3116

Legal Services Ombudsman
22 Oxford Court
Oxford Street
Manchester M2 3WQ
Tel. (0161) 236 9532

Legal Authority Ombudsman
(Contact your local authority for
details)

Office for the Supervision of
Solicitors
(OSS)
Victoria Court
8 Dormer Place
Leamington Spa
Warwickshire CV32 5AE
Tel. (01926) 820 082

Registry of County Court Judgments
173–175 Cleveland Street
London W1P 5PE
Tel. (0171) 380 0133

CONSTRUCTION PROFESSIONALS

Architects' Registration Council
73 Hallam Street
London W1N 6EE
Tel. (0171) 580 5861

Architects' and Surveyors' Institute
St Mary House
15 St Mary Street
Chippenham
Wiltshire SN15 3WD
Tel. (01249) 444 505

Association of Building Engineers
Jubilee House
Billing Brook Road
Weston Favell
Northamptonshire NN3 8NW
Tel. (01604) 404 121

Incorporated Society of Valuers and
Auctioneers (ISVA)
3 Cadogan Gate
London SW1X 0AS
Tel. (0171) 235 2282

Institute of Electrical Engineers
Savoy Place
London WC2R 0BL
Tel. (0171) 240 1871

Institute of Structural Engineers
11 Upper Belgrave Street
London SW1X 8BH
Tel. (0171) 235 4535

New Homes Marketing Board
(NHMB)
82 New Cavendish Street
London W1M 8AD
Tel. (0171) 580 5588

Royal Incorporation of Architects in
Scotland (RIAS)
15 Rutland Square
Edinburgh EH1 2BE
Tel. (0131) 229 7205

Royal Institute of Architects in Wales
(RIAW)
Midland Bank Chambers

75A Llandennis Road
Cardiff CF2 6EE
Tel. (01222) 762 215

Royal Institute of British Architects
(RIBA)
66 Portland Place
London W1N 4AD
Tel. (0171) 580 5533

Royal Institution of Chartered
Surveyors (RICS)
12 Great George Street
Parliament Square
London SW1P 3AD
Tel. (0171) 222 7000

TRADE ORGANIZATIONS/ USEFUL CONTACTS

Arboricultural Association
Ampfield House
Ampfield
Nr Romsey
Hampshire SO51 9PA
Tel. (01794) 368 717

Association of Relocation Agents
Premier House
11 Marlborough Place
Brighton
East Sussex BN1 1UB
Tel. (01273) 624 455

British Decorators' Association
32 Coton Road
Nuneaton
Warwickshire CV11 5TW
Tel. (01203) 353 776

British Wood Preservation and Damp
Proofing Association
6 The Office Village
4 Romford Road
London E15 4EA
Tel. (0181) 519 2588

Building Employers' Confederation
82 New Cavendish Street
London W1M 8AD
Tel. (0171) 580 5588

Buildings Research Establishment
Bucknalls Lane
Garston
Watford
Hertfordshire WD2 7JR
Tel. (01923) 664 664

Conservatory Council
Glass and Glazing Federation
44–48 Borough High Street
London SE1 1XB
Tel. (0171) 403 7177

Council for the Registration of Gas
Installers (CORGI)
1 Elmwood
Chineham Business Park
Crockford Lane
Basingstoke
Hampshire RG24 8WG
Tel. (01256) 372 200

Electrical Contractors' Association
(ECA)
ECA House
34 Palace Court
London W2 4JG
Tel. (0171) 229 1266

Electrical Contractors Association of
Scotland
Bush House
Bush Estate
Midlothian EH26 0SB
Tel. (0131) 445 5577

Federation of Master Builders
Gordon Fisher House
14–15 Great James Street
London WC1N 3DP
Tel. (0171) 242 7583

Guild of Master Craftsmen
166 High Street
Lewes
East Sussex BN7 1XU
Tel. (01273) 478 449

Heating and Ventilating Contractors'
Association
34 Palace Court

London W2 4JG
Tel. (0171) 229 2488

Institute of Plumbing
64 Station Lane
Hornchurch
Essex RM12 6NB
Tel. (01708) 472 791

National Association of Estate Agents
(NAEA)
Arbon House
21 Jury Street
Warwick CV34 4EH
Tel. (01926) 496 800

National Association of Plumbing,
Heating and Mechanical Services
Contractors
14–15 Ensign House
Ensign Business Centre
Westwood Way
Coventry
West Midlands CV4 8JA
Tel. (01203) 470 626

National Federation of Roofing
Contractors
24 Weymouth Street
London W1N 4LX
Tel. (0171) 436 0387

National Inspection Council for
Electrical Installation Contracting
(NICEIC)
Vintage House
37 Albert Embankment
London SE1 7UJ
Tel. (0171) 582 7746

Scottish Decorators' Federation
1 Grindlay Street Court
Edinburgh EH3 9AR
Tel. (0131) 221 1527

Subsidence Claims Advisory Bureau
Charter House
43 St Leonards Road
Bexhill on Sea
East Sussex TN40 1JA
Tel. (01424) 733 727

COMPANIES OFFERING INSURANCE BACKED WARRANTIES

Guarantee Protection Trust
27 London Road
High Wycombe HP11 1BW
Tel. (01494) 447 049

Independent Warranty Association
21 Albion Place
Northampton NN1 1UD
Tel. (01604) 604 511

National House Building Council
(NHBC)
Buildmark House
Chiltern Avenue
Amersham
Buckinghamshire HP6 5AP
Tel. (01494) 434 477

National Register of Warranted
Builders
14 15 Great James Street
London WC1N 3DP
Tel. (0171) 242 7583

ORGANIZATIONS SUPPLYING STANDARD SMALL WORKS CONTRACTS

CIP Ltd
(for JCT contracts)
Federation House
2309 County Road
Birmingham B26 3PL
Tel. (0121) 742 0824

Federation of Master Builders
Gordon Fisher House
14/15 Great James Street
London WC1N 3DP
Tel. (0171) 242 7583

Index

TITLES AVAILABLE FROM

GMC PUBLICATIONS

BOOKS

WOODWORKING

40 More Woodworking Plans & Projects	GMC Publications
Bird Boxes & Feeders for the Garden	Dave Mackenzie
Complete Woodfinishing	Ian Hosker
Electric Woodwork	Jeremy Broun
Furniture Projects	Rod Wales
Furniture Restoration (Practical Crafts)	Kevin Jan Bonner
Furniture Restoration for Beginners	Kevin Jan Bonner
Green Woodwork	Mike Abbott
Making & Modifying Woodworking Tools	Jim Kingshott
Making Fine Furniture	Tom Darby
Making Little Boxes from Wood	John Bennett
Making Shaker Furniture	Barry Jackson
Making Chairs and Tables	GMC Publications
Making Unusual Miniatures	Graham Spalding
Pine Furniture Projects	Dave Mackenzie
Security for the Householder: Fitting locks & other devices	E. Phillips
Sharpening Pocket Reference Book	Jim Kingshott
Sharpening: The Complete Guide	Jim Kingshott
The Incredible Router	Jeremy Broun
The Workshop	Jim Kingshott
Tool Making for Woodworkers	Ray Larsen
Woodfinishing Handbook (Practical Crafts)	Ian Hosker
Woodworking Plans & Projects	GMC Publications

WOODTURNING

Adventures in Woodturning	David Springett
Bert Marsh: Woodturner	Bert Marsh
Bill Jones' Notes from the Turning Shop	Bill Jones
Bill Jones' Further Notes from the Turning Shop	Bill Jones
Colouring Techniques for Woodturners	Jan Sanders
Decorative Techniques for Woodturners	Hilary Bowen
Essential Tips for Woodturners	GMC Publications
Faceplate Turning	GMC Publications
Fun at the Lathe	R.C.Bell
Illustrated Woodturning Techniques	John Hunnex
Keith Rowley's Woodturning Projects	Keith Rowley
Make Money from Woodturning	Ann & Bob Phillips
Multi-Centre Woodturning	Ray Hopper
Pleasure and Profit from Woodturning	Reg Sherwin
Practical Tips for Turners & Carvers	GMC Publications
Practical Tips for Woodturners	GMC Publications
Spindle Turning	GMC Publications
Turning Miniatures in Wood	John Sainsbury
Turning Wooden Toys	Terry Lawrence
Understanding Woodturning	Ann & Bob Phillips
Useful Woodturning Projects	GMC Publications
Woodturning Jewellery	Hilary Bowen
Woodturning Masterclass	Tony Boase
Woodturning Projects	GMC Publications
Woodturning Techniques	GMC Publications
Woodturning Wizardry	David Springett
Woodturning: A Foundation Course	Keith Rowley
Woodturning: A Sourcebook of Shapes	John Hunnex

WOODCARVING

Carving Birds & Beasts	GMC Publications
Carving on Turning	Chris Pye
Carving Realistic Birds	David Tippey
Decorative Woodcarving	Jeremy Williams
Essential Tips for Woodcarvers	GMC Publications
Essential Woodcarving Techniques	Dick Onians
Lettercarving in Wood	Chris Pye
The Art of the Woodcarver	GMC Publications
The Woodcarvers	GMC Publications
Understanding Woodcarving	GMC Publications
Wildfowl Carving - Volume 1	Jim Pearce
Wildfowl Carving - Volume 2	Jim Pearce
Woodcarving for Beginners	GMC Publications
Woodcarving Tools, Materials & Equipment	Chris Pye
Woodcarving: A Complete Course	Ron Butterfield
Woodcarving: A Foundation Course	Zoë Gertner

UPHOLSTERY

Seat Weaving (Practical Crafts)	Ricky Holdstock
Upholsterer's Pocket Reference Book	David James
Upholstery Restoration Projects	David James
Upholstery Techniques & Projects	David James
Upholstery: A Complete Course	David James

TOYMAKING

Designing & Making Wooden Toys	*Terry Kelly*	Making Wooden Toys & Games	*Jeff & Jennie Loader*
Fun to Make Wooden Toys & Games	*Jeff & Jennie Loader*	Restoring Rocking Horses	*Clive Green & Anthony Dew*
Making Board, Peg & Dice Games	*Jeff & Jennie Loader*		

DOLLS' HOUSES

Architecture for Dolls' Houses	*Joyce Percival*	Making Period Dolls' House Furniture	
Beginners' Guide to the Dolls' House Hobby	*Jean Nisbett*		*Derek & Sheila Rowbottom*
Dolls' House Bathrooms: Lots of Little Loos	*Patricia King*	Making Tudor Dolls' Houses	*Derek & Sheila Rowbottom*
Easy to Make Dolls' House Accessories	*Andrea Barham*	Making Victorian Dolls' House Furniture	*Patricia King*
Make Your Own Dolls' House Furniture	*Maurice Harper*	Miniature Needlepoint Carpets	*Janet Granger*
Making Dolls' House Furniture	*Patricia King*	The Complete Doll's House Book	*Jean Nisbett*
Making Georgian Dolls' Houses	*Derek & Sheila Rowbottom*	The Secrets of the Dolls' House Makers	*Jean Nisbett*
Making Period Dolls' House Accessories	*Andrea Barham*		

CRAFTS

Celtic Knotwork Designs	*Sheila Sturrock*	Embroidery Tips & Hints	*Harold Hayes*
Collage from Seeds, Leaves and Flowers	*Joan Carver*	Making Knitwear Fit	*Pat Ashforth & Steve Plummer*
Complete Pyrography	*Stephen Poole*	Pyrography Handbook (Practical Crafts)	*Stephen Poole*
Creating Knitwear Designs	*Pat Ashforth & Steve Plummer*	Tassel Making for Beginners	*Enid Taylor*
Cross Stitch Kitchen Projects	*Janet Granger*	Tatting Collage	*Lindsay Rogers*
Cross Stitch on Colour	*Sheena Rogers*		

VIDEOS

Drop-in and Pinstuffed Seats	*David James*	Classic Profiles	*Dennis White*
Stuffover Upholstery	*David James*	Twists and Advanced Turning	*Dennis White*
Elliptical Turning	*David Springett*	Sharpening the Professional Way	*Jim Kingshott*
Woodturning Wizardry	*David Springett*	Sharpening Turning & Carving Tools	*Jim Kingshott*
Turning Between Centres	*Dennis White*	Bowl Turning	*John Jordan*
Turning Bowls	*Dennis White*	Hollow Turning	*John Jordan*
Boxes, Goblets & Screw Threads	*Dennis White*	Woodturning: A Foundation Course	*Keith Rowley*
Novelties and Projects	*Dennis White*	Carving a Figure - The Female Form	*Ray Gonzalez*

MAGAZINES

WOODTURNING · WOODCARVING · TOYMAKING

FURNITURE & CABINETMAKING · BUSINESSMATTERS

CREATIVE IDEAS FOR THE HOME · THE ROUTER

The above represents a full list of all titles currently published or scheduled to be published. All are available direct from the Publishers or through bookshops, newsagents and specialist retailers. To place an order, or to obtain a complete catalogue, contact:

GMC Publications,
166 High Street, Lewes, East Sussex BN7 1XU United Kingdom
Tel: 01273 488005 Fax: 01273 478606

Orders by credit card are accepted